PERCEPTIONS of CHRISTIANITY
AMONG SOUTH ASIAN
MUSLIMS
IN AMERICA

PAUL S. BISWAS

WESTBOW
PRESS®
A DIVISION OF THOMAS NELSON
& ZONDERVAN

WestBow Press books may be ordered through booksellers or by contacting:

WestBow Press
A Division of Thomas Nelson & Zondervan
1663 Liberty Drive
Bloomington, IN 47403
www.westbowpress.com
1 (866) 928-1240

ISBN: 978-1-9736-9321-5 (sc)
ISBN: 978-1-9736-9320-8 (hc)
ISBN: 978-1-9736-9322-2 (e)

Library of Congress Control Number: 2020910736

Print information available on the last page.

WestBow Press rev. date: 07/10/2020

DEDICATION

I dedicate this book to my Christian coworkers and to those fellow Christians who strive to help Muslims embrace true perceptions of Christianity.

CONTENTS

FOREWORD

Dr. Ernie Beevers

I was honored when my good friend Paul Biswas asked me to advise him and help edit this book about the misperceptions of Christianity held by South Asian Muslims and how Christians can be more effective witnesses for Christ by understanding these misperceptions.

I can think of no one more suited to write on such a topic, both because of his interest and passion related to understanding how Muslims think about Christians and Christianity. He is the most knowledgeable person I know concerning Islam and Muslim beliefs and thoughts. He can speak ad-lib for hours about the history of Islam and carries a vast amount of related detailed information in his head.

He also has a passion and enthusiasm for expanding his knowledge about Muslim beliefs and thoughts and is particularly concerned to present an effective witness for Christ to them.

I was most impressed with his careful preparation for the interviews he conducted to collect firsthand data about South Asian Muslim perceptions of Christianity for the final chapters of this book. He was so careful in selecting not only the specific questions but also selecting those he interviewed to be sure they were a good representative sampling of South Asian Muslims in the Boston area, and he was meticulous in documenting and analyzing those interviews to show how their perceptions influence their convictions and attitudes toward Christians and Christianity.

(Dr. Beevers is a twenty-two years instructor and director of the New England Center for Southern Baptist Theological Seminary (now retired). He is emeritus missionary to Indonesia (served twelve years) with the International Mission Board (SBC).

* * *

Moussa Bongoyok, PhD

The academic study of Islam post 9/11 requires that scholars take extra caution. This is particularly necessary when a non-Muslim explores the Islamic beliefs and practices. The extreme sensibility on the part of both Muslim and non-Muslim populations ought to be taken into consideration in Islamic studies while maintaining academic standards of validity, reliability, and objectivity. Islam ought to be portrayed in such a way that most Muslims would agree with the description. At the same time, Christian scholars must have the freedom and the ability to examine what they observed in light of scholarly research and biblical teachings in order to draw the necessary implications for a respectful, loving, and yet faithful communication of the gospel to their Muslim neighbors.

This is exactly what Dr. Biswas did as he looked at how South Asian Muslims perceive Christianity. In order to go deeper into his study, he was wise enough to focus on the Muslim immigrants from South Asia who live in the greater Boston area (in Massachusetts, USA) and their descendants. The detailed presentation of the data he collected and his brief but helpful observations make his research important for future strategizing for Christian-Muslim relations or missiological approaches in this context.

Although a Christian, Dr. Biswas knows the South Asian culture perfectly, having been born and raised in that geographic context himself. His excellent knowledge of Islam and his solid background in Christian theology were also an asset. But above all, his long experience of ministry among Muslims both in Asia and in North America coupled with his excellent relational skills made it a little easier for him to approach his Muslim neighbors and interpret some cultural and religious values that are hardly perceived by outsiders.

Conducting such a study still carries a risk of subjectivity. In order to overcome that danger, he took on him the risk of sacrificing the beauty of a literary style in order to report as faithfully as possible the actual responses that come from his Muslim informants. We salute his courage as he offers valuable information that other scholars can further analyze using grounded theory or other relevant methods.

Furthermore, the way he approached the study and his comments and conclusions are also helpful for Christian practitioners, peacemakers, and development agents as they provide precious insights for Christian-Muslim relations, relief and development work in Muslim context, and Christian ministry in any similar Muslim context. For this reason, we strongly recommend this book to all who would like to have a better understanding of how Muslims perceive Christianity, to learn how to navigate Christian-Muslim relations, to develop strategies for holistic development in a Muslim context, or to present the gospel in such a way that it would clarify some of the major Muslim misconceptions and yet demonstrate Christian love for Muslims even when they are not very open to Christian beliefs and practices.

Moussa Bongoyok, PhD
President of Institut Universitaire de Développement International (IUDI)
Affiliated with the University of Maroua (Cameroon)

* * *

Drs. Michael and Adelle McKinney

Dr. Paul Biswas, in his work *Perceptions of Christianity among South Asian Muslims in America,* makes an excellent case for the reasons why the Christian church has neglected and has compromised the foundational principles of moral and spiritual ethics taught by Jesus Christ. This book was written to bridge this gap in the understanding and misunderstanding of how other religions view Christianity in America, and to build a bridge to counter their misconceptions. As you read this thorough and thoughtful analysis, which encompassed thousands of hours of research, you will find that it calls to attention, without meaning to, the failure of America's church to stand for the godly principles that made this nation the envy of the world. Dr. Biswas has excellently addressed these issues in his work, which should be an eye-opener to Christian colleges, seminaries, universities, churches, and missionary outreaches based in USA.

Men and women in the past dreamed of coming to America to experience religious freedom, liberty to worship God, and the desire to raise their children in an atmosphere of safety, respect, tolerance, and moral civility. Upon arrival, however, their vision of America as a Christian nation is clouded as they encounter images they see on television, people they meet on the street, and laws approved by the highest court in the land. It's time to bring America back to God.

Drs. Michael and Adelle McKinney
Cofounders: Promise Christian University
World for Jesus International Ministries
The Pastors Network of Southern California
The Promise Channel (R)

* * *

Dr. Terry W. Dorsett

In *Perceptions of Christianity among South Asian Muslims in America* Dr. Paul Biswas explores how immigrants from South Asia view Christianity. While most Christians think very highly of the society we built, many immigrants also see the negative aspects of how our faith has been applied. Dr. Biswas is not afraid to discuss both sides of this issue. This comprehensive book will be a real help to those Christians who want to be a better reflection of Christ to immigrants.

Dr. Terry W. Dorsett
Executive Director
Baptist Convention of New England, Inc.
Northborough, MA

* * *

Seong Hyun Park, PhD

I have appreciated the work of Dr. Paul Biswas both in the classrooms where he engages students and on the home-front where he hosts neighbors of Muslim faith. The appreciation now extends over the pages in this book where Dr. Biswas offers his findings from the qualitative research he has conducted on the perceptions of Christianity among the Muslim immigrants of South Asian origin in the Greater Boston area. Readers with interest in missiology and interfaith dialog will appreciate the subject of inquiry which has not received proper attention before.

Many will be prompted to ask the question, "What kind of neighbors are we?"

Seong Hyun Park, PhD
Dean of Boston Campus & Assistant Professor of Old Testament
Gordon-Conwell Theological Seminary

* * *

PREFACE

During many years of interacting with South Asian Muslims, I became aware of many misperceptions held by them, which seriously hinder their openness and receptivity to my efforts to share my Christian faith with them. This awareness led me to more intensive study of their perceptions of Christianity and inspired the research that culminated in the writing of this book.

The extensive research I conducted on the perceptions of Christianity among South Asian Muslims in Greater Boston was done from 2015 to 2017. Although this research was carried out in the Boston area; this population is generally representative of South Asian Muslims throughout America. Therefore, observations and insights from this research are applicable to South Asian Muslims throughout America as reflected in the title of this book.

A growing awareness of misperceptions among South Asian Muslims motivated me to explore the causes behind these misperceptions. Understanding these causes can help Christians who interact with Muslims to rectify these misperceptions.

The missiological research that is the basis for this book is related to my current missional work among South Asian Muslims, and in this book I endeavor to pass along insights and proven methods to my fellow Christians.

This book can further provide foundational material for academicians who wish to undertake further research in this area. Very little published work has been done specifically on South Asian Muslim perceptions of Christianity in America. This book seeks to address this deficiency.

ACKNOWLEDGMENTS

First of all, I give all glory and honor to God who granted me wisdom to write this book. Day by day I experienced His constant sustaining power, which was needed to complete this book.

I am indebted to many people for their encouragement and prayer support while writing this book, which is the result of my academic research and many years of ministry experience to Muslims. During this time, so many have contributed directly and indirectly to this effort that it will be impossible to name them all, but I want to extend my heartfelt gratitude to some individuals who contributed most by their valuable suggestions.

I express my profound gratitude to Dr. Ernie Beevers, my spiritual mentor and guide. He voluntarily came forward to help while I was desperately in need of a native English speaker who would be academically suited to this project. Because of his missionary experience in a Muslim country in Asia and his knowledge about Islam, he was the right person to understand and guide the expression of my ideas. I praise God for his patience. For over a year he worked with me, editing and reediting my many drafts and frequently interacting with me over the specific wording to make sure the expressed text captured the meaning I intended. His suggestions and editorial comments always kept me on the right track. He has been a channel of blessing for me especially with this project.

I also want to express my deep gratitude to Dr. Moussa Bongoyok, my professor and now colleague. He taught me about the importance of a correct theology of missions, which is such an important challenge the church faces today. He encouraged me in many ways by sharing his profound academic knowledge about Islam and insights from his long experience working among Muslim people groups in diverse cultural settings.

Under his mentorship, the research project I undertook for my doctoral study served as resource material for this book. I cannot find adequate words to fully express the extent of my deep appreciation and admiration for his patient encouragement. As my mentor, his openness and humble attitude have set an example for me to follow.

Throughout my forty years of ministry to Muslims, I have been blessed by many Muslim friends by their openness and interest in Christianity. For the South Asian Ministry in New England, we conduct two types of programs: one is intercultural get-together meetings and the other is Christian-Muslim interfaith dialogue meetings. In these meetings Muslim friends raise many sociocultural and ethical issues that they associate with Christianity. Their many misperceptions about Christianity challenged and inspired me to write this book.

I am thankful to all my coworkers and team members who encouraged me and supported me with their prayers. Lastly, I thank my family members whose unfailing support was so very helpful during my research and writing of this book.

I dedicate this book to my coworkers and those practitioners who witness to Muslim people groups in America and other countries. I pray this small effort will facilitate effective communication of the Christian gospel to Muslims.

INTRODUCTION

The word *perception* in the title is derived from the verb perceive, which means to grasp with the mind. So perceptions are the ways one thinks about or understands an idea, concept, or belief. Perceptions may be either positive or negative. By positive perceptions I mean correct or accurate perceptions; by negative perceptions or misperceptions I mean incorrect perceptions.

Perceptions are often reflected in beliefs held about a subject. In this book I refer to "perceptions of Christianity," meaning beliefs in the minds of South Asian Muslims about various aspects of Christianity including doctrines held by most adherents.

Perceptions that are frequently reinforced and seldom contradicted tend to be retained and more permanently established in the minds of an individual or group. Thus when a particular misperception about Christianity is repeatedly reinforced through teaching at the mosque by respected religious leaders, this misperception will tend to become more ingrained and firmly established in the mind of the Muslim adherent, and it is logical to expect such a perception to be more difficult to correct or modify.

Furthermore, perceptions are not static but dynamic, constantly being subject to modification based on new experiences and observations, new acquisition of facts, and interactions with non-Muslim neighbors, schoolmates, and workmates.

It might seem reasonable to assume that the perceptions found among Muslims in South Asia would be reflected in the perceptions held by Muslim immigrants from that same region; however, that is not necessarily true. For example, if 30 percent of Muslims in South Asia have a strong perception of Christians as infidels and as an enemy of Islam, this in itself might predispose that 30 percent not to leave their homeland and to be repulsed by the idea of moving to America, where Christianity is the predominant religion. Thus, it may be expected that the profile of perceptions of Christianity among immigrants will differ to some extent from their fellow South Asians who remain in South Asia.

The question naturally arises of how perceptions become changed or modified among those who immigrate. Those who immigrate to America will make decisions about the extent to which they and their children will integrate into the larger society in their new homeland. For the sake of their children's education, they usually have their children attend public schools and participate in school events with their American peers. Thus, the children of immigrants likely interact with Christian children in public schools, which might incline them to hold less strong perceptions of Christians as enemies of Islam.

The purpose of this book is to explore and articulate perceptions of Christianity among South Asian Muslims in America. The research I undertook for writing this book was focused on a specific ethnic group of Muslims (i.e., South Asians) and a particular geographical area, Greater Boston. South Asian Muslims in Greater Boston represent a significant percentage of Muslims in America. Throughout this book I also intend to explore the different misperceptions among the various ethnic groups of South Asian Muslims in America.

This book explores South Asian Muslim perceptions of Christianity from three fundamental perspectives: theological (doctrinal), sociocultural, and ethical (moral).

From the theological perspective, it explores the historical background of Islam in South Asia, the theological perceptions of major Christian doctrines among South Asian Muslims, and how Islam has had a significant impact on the development of perceptions of Christianity among South Asian Muslims. Muslim immigrants from that area bring these perceptions with them to this country.

From the sociocultural and ethical perspectives, this book shows how the perceptions of Christianity have been modified and shaped by these influences after they immigrate to this country.

Most of these perceptions of Christianity are incorrect; therefore, a primary focus of this book addresses what these misperceptions are and how these misperceptions prove to be a challenge to communicating the gospel to them.

There are always challenges when trying to witness to people from a different culture. One such challenge is exacerbated when facing prejudices and biases against Christianity. These prejudices and biases often grow out of misperceptions of Christian beliefs and teaching. This is particularly true when witnessing to Muslims.

Thus, it becomes important for Christian witnesses to know how the target people think and feel and what prejudices they have that must be overcome in order to effectively present the gospel to them. This includes witnessing to South Asian Muslims in America, which is the focal group for this book. In order to effectively communicate the gospel, it becomes imperative to know their perceptions of Christianity.

There is significant misinformation among South Asian Muslims in America about American culture and religious traditions, and many misperceptions specifically about Christianity.

Many misperceptions of Christianity derive from erroneous interpretation of major Christian doctrines held by South Asian Muslims. Related to this is the question about what the Qur'an (the holy book of Muslims, revealed to their prophet Muhammad) and Hadith (report of the words and deeds of Muhammad) teach regarding Christians, the Christian faith, and the Bible.

Often South Asian Muslims in America associate cultural, ethical, and moral issues in American society with Christian teaching because they tend to identify Christianity with Western culture.

Perceptions of Christianity among South Asian Muslims hinder interpersonal communication and congenial interaction, especially between Christian and Muslim; yet there are also some positive perceptions that can help in relationship building.

South Asian Muslims comprise the largest population of all Muslim immigrants in America. Carl Ellis states, "When we look at the ethnic diversity of the U.S. Islamic community, the largest group is African American—42 percent. South Asians comprise the next largest section—24 percent." (Ellis 2001, 39)

Today the population of South Asian Muslims in America is probably much higher, since the Ellis study was done in 2001. Comparing the statistical reports of different organizations over recent years, South Asian Muslims remain the largest group among Muslim immigrants in America.

This book focuses specifically on the South Asian Muslim population in America. This group is comprised mainly of first-generation immigrants, but also includes second-generation immigrants and those children born in America.

There is ongoing research on Muslims in Greater Boston called the Pluralism Project, based at Harvard University and led by Diana L. Eck. In 2010, the article "Islam in Greater Boston," stated:

> In Greater Boston, Islam encompasses a diverse group of over 50,000 adherents served by nearly 50 different Mosques, schools, and community organizations. Originally composed primarily of African-American converts, the Muslim population of Greater Boston has grown to include immigrants from the Middle East, North Africa, South Asia, and Southeast Asia, as well as converts of Euro-American descent and self-identified secular Muslims. (Pluralism Project 2010)

The largest Muslim population in the world is in South Asia and has a great deal of cultural and ethnic diversity. South Asian Muslims in Greater Boston are also ethnically and culturally diverse, even as they are in South Asia; however, their religious faith and beliefs are essentially the same as in their native lands.

A large percentage of South Asians in America are adherents of Islam because they came mainly from the Indian subcontinent (Bangladesh, Pakistan, and India). Both Bangladesh and Pakistan are predominantly Muslim, and although India is predominantly Hindu, the second-largest religion there is Islam. Phil Parshall stated:

> India, Pakistan, and Bangladesh together have a population of a quarter of a billion Muslims. This is about one-third of the world's Islamic population. These three countries, it must be understood, geographically and demographically, constituted one entity prior to 1947 [The British Colonial Era]. This must be borne in mind when the words *India* or *subcontinent* are used in a historical sense. (Parshall 1983, 32)

My involvement with two existing programs of South Asian ministry in New England (specifically "Intercultural Get-Together Meetings" and "Interfaith Dialogue with Muslims"), inspired me to undertake research on Muslim perceptions of Christianity. Through these programs I have been able to build relationships and network with many members of the South Asian Muslim community in New England.

In interaction with South Asian Muslims, many Muslim friends often raise cultural and ethical questions about American society, and I have noted they frequently identify these with Christianity.

As a native-born South Asian, I have observed that South Asian Muslims, while in their native lands, generally very seldom raise these sociocultural, ethical, or moral questions that they identify with Christianity. Furthermore, I have observed that the misperceptions generally held by South Asian Muslims are predominantly about Christian doctrines, rather than ethical, moral, and cultural issues.

Muslim immigrants from South Asia bring misperceptions about Christian doctrines with them to America. They also bring the predetermined idea that American culture is closely associated with the influence of Christianity. This presupposition that Christian influences are seen in cultural practices in American culture often causes Muslim immigrants to have a more negative bias against Christianity. However, the influence of Christianity on cultural practices has significantly diminished in recent years.

While it is true that much in American society has been influenced by Christianity, many things in American society today are against the teachings of Christianity. Unfortunately, most of these immigrants do not differentiate the elements in American society that have resulted from Christian influence and those that are against Christian teaching.

In the following paragraphs, I explain the procedures that guided my sociological research and the composition of this book.

The methodology used for the research was qualitative using an ethnographic study approach. The idea for using this approach came primarily from two sources. One was the article "Ethnography" by Mario Luis Small, a sociology professor at Harvard University (Small 2009). The other was the article "Interviewing for Research and Analysing

Qualitative Data: An Overview," by Martin Woods, published in 2011 by the School of Health and Social Services, Massey University (Woods 2011).

Concerning the importance of ethnographic study and research in various fields, Small stated:

> Today, ethnographers and qualitative researchers in fields such as urban poverty, immigration, and social inequality, face an environment in which their work will be read, cited, and assessed by demographers, quantitative sociologists, and even economists." (Small 2009, 5)

Ethnography emerged in the field of anthropology as a method for exploring how different cultures function and as a method for studying the meaning of the human experience as viewed through the lens of culture.

The ethnographic approach allowed me to analyze the perceptions about Christianity that South Asian Muslims brought with them as well as the perceptions acquired from experiences in America.

A qualitative method of data-gathering was employed. The nature of this type of research is exploratory and open-ended. The survey instrument for this research study was based on structured interviews. The main reason for using structured interviews was that this allowed me to ask participants detailed questions about specific topics relevant to this research. In structured interviews a predetermined list of questions is given to respondents, and their responses and comments are solicited.

The research for this book partly consisted of literary study and partly of personal interviews of South Asian Muslims living in the Boston area. This was further enhanced by my own experience as a Bangladeshi (Bengali) immigrant to America, coming from one of the dominant ethnic groups and Muslim countries in South Asia.

For the interviews I conducted, each respondent was presented with identical questions on a range of topics to elicit his or her perceptions from three perspectives: theological (doctrinal), sociocultural, and ethical (moral). Structured interviews were conducted one-on-one with appointments set up ahead of time by phone and email. This facilitated the collection of qualitative data from the participants for presentation and analysis.

The interviews involved a representative sample of fifty participants including intellectuals and nonintellectuals from the South Asian Muslim community in Greater Boston. Also included were participants from academic communities and from a variety of South Asian ethnic groups.

Once the interviews were conducted and data gathered from the responses and comments of the participants, these data were organized and presented in Chapter 4 and analyzed in Chapter 5. The objective of the data analysis was to discover typical patterns of perceptions among South Asian Muslims related to Christianity to determine the degree of agreement and disagreement.

I used a thematic approach for the data analysis wherein data are related according to common themes. Concerning the thematic approach, Jennifer Attride-Stirling pointed out:

> Thematic networks are web-like illustrations that summarize the main themes constituting a piece of text. The thematic networks technique is a robust and highly sensitive tool for the systematization and presentation of qualitative analyses. (Attride-Stirling 2001, 385)

Alhojailan Mohammad Ibrahim also states:

> Thematic Analysis allows the researcher to determine precisely the relationships between concepts and compare them with the replicated data. By using thematic analysis there is the possibility to link the various concepts and opinions of the learners and compare these with the data that has been gathered in different situation at different times during the project. All possibilities of interpretation are possible. (Ibrahim 2012, 10)

In the thematic approach, responses to a questionnaire provide data that are then analyzed. The thematic approach was the best method for analyzing these data because they lend themselves to being clearly presented and organized around the chosen theme: South Asian Muslim perceptions related to Christianity. It further facilitated classifying the data according to the related perspectives: theological, sociocultural, and ethical (moral) perceptions, as well as to differences of views according to ethnic groups.

There were some limitations related to the interviews. Current events in the Islamic world and in America doubtless affected the responses of the participants; however, good relationships within the Muslim community helped to overcome this limitation.

Some potential interviewees, out of fear of reprisals, as well as some more radical Muslims, declined to participate in the interviews.

The theory chosen for the research used for this book was development theory. The writing that most inspired me in this research was *Religion and Development,* edited by Gerrie ter Haar (2011), as the basis for my theoretical framework. The way Gerrie ter Haar and other scholars applied development theory for economic and social work is the same way it can be applied for outreach and evangelism.

The thesis statement for this book is: "Misperceptions of Christianity pose significant challenges to building harmonious relationships among South Asian Muslims in America and communicating the gospel to them."

The following questions are addressed throughout the book as supporting argument in favor of my thesis statement. There is one primary question and main hypothesis, followed by secondary questions and hypotheses.

The primary research question and the main hypothesis are:

> ➢ **Primary Research Question:** In what ways do misperceptions of Christianity pose a significant challenge to the communication of the gospel to South Asian Muslims in America?

> **Main Hypothesis:** In response to this primary question, my main hypothesis is that erroneous views and negative biases must be corrected before effective communication can proceed.

The secondary questions and related hypotheses are:

> ➢ **Question:** What are the ideological factors influencing South Asian Muslim perceptions of Christianity in America?

Hypothesis: Teachings by Muslim leaders and instructors about Christian doctrines predispose South Asian Muslims to negative perceptions of Christianity. Negative perceptions or misperceptions of Christianity are reinforced by interaction with different ethnic groups of South Asian Muslims in America.

➤ **Question:** How do experiences of discrimination within American culture influence South Asian Muslim perceptions of Christianity?

Hypothesis: South Asian Muslim perceptions of Christianity are influenced by their experiences of discrimination here in America, because they think most Americans are Christian and therefore believe that discrimination against them results from Christian influences within American society.

➤ **Question:** What are the effects of direct experiences with churches and Christians on South Asian Muslim perceptions of Christianity?

Hypothesis: Perceptions of Christianity may be improved through direct contact with churches and Christians within American society.

➤ **Question:** What are some ways that communication between Christian and Muslim can be improved despite negative perceptions of Christianity held by South Asian Muslims?

Hypothesis: Direct experience with Christians and churches may create more openness and trust between Christians and Muslims, so that genuine dialogue can take place. Direct experience with Christians and churches may lead to a greater willingness to work together on issues of common concern.

➤ **Question:** Are there sociocultural emphases and practices in American society that affect perceptions of Christianity among South Asian Muslims?

Hypothesis: Some cultural practices in America (e.g., same-sex marriage, living together outside marriage) foster negative perceptions of Christianity because South Asian Muslims associate these practices with Christian influence in society.

This book will be helpful for those who want to engage in social-development work among South Asian Muslims. It can also help to provide useful insights and methods for Christian workers such as pastors and church planters to develop tools for addressing and correcting misperceptions that South Asian Muslims often associated with Christianity.

Interaction in a cross-cultural context always has potential for conflict. This book is significant because it highlights the biases and misinformation that often lead to conflicts. Having a clearer understanding of and respect for Muslims, church workers and development workers can reduce conflicts and promote harmonious relationships and create a congenial environment for effective communication of the gospel.

I believe this book is unique because, to the best of my knowledge, no one else has done research in this specific area, although there are numerous general writings related to Muslim views of Christianity. This book can inspire further study into ways to build good relationships with South Asian Muslims and to effectively communicate the gospel to them.

It is my hope that this book will provide a better understanding of misperceptions about Christians and Christianity held by South Asian Muslims and stimulate practical suggestions as to how these misperceptions may be addressed and corrected.

CHAPTER 1

THEOLOGICAL PERCEPTIONS

OF CHRISTIANITY AMONG
SOUTH ASIAN MUSLIMS IN AMERICA

South Asian Muslims bring diverse theological perceptions of Christianity with them to America from their native countries. Most of these perceptions can be traced to early Islamic movements as well as to modern influences within Islamic societies. These perceptions are also reflected in the beliefs of South Asian Muslims about various major Christian doctrines.

The main objectives of this chapter are: (1) to examine the varied historical sources of these diverse perceptions of Christianity, (2) to survey the prominent misperceptions of major Christian doctrines held by South Asian Muslims, and (3) to show specifically how these perceptions are inherent in the Islamic faith and traditions.

This chapter is divided into two sections. The first section covers the theological influences that historically shaped perceptions of Christianity among Muslims in South Asia, which they bring with them when they immigrate to America.

The second section explores the theological perceptions of major Christian doctrines brought by South Asian Muslims when they immigrate to America. This section also clarifies the Christian doctrines about which South Asian Muslims typically agree or disagree.

Some of these perceptions of Christianity are held by nearly all South Asian Muslims; others by only a few. Also, the more conservative South Asian Muslims will embrace certain perceptions, while the more moderate or liberal will hold somewhat different views.

I also explore how firmly these perceptions of Christianity are retained by these immigrants after they immigrate to America. It is reasonable to expect some modifications to their perceptions of Christianity over time after they immigrate.

Even though there is wide diversity among Muslims in South Asia in language, culture, and ethnicity, there is typically much similarity in their religious beliefs and practices. This similarity is also found among South Asian Muslims in America in their religious beliefs and practices as well as their perceptions of Christianity. Many misperceptions and biases, which developed in their native countries, tend to be retained in how they perceive other religious groups, especially Christianity. The specific misperceptions and biases of Christianity vary considerably among individuals and cultural people groups.

It is obvious that what we find in the Muslims in South Asia will most likely be reflected in those who immigrate to America. There is much diversity in the practice of Islam in South Asia. This diversity is presented in this chapter by examining the varied theological influences that have shaped the perceptions of Christianity among South Asian Muslims. So we can expect to find similar diversity in America.

Today in every South Asian country there is a range of religious convictions, from radical to conservative Muslims, and it is reasonable to anticipate a similar variation in America.

For many centuries Muslims and Christians have coexisted in various parts of South Asia, and this proximity has affected the perceptions of Christianity, therefore the mere presence of Christian neighbors can be expected to influence the perceptions of Christianity among Muslims in America.

In South Asia, people groups tend to remain within their unique demographic regions, and this trend may be expected to some degree in the United States among immigrants from that region.

It is reasonable also to expect that many incorrect perceptions held by South Asian Muslim immigrants will be rectified to some extent over time because of their experiences with Christian neighbors in the context of America. This correction of misperceptions will doubtless affect attitudes and reduce negative biases toward Christianity.

Perceptions generally tend to change over time with exposure to new ideas and information, unless there is an environment of regular reinforcement. Therefore, it is to be expected that experiences of South Asian Muslims in their new homeland in America will obviously influence and modify their perceptions of Christianity over time.

First-generation South Asian Muslims hold many misperceptions of Christianity in common with their counterparts back in their native land. Yet it is reasonable to expect how strongly they retain these misperceptions is more likely to be modified by their experiences and observations in their new homeland.

It is also reasonable to expect the second- and third-generation South Asian children of immigrants to have perceptions of Christianity that are somewhat different from their parents and grandparents. For example, while the mosques in America continue the indoctrination of the children of South Asian Muslims, the fact that these children are educated in public schools clearly has an influence on their perception of Christianity. Since public schools obviously reflect the culture of the United States—and part of that culture includes Christian influences and views—and many classmates and new friends will be Christian, the children of South Asian Muslims generally may become better informed and more tolerant of Christianity and even less devout as Muslims.

THEOLOGICAL INFLUENCES THAT HISTORICALLY HAVE SHAPED PERCEPTIONS OF CHRISTIANITY AMONG SOUTH ASIAN MUSLIMS

This section explores theological influences that historically have imparted and shaped perceptions of Christianity among South Asian Muslims. These influences are varied, and perceptions are diverse; yet there are many perceptions of Christianity held in common among Muslims in South Asia and by South Asian Muslims in America.

In this section I include both positive and negative perceptions of Christianity among different Muslim groups in South Asia and how the various perceptions held by these groups were acquired historically. However, the majority of these perceptions are erroneous at least in some respects.

The theological influences considered here arose from various Islamic reform movements, such as Deobandi, Barelwi, Tablighi Jama'at, and Ahmadiyya, and from other sources of influence such as Sufism, including syncretism and folk Islam, and Islamism (radical elements of Islam). The influences examined here are not exhaustive but are representative of the major theological influences that have historically imparted perceptions of Christianity in the minds of South Asian Muslims.

Although perceptions of Christianity among South Asian Muslims have been imparted by these historical influences, these perceptions do not remain static but obviously change over time due to exposure to various influences within the social and religious environment.

For example, the effects of demography on perceptions of Christianity are discussed by Hugh Goddard. He points out that the way Christianity is viewed is quite different for the Muslim writer in India and the Muslim writer in Pakistan:

> The fact that within the South Asian subcontinent [India, Pakistan, Bangladesh] the Muslim and Christian communities in India are both minorities whereas in Pakistan there is a Muslim majority with a small Christian minority does something to explain the difference between the Indian Muslim and the Pakistani Muslim [literary] works about Christianity. (Goddard 1996, 174)

In South Asian Muslim society, religion exerts a significant theological influence even in Muslim-minority countries such as India, Sri Lanka, Nepal, and Bhutan. These religious influences historically have produced and shaped perceptions of Christianity in the minds of the South Asian Muslims. In societies where Islam is dominant, religion is interwoven with the government, culture, language, and ethnicity, and this has an even greater influence on shaping perceptions of Christianity.

A wide variety of theological influences in the history of Islam in South Asia have imparted and shaped the perceptions of Christianity among Muslims in this region. These influences have produced a composite of perceptions of Christianity that is quite consistent among the majority of South Asian Muslims, including those who have immigrated to America.

THE INFLUENCE OF ISLAMIC REFORM MOVEMENTS IN SOUTH ASIA

In the middle of the nineteenth century, some Islamic reform movements started on the Indian subcontinent, especially those native to the region. All these movements trace their origin to the eighteenth century when the Moghul Empire declined, and the British colonial era started. These movements originally began in reaction to the British presence, insisting on the superiority of Islam in comparison to other religions.

During the British colonial rule, misperceptions of Christianity increased among Muslims in South Asia because they identified Christianity with colonial imperialism, which they came to hate.

The modern missionary movement began in South Asia during the colonial era (1757–1947), and in many cases, Western colonial rulers provided freedom of access for Christian missionaries. George W. Braswell stated:

> Muslims regard the loss of political autonomy to "Christian" colonial powers as part and parcel of a continuing Christian Crusade. The Crusades, colonialism and Christianity are, for most Muslims, synonymous. Most Muslims in the Islamic Republics believe that Christianity is colonialistic, imperialistic, and political movement to dominate the world, including the lands of Islam. They have looked upon Europe and the U.S. as Christian entities whose government and foreign affairs have been improvised to dominate Muslim societies politically, economically, culturally, and religiously. They have seen Christian missionaries as agents of Western imperialistic societies. (Braswell 1996, 81)

In many cases, Christian missionaries themselves failed to differentiate between Christianity and colonial imperialism, although there were many notable exceptions.

In this section I discuss Muslim reformist groups and their activities in South Asia, especially in the socioreligious and political context of the Indian subcontinent. I further explain how these reform movements influenced Muslim society and exacerbated misperceptions of Christianity, which still today influence the perceptions of South Asian Muslims in America.

These reform movements mainly started among Sunni Muslims who were then the majority in South Asia and still are today. Shi'a Muslims are the minority in all South Asian countries. The specific movements included in this discussion are Deobandi, Barelwi, Tablighi Jama'at, and Ahmadiyya.

Deobandi. Deobandi is an Islamic reformist group established in 1887 and named after a town, Deoband, ninety miles north of Delhi, the capital of India. Deobandi became a strong Islamic reform movement in reaction to British colonial rule on the Indian subcontinent. In the minds of the South Asian Muslims, Christianity was typically associated with British colonial rule and British culture, which influenced their perceptions of Christianity.

In November 2009, the Combating Terrorism Center (CTC) in America published an article entitled "The Past and Future of Deobandism," written by Luv Puri, about the historical development of the Deobandi reformist group and their influence even in modern-day South Asia as well as in other Islamic countries. Luv Puri stated:

> The Deobandi school of Islam was founded in the latter half of the 19th century. It was part of a series of revivalist movements that were sweeping British India during the time … In 1867, Darul Uloom [Deobandi Seminary or training school] was founded in the town of Deoband as one of the first major seminaries to impart training in Deobandi Islam. By 1967, Darul Uloom had graduated 3,795 students from present-day India, 3,191 from Pakistan and present-day Bangladesh, and 431 from multiple other countries, such as Afghanistan, China, and Malaysia. (Puri 2009, 1)

The main objective of this reformist group was to guard the Islamic orthodox faith on the Indian subcontinent against the infiltration of any foreign culture or religion, especially Christianity. Although it was not the intention of the British colonial rulers to introduce Christianity into Islamic society, nevertheless there was the perception that this was their intent. It was rather the expansionist ambitions of the British East India Company that motivated them to come to India. John Keay states:

Coherent policies are hard to distinguish; it was the *ad hoc* and reactive nature of British expansion which convinced so many that dominion was fortuitous. But if coherence was lacking, cohesion was not. (Keay 2000, 385)

Christianity was already introduced into India long before Islam was introduced into India by the Arab invaders (711 AD), and well before the coming of the British colonialists in the eighteenth century. In fact, some historians have proposed that Christianity was first introduced to India in the middle of the first century by one of the twelve disciples of Jesus (Thomas) mentioned in the gospel of John 20:24–29. J. Herbert Kane points out:

The apostle Thomas is said to have reached India in A.D. 52 and labored there for twenty years before his martyrdom near Madras. The Mar Thoma Church in South India is named after him. (Kane 1978, 124)

Because the Deobandi extremists perceived the presence of Christianity as a threat to Islam, they were also in favor of jihad (holy war) to protect the Muslim people in all countries where Islam is practiced. Today in some regions of South Asia, orthodox and extremist Deobandis hold jihadi views.

This emphasis on jihad is characteristic of many Sunni who belong to the Deobandi reformist group. R. Upadhyay points out:

> Although, the Deobandi movement of Sunni Islam was initially launched against the British rule for restoration of Islamic power but gradually it hardened its interpretation of Islam to the extent that the first loyalty of the Muslim is to his faith and only then to the country of his abode. It maintains that the religious boundary of Ummah (Muslim community as a whole) is only the national boundary of the Muslims. They also prescribe that the Muslims have

a religious obligation to wage Jihad to protect the right of
Muslims in any part of the world. (Upadhyay 2010, 1)

This suggests that the Deobandi are against any teaching that
opposes their views; therefore, they perceive Christianity also as a
threat to Islam, which motivates them to guard against any influence
of Christianity.

As mentioned by Upadhyay, Deobandi reformists were Sunni
Muslims. They belonged to *Hanafi*, one of the schools of thought
in Islamic jurisprudence (*Madhhab*). John L. Esposito in the *Oxford
Dictionary of Islam* describes the Hanafi School as the "Most widespread
school of Islamic law, followed by roughly one third of the world's
Muslims." (Esposito 2003, 7) It is assumed that most South Asian
Sunni Muslims in America also embrace this Hanafi school of thought,
because the majority of Sunni Muslims in South Asia belong to the
Hanafi school of thought.

Ali S. Asani states:

> The vast majority of Muslims in South Asia are Sunni,
> relying on Sunni Ulama, or religious scholars, for guidance
> on matters of faith. Generally speaking, the Shafi'i school
> of jurisprudence prevails among Sunni communities in
> southern and southwestern India and Sri Lanka, whereas the
> Hanafi school is widespread elsewhere in the subcontinent.
> (Asani 2005, 4644)

From its inception, the Islamic Seminary in Deoband made a
sharp distinction between revealed or sacred knowledge and secular
knowledge. For that reason, the school excluded all learning that was
not obviously Islamic, forbidding Western style education and the study
of any subjects not directly related to the study of the Qur'an and
Hadith (collection of sayings and teachings of Mohammad) including
scientific studies. They associated Christianity with the Western style
of education and with colonial imperialism, which was the main reason
they rejected any Western or secular education and Christianity. Thus,
their perception of Christianity was that it is something repulsive to
them and to be rejected. Aminah Muhammad-Arif points out:

> Using teaching methods borrowed from the British, the
> Deobandi banned from their syllabus the teaching of English
> and "western" sciences, and taught instead the Qur'an, the
> *Hadis [Hadith]* and Islamic law and sciences. Urdu replaced
> Persian as the language of communication and of teaching.
> (Mohammad-Arif 2002, 21)

In America today, conservative South Asian Muslims reflect the influence of the Deobandi by bringing their children to the mosque to study the Qur'an and the Hadith for their religious education; however, the major part of their education is in the secular public school system.

The Deobandi oppose many practices of Sufism (mystical Islamic belief and practice), which is very popular among Muslims in many South Asian countries like Bangladesh. One of the practices of Sufism, the veneration of saints, which is also a practice of Catholicism, is vehemently opposed by Deobandi reformists. Thus, the Deobandi reformist would not only reject this practice of Sufism but also as practiced by Catholic Christians. Aminah Mohammad-Arif points out:

> The Deobandi movement drew its membership mainly from
> the Muslim elite of the day and was rooted in the tradition of
> some Sufi [Chistia] orders. It emphasized individual spiritual
> discipline, gained through the influence of a spiritual
> master, but was firmly opposed to any veneration of saints.
> (Mohammad-Arif 2002, 21)

In the following section I will be discussing Sufism in more detail. There was a growing misperception of Christianity among the Deobandi reformists that British colonial rulers in India were all Christians. In most cases the Christian missionaries in India, whose objective was to convert Muslims to Christianity, were under the protection of the colonial rulers. The South Asian Muslims in India had the accurate perception that the intent of the missionaries was to convert them away from Islam.

In America today, many South Asian Deobandi Muslims still retain the fear that their Christian neighbors want to convert them away from Islam, which is true of many of their Christian neighbors.

Even as Deobandi Muslims associated Christianity with British culture in South Asia, the South Asian Muslim immigrants to America associated Christianity with American culture.

It is my personal observation that among Sunni Muslims in South Asia, especially in India, Pakistan, and Bangladesh, people still have much respect for the Deobandi group. My interviews reveal that there is also much respect for the Deobandi among conservative South Asian Muslims in America.

After the partition of India in 1947, many graduates from the school in Deoband (Dar ul-Ulum), immigrated to Pakistan, where Islam was the dominant religion. Deoband is located in a region in India that became Hindu dominated. These graduates established many *Madrasas* (Islamic schools) on their own initiative, teaching the fundamentalist ideology of Deobandi. Later Islamic fundamentalist political parties in Pakistan patronized and gave funds to establish Deobandi Madrasas in different parts of the country.

In present-day Pakistan, these Madrasas promote anti-Christian teachings in their curriculum. They are not only against Christianity but also other versions of Islam. These Madrasas are only based on the Qur'an as they interpret it, and the Deobandi version of shariah (Islamic law). Modern-day Taliban is a product of these Madrasas. (*Kabir*, documentary on YouTube, posted 2013)

They are against Western influence and secular education, because these Madrasas are governed by extreme Deobandi groups who associate secular and Western education with Christianity.

Most of the senior leaders and teachers of these Madrasas were taught this extreme ideology from their indoctrination at Darul-Ulum (Seminary).

Thus, a negative perception of Christianity is promoted by extreme Deobandi in Pakistan that encourages anti-Christian activities. An example of this is the bombing at an Easter sunrise service in Lahore in 2016.

Immigrants from these areas also come to live in America and bring with them the anti-Christian attitudes and negative perceptions of Christianity absorbed while they were in their native lands.

Fundamentalist Muslims in modern-day South Asia have negative perceptions of Christianity instilled by Muslim indoctrination before they immigrate to the United States and hence bring these misperceptions with them. Their misperception is that America is a Christian nation, and therefore they have many negative impressions about Christianity associated with secular emphases and behavior they observe in America. They still associate America with imperialism, which they came to fear and hate back in South Asia, and still associate Christianity with these memories.

Originally Deobandi reformists did not support violence or any extremist activities in defense of Islam, but at the same time they were not open to other religious groups. The idea of the supremacy of their version of Islam was always in their minds. Deobandi in South Asia still associate Christianity with Western culture and civilization.

South Asian Muslims bring these misperceptions with them when they immigrate to the United States. In my experience through interfaith dialogues with South Asian Muslims in America, I have observed that this misperception is still common among South Asian Muslims, especially among the first and second generation.

Barelwi. Barelwi or Barelvi (Urdu pronunciation sounds the v. Urdu is one of the major languages in South Asia) arose as a Sunni Islamic movement in South Asia at the end of the nineteenth century (c. 1880), and was affiliated with the Hanafi School (one of the four major Islamic schools of jurisprudence or legal thought). The name itself traces its roots to the Indian town of Bareilly, the birthplace of the founder of the Barelwi movement, Ahmed Raza Khan Bareilly.

The Barelwi movement arose in reaction against the Deobandi opposition to British rule. The Barelwi also rejected the idea of a close association of Christianity with the British colonial authorities that was held by the Deobandi.

Also in contrast to the Deobandi, the Barelwi held a unique emphasis on *pirs* (spiritual masters, authoritative spiritual guides), shrines, and the veneration of saints.

Alex Philippon points out:

> Often overlooked by scholars, this theological school [Barelwi] was founded in the nineteenth century in colonial India in

reaction to "orthodox" assaults of reformist movements such
as the Deobandi and *Ahl-i Hadith*. Usually presented merely
as a counter-crusade against the repeated attacks against *pirs*
and shrines, or as a passionate defense of Sufi status-quo,
this phenomenon can also be considered a reform movement
in its own right. (Philippon, 2012, 111)

The Barelwi emphasized the uniqueness of Muhammad and gave
Muhammad a near divine, elevated status, which is highly criticized by
the Deobandi and orthodox Muslims. The Barelwi also commemorate
Muhammad's birthday (*Mawlid or Maulid*), which is a popular practice
among South Asian Muslims. The elevation of Muhammad's status is
unique to the Barelwi, and this can be seen as a possible parallel to
Jesus's divine status and the Christian observance of the birth of Christ
at Christmas. Aminah Mohammad-Arif points out:

> The role of saints and spiritual masters as intercessors to
> God; and the celebration of popular festivals [in particular
> *Maulid*, which commemorates the Prophet's birth]. The
> Deobandi contest these principles strongly: they condemn
> the veneration of saints, but above all the near-divine status
> given by the Barelwi to the Prophet. (Mohammad-Arif 2002,
> 21–22)

The Barelwi belief in Muhammad's uniqueness and divine nature
is in contradiction to major Christian doctrine, which embraces the
unique divinity of Jesus and makes no mention of Muhammad or any
other person being divine. The Qur'an also does not mention any notion
of Muhammad having a divine nature.

Describing their beliefs and practices, and the present-day growth
of this group, John L. Esposito states in the *Oxford Dictionary of Islam:*

> [The Barelwi movement] emerged as part of the religious
> debate among Islamic legal scholars as to how Muslim identity
> and action should be used to redeem India. Emphasizes
> primacy of Islamic law over adherence to the Sufi practices
> and personal devotion to the Prophet Muhammad. Since
> partition of India and Pakistan in 1947, has addressed leading

political issues for Muslims. Largely rural phenomenon when begun, but currently popular among urban educated Pakistanis and Indians. (Esposito 2003, 10)

The majority of Muslim adherents in South Asia (mainly on the Indian subcontinent) are Sunni Muslims who are divided into two subgroups (schools of thought), one is Deobandi and the other is Barelwi. It is reasonable to assume this division is also reflected in the South Asian Muslim population in America.

In recent years in Pakistan, the largest Muslim country in South Asia, a faction of the Barelwi group is becoming more extreme and fanatical. They commit a variety of violent attacks against non-Muslims, especially against Christians in Pakistan. They have taken advantage of the "Blasphemy Law" by bringing false accusations against Christians and have persuaded the government to persecute Christians.

The article "Pakistan's Blasphemy Law," written by Aakar Patel, published in the *Express Tribune* on August 26, 2012, stated that in 1982, President Ziaul Haq introduced an addendum to the original ordinance about blasphemy: "Whoever wilfully defiles, damages or desecrates a copy of the Holy Qur'an or of an extract therefrom or uses it in any derogatory manner or for any unlawful purpose shall be punishable with imprisonment for life." (Patel 2012, 1)

This addendum was further amended in 1986 under Prime Minister Muhammad Khan Junejo:

> Whoever by words, either spoken or written, or by visible representation or by any imputation, innuendo, or insinuation, directly or indirectly, defiles the sacred name of the Holy Prophet Muhammad [peace be upon him] shall be punished with *death*, or imprisonment for life, and shall also be liable to fine. (Patel 2012, 1) (Emphasis mine.)

These amendments to the blasphemy law made it legal to severely punish those convicted of blasphemy. Blasphemy was defined by the first amendment to mean anything that disrespects the Qur'an and by the second amendment as disrespecting the Prophet Muhammad, and the punishment could be a death sentence.

The definition of blasphemy can include the declaration that Jesus is God or saying something derogatory against Muhammad and the Qur'an, so Christians can be accused of blasphemy because they claim Jesus was God. In many cases this "blasphemy act" is used today to persecute Christians in Pakistan.

In 2011, Muhammad Ismail Khan, in his article "The Assertion of Barelvi Extremism," (published by the Hudson Institute in America), describes how Barelwis in Pakistan embrace extremism and violence through enforcing the shariah law regarding "blasphemy." Muhammad Ismail Khan stated:

> On January 4, 2011, Salman Taseer, the governor of the Pakistani province of Punjab, was shot to death in the capital city of Islamabad by one of his bodyguards, Malik Mumtaz Qadri. In his confession statement, Qadri said that he committed the cold- blooded murder to avenge the governor's public criticism of Pakistan's blasphemy law. The controversial law provides for punishments, ranging from fines to death sentences, for those found guilty of desecrating religion. Governor Tasser emerged as an outspoken critic of the law through his advocacy of leniency in the case of Aasia Bibi, a poor Christian woman convicted to death on November 11, 2010, for allegedly speaking "ill" against the Prophet Muhammad [a charge that Aasia Bibi flatly rejected], ... yet, two days after Taseer's murder, over five hundred Barelvi scholars from an organization called the *Jamaat Ahl–e-Sunnat Pakistan* (JASP) issued a statement that explicity warned mosque leaders not to offer Islamic funeral prayers for Salman Taseer. (Khan 2011, 1)

The founder of the Barelwi movement, Ahmed Raza Khan Bareilly did not associate Christianity with British colonial rule or with the idea that non-Muslims are infidels (enemies of Islam). Muslim extremist groups consider non-Muslims, especially Christians, infidels. Bareilly had a positive view of British rule in India and also did not support jihad (holy war) against the British colonialists. For that reason, he was accused of being a British agent.

Smith Paul in his *Facebook* blog, "A British Agent," wrote:

"[When the] British came to India, they brought forward some individuals to divide the Muslims and strengthen their rule. Mirza Ghulam Ahmed Qadyani and Ahmed Raza Khan Beralwi [Barelwi] were among those individuals. Both gave fatwas [legal ruling] that it is haram [forbidden] to fight the British." (Paul 2013, 1)

This means that the founders of both the Ahmadiyya movement and the Barelwi movement forbid fighting against the British.

Today in some countries and regions of South Asia, many Barelwis have departed from their original beliefs in and practices of jihadism (militant violence).

Barelwis are in modern day Pakistan, and in certain regions of India, such as Kashmir, as well as in Bangladesh. A small percentage of Barelwi Sunni Muslims in Bangladesh call themselves *Ahl al-Sunnah wa'l-Jamaah* (People of the Prophet's Way and Community) and this group does embrace the extreme jihadi idea with the objective of establishing Islam in every area of life, even through violent strategies and methods. It is reasonable to assume this same ideology is embraced by many South Asian Sunni Barelwi Muslims who immigrate to America. This ideology reflects their perception of Christians as infidels (enemies of Islam).

In 2011, Muhammad Ismail Khan, a noted Pakistani Islamic writer, gave a demography report in the article "The Assertion of Barelvi Extremism," published by the Hudson Institute in America: "According to one estimate, 15 percent of Pakistani's Sunni Muslims would consider themselves Deobandi and some 60 percent are in the Barelvi tradition" (Khan 2011, 1). It is almost impossible to determine the percentage of South Asian Barelwi Muslims in America who hold to the jihadi idea (militant force) of the Barelwi group named Ahl al-Sunnah wa'l-Jamaah. However, estimates clearly indicate a majority of South Asian Muslims are Barelwi, and it is reasonable to expect that the influence of the Barelwi movement will be exerted on South Asian Muslims in America.

The interviews conducted as part of the research for this book include questions about Barelwi perceptions of Christianity.

The Barelwi movement has had a significant influence on the diversity of perceptions of Christianity in South Asia through its teachings and ideology; however, many of their perceptions are negative, and their teaching opposes important Christian doctrines. This same influence can be found also in America among the South Asian Muslims.

Tablighi Jama'at. The Tablighi Jama'at (Society for spreading faith), was established in the twentieth century in India as a revivalist and Islamic missionary movement among Sunni Muslims. Tablighi Jama'at remains closely connected with Deobandi, but with a reformist emphasis on spreading the faith of Islam. In 2010, the Pew Research Center published an article, "Tablighi Jama'at," about the beginnings of the Tablighi Jama'at movement on the Indian subcontinent. The article states:

> Theologically, the Tablighi Jama'at movement is closely tied to the scriptural [the Qur'an], conservative Deobandi school of Sunni Islam, which emphasizes strict adherence to religious orthodoxy. Most of the religious scholars and leaders associated with Tablighi Jama'at are followers of Deobandism. (Pew Research 2010, 1)

This movement emphasizes spiritual renewal for every individual Muslim in faith and practice. Aminah Mohammad-Arif also states, "Its main aim was to encourage Muslims to purify their religious practices and create an Islamic environment" (Mohamad-Arif 202, 21).

Since the beginning, Tablighi Jama'at has an aggressive zeal for spreading Islam. To proselytize people from other religions through preaching Islam is one of its objectives. Their methodology is called *Da'wah* (invitation) to embrace Islam. Muslims (both practicing and nonpracticing) believe that Islam is the only true religion. The teaching of Tablighi Jama'at goes beyond that belief, to stress that every individual Muslim has an obligation to share the faith with non-Muslims and invite them to embrace Islam. In September 2016, the Pew Research Center republished the article "Tablighi Jama'at," to include the teachings and practices of Tablighi Jama'at. This article states:

> The *Tablighi Jama'at* [Society for spreading faith] is a global educational and missionary movement whose primary purpose is to encourage Muslims everywhere to be more religiously observant. According to the teachings of Tablighi Jama'at, the reformation of society is achieved through

personal spiritual renewal. To this end, the group encourages its followers to undertake short-term preaching missions, known as *Khuruj*, in order to reinforce the religious norms and practices that, in its view, underpin a moral society. (Pew Research 2016, 1)

Tablighi Jama'at is a growing Islamic missionary organization and has spread not only on the Indian subcontinent but also to North America. Concerning the Tablighi Jama'at expansion, Aminah Mohammad-Arif points out, "The Tablighi Jama'at grew under the leadership of Ilyas' son Muhammad Yusuf (1917–65), spreading not only through the subcontinent, but also to the rest of the world, and especially to North America" (Mohammad-Arif 2002, 21).

Although Tablighi Jama'at claims to have no political ambition, they cooperate with Jama'at-i-Islami in political activities. Aminah Mohammad-Arif wrote:

> Founded by Muhammad Ilyas (1885–1944) between 1925 and 1927, this movement (Tablighi Jama'at) and the Jama'at-i-Islami [the largest Islamic militant and political organization in South Asia] together make up the two largest Islamic organizations created in the twentieth century in South Asia. (Mohammad-Arif 2002, 21)

In 2016, the United States Institute of Peace published an article, "Islamist Networks: The case of Tablighi Jama'at," about the influence of Tablighi Jama'at within the Islamic society in South Asia and in the West. This article states:

> South Asia is by far the most significant region for the group [Tablighi Jama'at], with Mecca and Medina also serving as important geographical symbols. The organization is diverse and includes persons from nearly every sector of society across the countries of South Asia and beyond. Within South Asia, members of the lower-middle class and the business community have joined the group and some members even hold government posts. In the West, second and third generation Muslim diaspora make up the main pool of

Tablighis. This demographic usually has little knowledge of Islam but are also not fully assimilated to culture in the West. (The United States Institute of Peace 2016, 1)

In Bangladesh, one of the South Asian Muslim countries, Tablighi Jama'at is very popular. Yogindar S. Sikand mentioned that Tablighi Jama'at "is undoubtedly one of the most popular Islamic movements in contemporary Bangladesh" (Sikand 2007, 1).

I have the impression that the methodology of Tablighi Jama'at is similar to that employed by some evangelical Christian churches in America. They train and engage individual Muslims in house visits where *da'wah* (invitation to embrace Islam) is employed to encourage non-Muslims to come and learn about Islam. Whether or not Tablighi Jama'at leaders are aware that their methodology is similar to that of conservative evangelical Christians is an open question. Even if they are aware of this, there remains the competition for the allegiance of adherents, and the perception of Christianity as a competitor with contradictory doctrines is clearly held by the Tablighi Jama'at.

Inasmuch as the Tablighi Jama'at movement strongly associates Christianity with some immoral practices in American society, they would also, in response to this perceived threat, redouble their efforts to recruit followers.

In their new home in America, many South Asian Muslims perceive a threat to their traditional values and religious practices and associate Christianity with the offensive practices they observe in their new surroundings. They have a clear perception that Christianity and Christian influences in their social environment in America are antithetical to their beliefs. This may cause them to become more rigorous in their observance of Islam, especially when they first arrive here. This makes them prime targets for Tablighi Jama'at recruitment.

Khalid Duran and Daniel Pipes have made a study of the religious life of Muslim immigrants:

> Do immigrants become more religious or less so on arrival in the United States? Those who embrace the freedoms America offers and become religiously less observant [or even convert out of Islam], are acting out what they could not express in

> the home countries. In contrast, about one third of Muslim immigrants say they have become more religious in the United States. Their increased piety has two main sources, cultural and moral. On the cultural level, immigrants respond to the strangeness of a new land by emphasizing familiar rituals and spending time at the mosque. On the moral level, they respond to the radical oneness of American life by emphasizing their hitherto neglected faith. (Duran and Pipes 2002, 1)

In conclusion, the perception of Christianity among Tablighi Jama'at is that Christianity is a competitor of Islam. Christians try to proselytize non-Christians including Muslims. Tablighi Jama'at also seeks to proselytize non-Muslims. Thus there is competition for adherents. The Tablighi Jama'at response is to perceive Christianity as an enemy of their particular brand of Islam, and to try to counter the influences of Christianity in their community. In order to protect their faith and practices of Islam, they urge every individual Muslim to propagate his/her faith and invite non-Muslims to embrace Islam.

Ahmadiyya. The Ahmadiyya movement started as a liberal, progressive Islamic movement on the Indian subcontinent during the British colonial rule in the nineteenth century. The founder of this group was Mirza Ghulam Ahmad. He was born in Qadian, which is now a part of the Indian state of Punjab. This movement was named after him. The group was also called Qadiani because the founder was born in Qadian.

After the partition of India in 1947, many of Ahmad's followers and his successors immigrated to Pakistan and claimed to be a separate sect of Islam. Aminah Mohammad-Arif points out:

> Alongside the Sunni and Shi'a [the two mainline Islamic sects], a third strand of Islam [Ahmadiyya] has emerged in South Asia. This sect is similar to Sunni Islam but presents certain characteristics which put it in its own category. (Mohammad-Arif 2002, 28)

From the beginning, this group and its founder Mirza Ghulam Ahmad have been strongly criticized by both Muslims and Christians. Ergun Mehmet Caner and Emir Fethi Caner state:

After his death in 1908, the movement continued, both in mission activity and opposition [to orthodox Islamic groups]. In 1974, after an examination of all the evidence presented for and against the Qadians (Ahmadiyya), the Muslim World League [*Rabita Alame Islami*] passed a unanimous resolution declaring that the Qadiani movement and its leaders were apostate and outside the fold of Islam. (Caner and Caner 2002, 170)

The Muslim World League is a collaboration of orthodox Muslim groups. The Ahmadiyya group is still considered as heretical by orthodox Muslims from the mainline Islamic sects in Pakistan and other countries of South Asia. Beginning in 1974, the Ahmadiyya also have faced opposition from the government of Pakistan. Aminah Mohammad-Arif points out:

Since the 1950s they [Ahmadiyya] have been attacked by "orthodox" Muslims. In 1974 they were declared, in an amendment to the constitution, to be non-Muslim, and since then they have been seen as a minority, and regularly persecuted. (Mohammad-Arif 2002, 29)

There are two main reasons why Ahmadiyya adherents are not recognized as Muslim by the main Islamic sects, Sunni and Shi'a. The first reason is that the founder of Ahmadiyya claimed to be a prophet, declaring that he fulfilled all the qualifications of prophethood. Another claim was that he is the promised Messiah (*Mehdi or Mahdi*) of Christian and Shi'a teaching. Islamic doctrine holds that only the prophets mentioned in the Qur'an are legitimate. Moreover, according to the Qur'an, Muhammad is the final prophet. After Muhammad, there are no other prophets. "Mohammad is not the father of any man among you, but a messenger of God, and the seal of the prophets. God has knowledge of everything" (Surah 33:40). Aminah Mohammad-Arif states:

Prophetology lies at the heart of Ahmadi doctrine, and is also the main cause of hostility from its opponents. Ghulam Ahmad reckoned that he possessed the spiritual qualities required of a Prophet and considered himself to be one. This allegation contradicted Sura 33:40, which calls Muhammad the "seal of the prophets" [khatam al-anbiya], and it has therefore been opposed by the Sunni from the start. (Mohammad-Arif 2002, 29) ("Seal of the prophets" means the final prophet.)

The second reason that Ahmadiyya are not recognized as Muslim by the main Islamic sects is because they believe that Jesus was crucified. This claim is against Islamic teaching and the Qur'an even though it is in basic agreement with Christian doctrine.

However, although Ahmadiyya believe Jesus was crucified, they believe that Jesus did not actually die on the cross, but rather swooned and soon revived and continued his work, only to die a natural death later. This is not in agreement with either Islamic or Christian teaching.

The Qur'an declares that Jesus did not die, and also that there was no Crucifixion, but Jesus was lifted directly up to heaven by God. "But God raised him [Jesus] up [in position] and closer to Himself; and God is all-mighty and all-wise" (Surah 4:158). Mainline Islamic sects have denounced the Ahmadiyya movement as deviating from the true teachings of Islam concerning Jesus's death.

The founder of Ahmadiyya, Mirza Ghulam Ahmad, further taught that in order to continue his work on earth, Jesus traveled to Srinagar (Kashmir), India, where he died and was buried.

Ahmad wrote the book *Jesus in India,* in Urdu in 1899 (translated from Urdu to English, fully revised in 2003), in which he stated:

> The innocence of Jesus has not only been proved a priori but also a posteriori. For hundreds of thousands of people have, with their own eyes, seen that the tomb of Jesus lies in Srinagar, Kashmir. As Jesus was crucified at Golgotha or the site of the skull, his tomb too has been found at the site of the skull i.e. Srinagar. That the word *sri* [in Hindi means skull] should occur in the names of both places is a strange coincidence indeed. (Ahmad 2003, 61–62)

The claim that Jesus traveled to India and finally died there obviously has no historical or archeological evidence. Jocelyne Cesari points out:

> These [Ahmadiyya] claims also further undermined
> Christian doctrine, a move further exemplified in Ghulam
> Ahmad's assertion that Jesus died in Srinagar, India, rather
> than on the cross. (Cesari 2007, 28)

Since Sunni is the predominant Islamic sect in South Asia, it can be assumed they are probably the majority among South Asian Muslims in America. Ahmadiyyas are very much a minority community in South Asia.

Beginning in 1960, In order to avoid persecution, an increasing number of Ahmadiyya, especially from Pakistan, started immigrating to America. The Ahmadiyya group has a strong missionary zeal to proselytize people outside their faith including Christians.

In 2014, the Pluralism Project of Harvard University, directed by Diana L. Eck, updated their online post, "World Religion in Greater Boston," to include the migration of Ahmadiyyas to the United States, especially to Massachusetts, and on their mission to proselytize: "Ahmadia [Ahmadiyya] Muslims came to the United States on formal proselytizing missions in the 1920s" (Pluralism Project 2014, 1).

Their objective of proselytizing Christians implies their perception of Christianity as those in need of being converted to Islam, hence obviously Christians are seen by Ahmadiyya as unbelievers (infidels). However, compared to other Islamic fundamentalist groups, Ahmadiyya are more willing to dialogue with Christians about matters of faith. Even though they see Christians in general as infidels, they nevertheless advocate open dialogue between Christian and Muslim.

Ahmadiyya also believe in jihad (struggle) against those who are outside the Islamic faith (their unique interpretation of Islam) including Christians. But their idea of jihad emphasizes nonviolence. In 2007, John H. Hanson wrote an article, "Jihad and the Ahmadiyya Muslim Community: Nonviolent Efforts to Promote Islam in the Contemporary World," in *Nova Religio: The Journal of Alternative and Emerged Religions*:

> Ghulam Ahmad also claimed as the spiritual manifestation
> as the Messiah and Mahdi to usher in a new era in which
> nonviolent activities alone defined jihad. These arguments

have not persuaded most Muslims, but the Ahmadiyya Muslim
community continues to stress jihad of the pen, that is, efforts to
promote and defend Islam in various media. (Hanson 2007, 77)

It should be noted that the word *jihad* is used in two different senses.
One meaning is the familiar "holy war," which implies violent force. The
other meaning is "struggle," which suggests a possible nonviolent use
of the term.

In conclusion, the founder of the Ahmadiyya movement, Mirza
Ghulam Ahmad, promoted a reform of Islam, advocating anti-Christian
doctrines, such as the swoon theory, and claiming himself to be
the promised Messiah. His claims not only went against Christian
doctrines, but Qur'anic teachings about Jesus as well. Hence, he faced
the opposition of both Christian and mainline Muslim. Ahmadiyya
obviously have a wrong perception of the Christian doctrines of the
Crucifixion and Resurrection, as well as the promised Messiah.

THE INFLUENCE OF SUFISM ON
PERCEPTIONS OF CHRISTIANITY

In this section, first of all I explore the definition of Sufism from scholarly
perspectives, in order to show the differences between ideologies of
Islamic reform movements and Sufi philosophy. I then present a brief
historical background of Sufism in South Asia. I further discuss the
development of syncretism within Sufism in South Asia and how this
syncretism, mixed with folk Islam, shapes perceptions of Christianity
among Muslims in South Asia. This, in turn, is reflected among South
Asian Muslims in America.

Definition of Sufism. When we think about mysticism in Islam,
Sufism first comes to mind. R. Upadhyay defines Sufism as:

> Mystic interpretation of Islamic life within the bonds of
> religious orthodoxy is known as Sufism, which was initially
> launched by God fearing people of the Perso-Arab world.
> They renounced the world and devoted themselves to His
> service. (Upadhyay 2004, 924)

In *the Oxford Dictionary of Islam* John L. Esposito defines Sufism:

> Islamic mysticism often referred to as the internalization and intensification of Islamic faith and practice. Sufis strive to constantly be aware of God's presence, stressing contemplation over action, spiritual development over legalism, and cultivation of the soul over social interaction. In contrast to the academic exercises of theology and jurisprudence, which depend on reason, Sufism depends on emotional and imagination in the divine-human relationship. (Esposito 2003, 302)

Sufism emphasizes God's love and a love relationship between the devotee and God. Phil Parshall describes Sufism:

> The Muslim mystic hopes, even in this mortal life, to win a glimpse of immortality. This is done by passing away from self into an absorption in the consciousness of God. He feels confident this experience will lead him, after death, to enjoy an eternity with his Lord and with the angels and prophets. The Sufi generally places more emphasis on his relationship to God in this life than on that which is to come. (Parshall 1983, 27)

Although militant Islamists dominate the headlines, the Sufi ideal of nonviolence has captured the imagination of many Islamic adherents. Sufism played an important role in the spread of Islam, particularly on the Indian subcontinent. John Bowker describes Sufism:

> Sufism is usually treated as a single phenomenon, although it is made up of different strands and styles. Sufism is a major part of Islam, and Sufis have been particularly important in the spread of Islam. In the eighteenth and nineteenth century, at least half [perhaps as many as three quarters] of the male Muslim population was attached in some sense of Sufi *tariqa* [order]. (Bowker 1997, 925)

Sufism is a form of Islam that places more emphasis on a personal relationship with God. Wilfred Cantwell Smith has pointed out, "Sufism stresses the individual rather than society, the eternal rather than the historical, God's love rather than His power, and the state of man's heart rather than behavior" (Smith 1957, 44–45). Thus, Sufism in these respects is closer to Christian emphases than mainline Islam.

There are several ways Sufism has similar emphases to Christianity: emphasis on God's love, on the personal relationship with God, on eternity as more important than this life, on what is in the heart as more important than external observance of law (works), and on inner cleansing being more important than outward cleansing, on the awareness of God's presence, etc. These Sufi emphases are similar to those found in Christianity, but are not typical of the mainline Islamic sects.

The Sufi emphasis on the veneration of saints is also comparable to Catholicism, and the emphasis on pirs (authoritative spiritual guides) is similar in some respects to Catholic priests; however, these emphases are not generally comparable to Protestantism.

Sufism also focuses on the transformation of the inner being. Phil Parshall stated:

> The Muslim mystic hopes, even in this mortal life, to win a glimpse of immortality. This is done by passing away from self into absorption in the consciousness of God. He feels confident this experience will lead him, after death, to enjoy an eternity with his Lord and with the angels and prophets. The Sufi generally places more emphasis on his relationship to God in this life than on that which is to come. (Parshall 1983, 27)

Radical or fundamentalist Muslims criticize Sufis. They say that Sufism is against Islamic law (Shariah). John Bowker wrote, "The Sufi experience of absolute reality [*haqiqa*] is not opposed to Shari'a [or shariah] [Islamic law], but is its foundation" (Bowker, 1997, 925).

Sufism emphasizes more the cleansing of the inner self rather than the performance of ritual outer cleansing. John A. Subhan, a former Sufi converted to Christianity, has commented, "Sufism, like other forms of mysticism, emphasizes not the performances of external ritual, but rather the activities of the inner self" (Subhan 1938, 6).

Some practices of Sufism distinguish them from the mainline orthodox Muslims. David W. Shenk comments on Sufism he observed in his extensive travels:

> In Muslim communities across the African Continent saint veneration and mysticism abound. Recently I visited central Java, Bangladesh, and southern Yugoslavia, and found that in these widely diverse Muslim communities, saint veneration and mysticism are persistent. And the experience and practice of saint veneration were amazingly consistent. This is especially remarkable, because in each community the orthodox institutions are always in tension with this widespread popular expression of Islam. (Shenk 1981, 1)

So based on these definitions by scholars, we can conclude that Sufism is not specifically a separate sect of Islam. Rather it is a mystical movement overlaying the two mainline Islamic sects (Sunni and Shi'a) as well as being practiced in some other Islamic organized movements. Any Muslim can be Sufi. It's a spiritual movement within Islam. It can be compared with Pentecostal influence in the United States, spanning a wide range of denominations.

Historical Background of Sufism. In the early part of the eighth century, Arab invaders came into South Asia with the objective of introducing Islam. These invaders were followed by Arab traders and later by Sufi missionaries, who preached Islam to the local people.

The Arab invaders who came to South Asia first invaded Sindh, a province of modern-day Pakistan. Anjana Narayan and Bandana Purkayastha have pointed out:

> Sindh is known as *Bab-ul-Islam*, the Gateway to Islam, as Islam entered India and South Asia through Sindh. In 711 A.D., Sindh was conquered by the famous Arab conqueror, Mohammad Bin Qasim. (Narayan and Purkayastha 2009, 72)

When Islam came to India, the majority of people in India of that time were Hindu. The main resistance against Islam and the Arab invaders came from the ruling class and from higher-caste Hindus. Most Hindus resisted the imposition of a foreign religion and culture on them. So few local Hindu willingly converted to Islam.

Sufism originated outside of South Asia. It is thought the movement originated in Iraq and Iran. On the Indian subcontinent today, there is a strong influence of Persian (Iranian) Sufism. Quoting from the book *The Persian Presence in the Islamic World,* edited by Richard G. Hovannisian and George Sabagh, Clinton Bennett wrote, "Many scholars label Sufism an 'essentially Persian [Iranian] product,' drawing on ancient Iranian mystical traditions" (Bennett 2012, 18).

The movement started as an ascetic movement, and it came to the South Asian region, mainly the Indian subcontinent, in the twelfth century. Rajib Singh in his article "Bhakti (devotion) and Sufi Movement" points out "Sufism reached India in the 12th century A.D. Its influence grew considerably during the thirteenth and fourteenth centuries" (Rajib Singh 2014, 1).

Although Christianity was introduced into India in the first century AD, it was concentrated in a very limited geographical area in South India. Christianity did not expand its efforts into other parts of India until the sixteenth century when Portuguese traders and Catholic missionaries began to have an influence. J. Herbert Kane points out:

> The Apostle Thomas [one of the twelve apostles of Jesus] is said to have reached India in A.D. 52 and labored there for twenty years before his martyrdom near Madras. The first Jesuit [one of the Catholic orders] missionaries landed in India in 1542. (Kane 1978, 124)

Sufism came to have a significant influence on the Indian subcontinent through its method of nonviolent persuasion. Phil Parshall has pointed out:

> After the military conquest of northern India, Sufis began to pour into the country. This peaceful and tolerant element of Islam impressed the conquered Hindus, whereas the more fanatical and militaristic orthodox Muslim priests were feared and hated. Almost all willing conversions were the result of the preaching of Sufi missionaries. (Parshall 1983, 33)

Today Sufism has come to have a wide influence in South Asia, especially on the Indian subcontinent. Sufism flourished in South Asia, and from there it expanded even as far as the United States.

Sufi emphases are distinct from the rigid doctrinal teachings of the traditional sects of Islam (Shi'a and Sunni). Kenneth Cragg states that "mystics [Sufis] are well known for their relative detachment from canons of orthodoxy and for the way in which they are apt to become doctrinally, a law unto themselves" (Cragg 1959, 80).

Sufism within Islam is not limited to one particular Islamic sect, but its emphases and practices are found in various sects and groups. Sufism is like an overlay among Sunni and Shi'a, as well as Deobandi, Barelwi, and some other reform movements. It can be compared to the charismatic influence across many denominations in the United States.

Sufism is a more inclusive form of Islam. Clinton Bennett has stated:

> Often described as the soul of Islam, Sufism is one of the most interesting yet least studied facets of this global religion. Sufism is the softer, more inclusive, and mystical form of Islam. Ethnographic compilations have presented research carried out in Europe and North America while the Sufi heartlands have attracted less attention. Yet nowhere in the world is the handprint of Sufism more observable than South Asia. Not only does the largest Muslim population of the world reside there but also the greatest concentration of Sufis. (Bennett 2012, 1)

Syncretistic Nature of Sufism Shapes Perceptions of Christianity. Sufism initially began as a spiritual revolt against worldliness and materialism in Islam. The Sufi movement not only grew into an established system of faith and worship within Islam, but also Sufism was noted in South Asia for its adaptation to the dominant existing social and religious milieu. This shows the syncretistic nature of Sufism and accounts for its popular appeal to the non-Muslim populous.

Syncretism was one of the major factors in the growth of Sufism in South Asia, especially on the Indian subcontinent. Because of the emphasis on syncretism, the Sufis are more tolerant of other religions, including Christianity. This further suggests that their perception of Christianity is different from the major Islamic sects that embrace the legalistic Islam (strict observance of shariah law) and reformist Islam, such as Deobandi, Tablighi Jama'at, and extremist Barelwi. Clinton Bennett points out:

> Elsewhere in the Muslim world, for example in much Arab space, legal Islam and reformist Islam totally reject Sufism. In the Subcontinent, the relationship between Sufism and reformist Islam is complex, complicated, even confusing, but they are not completely polarized. (Bennett 2012, 7)

Their emphasis on syncretism motivated Sufis to blend into the established indigenous culture and existing religious structures of the local people. This syncretism and inclusiveness of Sufism impressed the indigenous people, which helped the growth of Islam in the South Asian region, especially on the Indian subcontinent, in the twelfth century. Peter G. Gowing and William Henry Scott have described the effectiveness of syncretism in the methodology followed by Sufi missionaries:

> Are the "foreign" agents of religious acculturation insistent about the features of their own religion? Do they permit the indigenous population to combine some of their native religious beliefs with the new religious beliefs being introduced? This is a very crucial factor affecting what happens to the product: if sufficient force is used to keep the new religion "pure", the indigenous population may not accept any of it, because it is not offered in a permissive atmosphere. (Gowing and Scott 1971, 12)

In South Asia, Sufi syncretism is much closer to Christian Pietism in Europe. Because of the similar ascetic practices of Christian Pietists, many positive perceptions of Christianity developed among Sufis in South Asia. Larry Poston comments on this similarity:

> Just as pietist Christians were able to bypass the external institutional missiology of their time through the adoption of an internal-personal approach, Islamic history has developed a vehicle in Sufism capable of accomplishing a similar function. Islamic Sufism focuses upon internal

experience rather than external observances, advocates an
activist approach to sanctification. (Poston 1992, 62)

The syncretistic practices of Sufism make Sufis in South Asia more
tolerant of other religions, including Christianity. This Sufi tolerance
of Christianity is also reflected in the perceptions of Christianity by
many South Asian Muslims in America. This is demonstrated in the
interviews presented in this book.

Part of the emphasis on syncretism relates to how Jesus is perceived.
Jesus is portrayed as the "Perfect Man" by many Sufi poets, among
whom Ibn al-Arabi and Jalaluddin Rumi are prominent.

Milad Milani researched contemporary Sufism. In 2012, he wrote
an article, "Representation of Jesus in Islamic Mysticism: Defining Sufi
Jesus," in which he analyzed the views of two poets, Ibn al-Arabi and
Rumi Milad Milani states:

> Ibn al-Arabi's treatment of Jesus facilitates an important
> parallel between the life-giving power of Jesus, through his
> breath, and the way Jesus was conceived. Furthermore, Ibn
> al-Arabi asserts a particular harmony between the Qur'anic
> Jesus son of Mary [Isa ibn Maryam] and the biblical Jesus
> son of God. He [Ibn al-Arabi] suggests: "as the son of Mary,
> Jesus is human; but one who could revive the dead, Jesus
> was of God of Spirit." Both Ibn al-Arabi and Rumi perceived
> Jesus to be at the centre of the human imaginative and
> creative process, which was directly linked to God through a
> perception of him as the Perfect Man and the breath of God.
> It is obvious that the mystics carried the meaning of Jesus
> well beyond what we would normally identify as Islamic
> norms, and well beyond what was required of a prophet,
> whereby Jesus is imagined differently as having a special
> capacity to renew and transform human lives, to render them
> whole and complete. (Milani 2012, 45–65)

Concerning the Sufi treatment of Jesus, James Roy King wrote:

> What is unique about the treatment of Jesus across the vast
> corps of Sufi materials is that he is for them, emblematic

of several important qualities: purity, perfection, love, and healing. As a result, Jesus has maintained a consistent role in both orthodox and heterodox forms of Sufism.

Many ideas about Jesus in Sufi teaching are not found in the Qur'an or in the Bible. For example, Sufis accept the Qur'anic view that Jesus was taken to heaven, but Sufis added a further teaching that after being lifted into heaven, he became an angelic being. Irfan A. Omar edited the book *A Muslim View of Christianity: Essays on Dialogue by Mahmoud Ayoub*. Omar quotes Ayoub:

> Jesus was taken to heaven because his entrance into worldly existence was not through the gate of lusts; therefore, his departure from it was not through the gate of death. He rather entered through the gate of power [*qudrah*] and departed through the gate of majesty ['*izzah*]. [In heaven] God gave him wings and clothed him with light and removed from him the desires for food and drink, thus he flies with angels, and is with them around the throne. For he is human and angelic, heavenly and earthly. (Omar 2007, 179)

Sufis believe in Jesus's Second Coming, which is similar to the general beliefs of both Muslims and Christians. But the traditional Muslim theological perception differs from Christian doctrine about the role of Jesus after his Second Coming. According to Islamic teaching, after his Second Coming, Jesus will become a part of the Islamic community (*ummah*). Irfan A. Omar quotes Mahmoud Ayoub, in *A Muslim View of Christianity: Essays on Dialogue by Mahmoud Ayoub*, concerning Jesus's Second Coming:

> He shall return in the end to be a sign for the hour ['*ilm li sa'a*], that is, the Day of Resurrection and the seal of general *walayah* [saintship]. For after him, there is no *wali* [saint or friend of God] with whom God would close the Muhammadan cycle [*al dawrah al-Muhammadiyyah*]. [For in this] is its great ennoblement, in that it will be closed by a prophet-messenger who will be subject to the *Shari'ah*. Both Jews and Christians will believe in it [that

is, Islam]. Through him [Jesus] God will renew the age of prophethood for the community [ummah]. He shall be served by the *Mahdi* and the men of the cave. He shall marry and beget children. He shall be one of the community for Muhammad as the seal of his *awliya'* and heirs with regard to *walayah*. [Sufi theology posits two concentric cycles of prophethood and *walaya,* beginning with Adam and ending with Muhammad, the seal of the prophetic cycle. That of walayah will continue until the end of time. Jesus, however, will have the great privilege of culminating both cycles, being the perfect *wali* and perfect prophet]. For the spirit of Jesus is the manifestation of the greatest name, and an effulgence of divine power … ; he is the manifestation of the universal divine name, primordial inheritance. (Omar 2007, 179–80)

Concerning the divinity of Jesus, the perception of Sufis is similar to the views of Muslims in general. They consider Jesus as a "Slave of God." The same title was given to Muhammad in the Qur'an. Javad Nurbakhsh in his book *Jesus in the eyes of Sufis* points out:

God has privileged only two of His prophets by addressing them as His slaves: Muhammad and Jesus. In reference to Muhammad, the Qur'an says: "*When the slave of God stood up*" (72/19). The Qur'an also quotes Jesus as declaring from the cradle: "*I am the slave of God. He has given me a book of Scripture*" (19/30). Sufis believe that "slave of God" denotes the perfect devotee; the most complete of slaves on whom God has manifested all of His names. On account of having realized the name "Allah", which is God's Greatest Name and the All-embracing Name that encompasses all His attributes, he reaches the loftiest of stations and the most sublime degrees of human perfection. (Nurbakhsh 1983, 146)

As seen from this statement, Sufis consider Jesus "the perfect devotee." Sufis also believe that Jesus maintained a purely ascetic life. In this respect, Jesus was seen as a devout Sufi. Javad Nurbakhsh further comments:

Jesus was the acetic among the prophets, and attained such level of perfection in renunciation that he became completely detached from the whole world. Jesus liked poverty, which he understood as possessing nothing but God, and he has come to represent the epitome of this manner of devotion. (Nurbakhsh 1983, 150)

There are some common practices among all orders of Sufism such as veneration of saints, visiting tombs of saints, and use of music, meditation, and chanting the name of God or his attributes (*Dhikir or Zikr*). Similar practices exist also among some Christian groups in South Asia. A. M. A. Shushtery researched the origin of these practices of veneration of saints and visiting tombs of saints by Sufis:

The Prophet [Muhammad] was said to have given warning against making tombs a place of worship. Still, such veneration started very early among Muslims. This may have been due to the influence of then-prevalent Christian saint-worship in Syria and Egypt. The practice soon spread in Iran, where today more than a thousand known and unknown persons are worshiped [as saints]. (Shushtery 1938, 230)

Shushtery's research implies the adoption of these practices from some ancient Christian groups, although there is no biblical teaching supporting these particular practices. Sufi perception of Christianity is reflected in some of their practices.

Sufis have some practices in their worship similar to some found in Christian churches such as meditation, using loud music in worship, chanted recitation of scripture, charismatic dancing, as well as whooping and shouting. Currently there is no South Asian Sufi center organized by South Asians in America, but many South Asian Muslims in America embrace emphases and practices of Sufism brought by immigrants from South Asia.

In recent interviews with South Asian immigrants, I have found many who respect Sufism but do not strictly follow any Sufi order. They appear to me to be more open to attend charismatic Christian church services. At least four of those interviewed shared their opinion that veneration of saints in Sufism is a Catholic influence.

FOLK ISLAM AND ITS INFLUENCE ON PERCEPTIONS OF CHRISTIANITY

Folk Islam is a popular form of religious practice in Islam. Folk Islam is another modification of Sufism in South Asia, which has had a substantial influence in Islamic society and religious practice in that region.

In the South Asian region, many of the practices of folk Islam are intermingled with Sufism. Orthodox Muslims do not consider folk Islam as an acceptable part of Islam. They think this is animistic and occultist. William J. Saal points out, "Folk Islam shares much in common with traditional occultism; it is essentially animism with an Islamic veneer" (Saal 1993, 56).

Some of the characteristics of the practice of folk Islam include belief in *jinn* (supernatural creatures or demons), teachings found in early Arabian folklore and later Islamic mythology and theology. Jinn is associated with demons, magicians, fortune-tellers, healers, spiritual guides known as pirs, celebration of *urs* (anniversaries of the death of pirs and saints), and getting help from sorcery.

Folk Islam emphasizes the spirit world, including belief in demonic as well as good spirits. It is a common belief of ordinary people who practice folk Islam that their lives are regulated by the spirit world. Concerning the influence of folk Islam, William J. Saal writes:

> Every aspect of daily life, from birth to death, is governed by the spiritual realities of this [spirit] world. Ordinary Muslims regularly turn to the practice of folk religion to meet felt needs while considering themselves to be genuine followers of Islam." (Saal 1993, 51)

In Sufism as well as in folk Islam, the role of pirs (spiritual guides or mentors) is prominent in Muslim religious practice in South Asia. This emphasis on pirs may not directly relate to the Sufi or folk Islam perception of Christianity either in South Asia or in America. It is even suggested historically that ancient Christian practice in Asia was an influence on the development of the idea of pirs, although modern-day Sufis may have no association of that practice in their perception of Christianity. However, there are some striking similarities between Sufi pirs and Catholic priests:

> Both are officially recognized and usually held in high regard by the average adherent.
> Both are respected as influential counselors and guides in spiritual matters.
> Both are seen as mediators between the adherent and God.

Perhaps pirs are regarded by Sufis as having an even higher status than Catholic priests. For example, pirs are often considered to be saints. Pirs are revered human mentors and authority figures, who play an important role in Muslim religious practice and in society in South Asia. This is a direct influence of Sufism. Every family chooses their own Pir. Phil Parshall points out:

> In fact, the *pir* becomes a little god. He is to be followed in blind faith. The least word of a pir is absolute law to the disciples. Even if the *pir's* commands contravene the letter of the law, they must be fulfilled. Such is the overwhelming power of saint over devotee. The pact between saint and disciple can never be dissolved unilaterally by the will of the devotee. (Parshall, 1983, 57)

In the interaction between Sufi and Christian, the subject of pirs may arise and can be compared and contrasted with Catholic priests as a basis for dialogue and may help to clarify and modify some misperceptions of Christianity among Sufi Muslims.

One of the five pillars of Islam is the pilgrimage to Mecca (*Hajj*). When Muslims go to Mecca on a pilgrimage, they must perform certain rituals. William J. Saal, a scholar on Islam, associated these rituals with folk Islam:

> Folk practices and beliefs are often entwined with Islam's obligatory duties. For example, at the time of the pilgrimage,

the Black Stone in the Ka'aba is venerated; pilgrims press against the area between the stone and the door in the side of the Ka'aba. They hug the curtain and call upon God. They throw stones at a pillar that symbolizes demonic power. They take water from a sacred well to anoint the sick or dying. (Saal 1993, 52)

Saal's comments suggest that some of the rituals practiced by the pilgrims during the Hajj are associated with folk Islam. However, mainline Islamic sects do not accept Saal's views associating folk Islam with the observation of Hajj, because all these rituals during Hajj have become formalized as obligatory duties.

Both Sufis and practitioners of folk Islam believe in the intercessory role of Muhammad especially on the final judgment day, which compares to the Christian view of the role of Jesus Christ (Romans 8:33–34; Hebrews 7:25). According to this teaching, Muhammad will be an advocate for all Muslims on that day. Reynold Nicholson points out, "Sufis claim this assistance from Muhammad as part of their heritage ... The ideas developed in later folk Islam concerning the person of Muhammad show a remarkable likeness to what is known in Christian theology as the doctrine of a mediator" (Nicholson 1976, 66–67). However, the Qur'an is not clear about any intercessory role of Muhammad on judgment day; rather, the Qur'an makes it clear that no one can intercede: "on that day no intercession will matter other than his [Allah's] whom Ar-Rahman [one of the attributes of Allah as merciful] grants permission and accepts" (Surah 20:109).

This Sufi idea of the intercessory role of Muhammad came later, as a parallel to the idea of Jesus's intercessory role written in the Bible.

It is my impression, based on personal interviews, that while many South Asian Muslims in America believe in folk Islam, the practice of folk Islam in America is not as strong as in their native countries. But when they visit their homeland, many South Asian Muslims go to their own pirs in order to receive blessings and guidance, celebrate urs, and visit the tombs (mazars) and shrines of Sufi saints (dargahs). Based on interviews with South Asian Muslim friends in America, this is apparently a common practice.

In personal interviews, I have found at least ten Bangladeshi Muslims in America who are adherents of Sufism and engage in some practices of folk Islam. These people are more open to Christianity, compared to Orthodox Muslims. Their perception of Christianity is that Sufism and Christianity are very close, and they see Jesus was the great Sufi. However, they still perceive Christians as outside the fold of their true faith of Islam and as targets for proselytism. They do not consider Christians as enemies of Islam (*Kafir*). They understand that there are some doctrinal differences between Islam and Christianity, but they would agree that misunderstandings can be eliminated through learning truths about Christianity and through interaction and dialogue with knowledgeable Christians.

The teaching of Sufism is more inclusive than orthodox Islamic sects, and for that reason Sufism became very popular in the eastern part of Bengal, which is modern-day Bangladesh. Sufism was instrumental in spreading Islam in this part of India. Most Muslims in Bangladesh still have great respect for Sufi missionaries, who also significantly contributed to the spread of Islam on the Indian subcontinent. Clinton Bennett states:

> Bengali-flavored Islam, due to resonance with certain aspects of indigenous culture, brings to the fore important principles and potentialities in the Qur'an ... Iran, of course, also contributed to the way that Islam developed in Bangladesh, especially through Sufi thought. (Bennett 2012, 211–12)

The majority of Bangladeshi Muslims in America demonstrate a favorable view of Sufism. Sufism is also attractive to many Americans because of its inclusiveness and nonviolent nature. Many Americans have adopted some Sufi practices as part of a New Age Movement. Famous Sufi poets Jalaluddin Rumi, Inayat Khan, and Idris Shah are very popular in the United States. Their emphasis on universalism and tolerance, as well as their message of love and nonviolence, are attractive to many Westerners. These emphases reveal their objective of proselytizing Christians, which shows their perceptions of Christians as outside the true faith of Islam.

In conclusion, there is a great diversity of theological perceptions of Christianity among South Asian Muslims, which are somewhat different from Muslims in other parts of the world. Sufi emphasis on nonviolence and openness to interrelate with Christians helps to establish more congenial relationships. While Sufis are more open to interaction with Christians, they nevertheless perceive Christians as not true believers and targets for proselytism to Islam. Compared to other Islamic reform groups, Sufis have more positive perceptions of Christianity, which facilitates communicating the gospel to South Asian Muslims in America.

THE INFLUENCE OF ISLAMISM ON PERCEPTIONS OF CHRISTIANITY

In this section, first of all, I define the terms Islam, Islamism, and Islamist, and show the differentiation among these terms. Then I explore the Muslim groups that embrace the ideology of Islamism (called Islamists) and their ideological influence among South Asian Muslims in America. I further explore how the ideologies of Islamist groups affect perceptions of Christianity held by these immigrants.

Comparison of Islam and Islamism. Islam is a religion that teaches its followers to have complete submission to the Creator (Allah) and practices certain religious duties as a daily routine. The word *Islam* means submission and refers to submission to the will of God. Timothy George wrote, "The word *Islam* literally means 'submission' or 'surrender.' It comes from the Arabic root word *s-l-m*, which connotes peace in Semitic languages—as in Hebrew greetings *shalom* ..." (George 2002, 20) However, this is a mistaken idea of the definition of Islam.

The Arabic words *Salam* (peace) and *Islam* (submission) are derived from the same root word in Arabic; however, this does not mean they are closely related in meaning. Today many Islamic writers and Muslim clerics suggest a connection between these two words, insisting that the meaning of the word *Islam* is peace. This is incorrect. This is an attempt to present Islam as a peaceful religion; however, this is a misrepresentation of the way Islam is practiced and the violent elements and emphases in the religious practice. Through complete submission to God, one may achieve an inner peace, but the word *Islam* does not mean peace. In its common usage among Muslims, the term only refers to the Islamic religion.

Hammudah Abdalati states:

> In the religious sense the word Islam means submission to the will of God and obedience to His law. The connection between the original and the religious meanings of the word is strong and obvious. Only through submission to the will of God and by obedience to His Law can one achieve true peace and enjoy lasting purity. (Abdalati 1975, 7)

There is a significant difference between the terms *Islam* and *Islamism*. In the Western world, *Islamism* and *Islamists* are commonly used terms, and people understand that these two terms refer to the radical elements of Islam as a religion. Islamists are simply those who follow the ideology of Islamism. Islamism demands more than total surrender to God, rather also a commitment to a radical ideology. But the question arises, what is that ideology? In answer to this question, Daniel Pipes states:

> Islamism is an ideology that demands man's complete adherence to the sacred law of Islam and rejects as much as possible outside influence, with some exceptions [such as access to military and medical technology]. It is imbued with a deep antagonism towards non-Muslims and has a particular hostility towards the West. It amounts to an effort to turn Islam, a religion and civilization, into an ideology. Islamism is, in other words, yet another twentieth-century radical utopian scheme. Like Marxism-Leninism or fascism, it offers a way to control the state, run society, and remake the human being. It is an Islamic-flavored version of totalitarianism. The details, of course, are very different from the preceding versions, but the ultimate purpose is very similar. (Pipes 1998, 1)

Moussa Bongoyok agrees that Islamism is an ideology. He points out: "Islamism ... is the ideology held by fundamentalist and conservative Muslims that all of life, including the political and social realms, should be regulated by the way of God" (Bongoyok 2008, 298).

On January 27, 2010, Soner Cagaptay wrote an article, "Muslims vs. Islamists," published on *Hurriyet Daily News,* a leading news source in Turkey:

> While Islam is the faith of 1.4 billion people, Islamism is not a form of the Muslim faith or an expression of Muslim piety; it is, rather, a political ideology that strives to derive legitimacy from Islam. Islam and Islamism are not synonymous, and there is even a tension between the two. So, if Islam is a faith, then what is Islamism? It can be best described as an anti-ideology, in the sense that it defines itself only in opposition to things. That is, Islamism stands not for but against. Islamism is also anti-Christian, having a perverted view of the religion as well. (Cagaptay 2010, 1)

The author's comments still apply even though the current Muslim population in 2017 is 1.7 billion. (See Joshua Project.)

In writing about Islamism, Olivier Roy points out:

> Islamism was created both along the lines of and as a break from the *salafiyya.* The Islamists generally adopt Salafist [one of the Islamic schools of thought] theology: they preach a return to the Quran, the Sunna [Sunnah], and the *sharia* [shariah] [the Islamic law] and reject the commentaries that have been part of the tradition [the gloss, the philosophy, but also the four major legal schools, the *madhabib*] ... Three points clearly separate the Islamists from the fundamentalism of ulamas [theologians who interpret Islamic law]: political revolution, the *sharia,* and the issue of women. Islamists consider that the society will be Islamized only through social and political actions: it is necessary to leave the mosque ... The economy and social relationships are no longer perceived as subordinate activities that grow out of pious acts or the *sharia,* but are considered key areas. (Roy 1994, 35–36)

Roy further describes Islamists:

> For Islamists, the political detour is not an illusion, resulting in return to the point of departure: it is the means by which

a new conversion of the individual will occur. The political phase is the experience of total commitment, of a militancy inscribed within a psychological agenda. Respect for the *sharia* [Islamic law] is not the mechanical application of a formalist legalism; it is the translation of true virtue into human behavior. (Roy 1994, 65)

In the Western world, the word *Islamism* is understood to mean Muslim extremism, but some Muslims argue that Islamism is not necessarily extremism. In 2012, Maidul Islam, in his doctoral thesis, "Limits of Islamism: Ideological Articulations of Jama'at-i-Islami in Contemporary India and Bangladesh," explained Islamism in this way:

All "Islamic" people are definitely "Muslims" but not necessarily "Islamists", and all "Islamists" are certainly both "Muslims" and "Islamic." The examples of *Islamic* organizations are Tablighi Jamaat, Jamiat-Ulema-i-Hind, etc., while Jamaat-e-Islami [Jama'at-i-Islami], Al-Qaeda, Taliban, Hamas, Hezbollah, and the Muslim Brotherhood etc. can be categorized as *Islamist* organizations. However, Islamist organizations form a broad political spectrum, and we can differentiate them into three distinct groups in terms of operational strategies and attendant tactical questions related to the modes of capturing political power: 1) Moderate Islamists, 2) Mainstream Islamists, and 3) Extremist Islamists. The moderate Islamists generally choose parliamentary democratic methods like participation in elections and mass mobilizations, *Mainstream* Islamists use both parliamentary method and armed violence and *Extremist* Islamists, however, use only violent and terroristic methods. (Islam 2012, 7) (Emphasis mine.)

Although Maidul Islam includes one classification as "moderate Islamists," because they participate in the democratic process when it works for them; nevertheless, I personally disagree with this classification because when they cannot achieve their goal of Islamization through democratic means, they resort to more radical and militant means. Furthermore Jama'at-i-Islami cannot be seen as moderate because they engage in so many extremist activities in South Asia. Maidul Islam even admits that mainstream Islamists use armed violence and does not claim in so many words that even moderate Islamists oppose violence and militant methods.

In 2007, Mehdi Mozaffari published an article, "What is Islamism? History and Definition of a Concept." He pointed out:

> Islamism is a complex phenomenon with multiple dimensions and various ramifications. Like other political doctrines, Islamism, in its contemporary shape, is an "ideology," a movement, organization, and a form of government. (Mozaffari 207, 17)

So Islamism can be seen as a religio-political ideology associated with the radical practices of Islam, which generally refer to militant methodologies. The main goal of this ideology is to establish Islamic states in which Islam will dominate in every sphere of life. In order to implement such a goal, Islamists often justify force or violence to impose their ideology on others who do not embrace their ideology.

Islamist Groups among South Asian Muslims in America. There are several active Islamist groups and organizations among South Asian Muslims in America. Many of these groups originated in South Asian countries with different names. Their objective is to establish their particular version of Islam in every sphere of life (Islamization) in societies where they live. Adherents of these groups immigrate to America and bring this ideology with them. Here in America they do not usually publicly manifest their violent and radical nature; rather they try to indoctrinate and impose their ideologies through teaching in small groups and mosques. Among these South Asian Islamist groups, Jama'at-i-Islami is the most influential among South Asian immigrants in America.

During sixteen years of ministering among South Asian Muslims in America, I have observed that Jama'at-i-Islami have organized several Islamist groups in this area. Among these the Muslim Student Association and the Islamic Circle of North America are the most prominent. There are many other Islamist groups active in South Asia; however, these have very little influence in the United States today. In this section, my aim is to explore the ideologies of the most prominent and influential Islamist groups in America, and their influence among South Asian Muslims in this area, including their perception of Christianity.

Jama'at-i-Islami. Jama'at-i-Islami is the largest Islamist group in South Asia. It was founded on the Indian subcontinent in 1941 by Abu'l A'la Maududi, during the British colonial era. Originally it was a fundamentalist religious and social organization, but it quickly became politicized. According to the founder, the main objective of Jama'at-i-Islami is to establish Islamic states based on shariah law (strict Islamic law based on the Qur'an and Sunnah). John L. Esposito in the *Oxford Dictionary of Islam* defines Sunnah: "Established custom, normative precedent, conduct, and cumulative tradition, typically based on Muhammad's example" (Esposito 2003, 305). Another way of stating this objective of Jama'at-i-Islami is: the Islamization of the society and the country where they reside.

Concerning the founder of Jama'at-i-Islami, Aminah Mohammad-Arif states:

> The British presence in India led him [Abu'l A'la Maududi] to give a political dimension to his understanding of Islam. He eventually founded the *Jama'at-i-Islami*, a politico-religious party, made up of a disciplined elite trained according to the Maududian ideal. The party was to infiltrate the political and social spheres, the ultimate objective being the establishment of a divine order on Earth through an Islamic state. (Mohammad-Arif 2002, 22)

At the end of the British colonial era in 1947, the partition of India took place, and India was divided into two countries—India and Pakistan. Although he did not strongly favor the idea of partition, Maududi immigrated to Pakistan and organized Jama'at-i-Islami as a Muslim fundamentalist political party, in order to establish an Islamic state where shariah law would be the norm. His main objective was the Islamization of this new country.

Jama'at-i-Islami is strong and active on the Indian subcontinent (India, Pakistan, and Bangladesh), but at the same time they attempt to influence South Asian Muslims in all other countries where they reside, including the United States. In a recent interview with four Bangladeshi

Muslims in America, they all stated that there is a growing influence of Jam'at-i-Islami among Bangladeshi Muslims in America. Jama'-at-i-Islami has a political agenda, and in Bangladesh and Pakistan they are even recognized as a registered political party.

Jama'-at-i-Islami strives to impose shariah law in the countries where they live. In most cases this results in political violence and even causes the death of innocent people. Aminah Mohammad-Arif points out, "In Bangladesh there has been for some years a growth in fundamentalist movements, among them the local Jama'at-i-Islami" (Mohammad-Arif 2002, 22).

The Jama'-at-i-Islami and the other militant Islamist groups all have a similar ideology. One example is the Muslim Brotherhood in Egypt. Jama'at-i-Islami and the Muslim Brotherhood have many similarities in their ideologies.

The Pew Research Center found in their research about the common ideology between Muslim Brotherhood in Egypt and Jama'-at-i-Islami on the Indian subcontinent:

> The Muslim Brotherhood and Jama'at-i-Islami are separate movements that tend to draw the bulk of their members from different ethnic groups [Arabs and South Asians, respectively]. Nevertheless, both groups are rooted in a political ideology, frequently described as "Islamist," that calls for the establishment of a distinctly Islamic system of government. (Pew Research Center 2010, 1)

In Pakistan, Jama'at-i-Islami has achieved some measure of reaching their goal of Islamization, through participation in the democratic process. In Pakistan, they are quite successful promoting Islamization through collaboration with both the military and the civil government. Specific accomplishments toward Islamization in Pakistan include:

➤ Imposing *shariah* law in Pakistan
➤ Getting the Blasphemy Act passed by the Parliament
➤ Getting Ahmadiyya officially banned by the government
➤ Supporting the Taliban by collecting funds to finance the freedom movement in Afghanistan against the Soviet occupation

Since Islamization is the ideology of Jama'at-i-Islami, they perceive other religious groups, including Christianity, as enemies of Islam. This indicates their perception of Christianity. But many Islamic scholars and moderate Muslims in South Asia do not agree that Christianity is an enemy of Islam. This perception of Christianity as an enemy of Islam is the direct influence of Saudi Wahhabism on Jama'at-i-Islami.

Wahhabism is a fundamentalist, revivalist movement in Saudi Arabia with the objective of socio-moral reconstruction of the Arabian society with strict interpretation of the Sunnah (customs of the Prophet Muhammad). PBS *Frontline* in its analysis of Wahhabism, stated:

> For more than two centuries, Wahhabism has been Saudi Arabia's dominant faith. It is an austere form of Islam that insists on a literal interpretation of the Koran (Qur'an). Strict Wahhabis believe that all those who don't practice their form of Islam are heathens and enemies. (PBS *Frontline* 2014, 1)

Perceiving Christianity as the enemy of Islam is also found among the Jama'at-i-Islami in America. In America, although it is part of their ideology and methodology, they do not yet employ their extremist and militant tactics; rather they collaborate with Tablighi Jama'at and other established Islamist groups in America. This is demonstrated in the interviews conducted with South Asian Muslims presented later in this book.

Among South Asian Muslims, those who are strongly influenced by the ideology of Jama'at-i-Islami tend to avoid any interaction with mainstream non-Muslim Americans, especially Christians. This is because they associate Christianity with immoral practices they observe in America, which indicates their negative perception of Christianity. Within the Muslim communities in America, they try to separate themselves from those who do not support their ideology, even from other South Asian Muslims, and from those who are more progressive-minded, which implies their perception of Christianity as something to be avoided at all costs.

In the South Asian region, especially in Pakistan and Bangladesh, in order to accomplish Islamization in the name of the religion of Islam, Jama'at-i-Islami employ extremist methods, including jihad (holy war), against people outside their ideology. In this endeavor, they collaborate with many Islamic jihadi groups and terrorist organizations. A human rights activist and renowned writer in Bangladesh, Shariar Kabir, in his documentary on YouTube, "The Ultimate Jihad," describes many atrocities of Jama'at-i-Islami (Kabir, documentary on YouTube, posted 2013).

In interviews I have conducted with South Asian Muslims in America, many of the participants shared their opinion that there are many active Islamist organizations and associations in America that collaborate with Jama'at-i-Islami.

The perception of Christianity held by Jama'at-i-Islami and other Islamist groups is that Christianity deals only with spiritual matters, while to them Islam covers every area of human life. A notable politician, philosopher, and poet in South Asia, Sir Muhammad Iqbal, had a great influence over Maududi, the founder of Jama'at-i-Islami. Quoting from the writings of Muhammad Iqbal, Iqbal Singh Sevea points out:

> Contrasting Islam with Christianity, Iqbal described the latter as a purely monastic order which had gradually developed into a vast church organization. Unlike Islam Christianity is not a polity. Unlike Christianity, Islam is a civil society from its origins. (Sevea 2012, 115)

Jama'at-i-Islami also has a negative perception of the Christian Bible. In his book *Towards Understanding of the Qur'an,* Maududi divided the Bible into two parts: the first part, he argued, was authored by either Jews or Christians and therefore is not divine. The second part of the Bible consists of portions that are inspired by God. That section, he argued, "is in tune with the message of the Qur'an, but suffers from the tampering of translators, scribes, and exegetes, and the errors of oral transmitters" (Maududi 1992, 178–79). Jama'at-i-Islami teaches the beliefs of Maududi concerning the Bible.

Jama'at-i-Islami perceives that the doctrine of Jesus as the Son of God, held by Christians, is simply an interpretation derived from false philosophy and superstitions. Maududi points out, "The real error of the Christians lies in considering Jesus to be the son of God and a partner in His godhead, rather than His servant and Messenger" (Maududi 1992, 178–79). Maududi clearly rejected Christian sources as unreliable and considered the Qur'an the only authentic source regarding the life of Jesus Christ.

In conclusion, racial prejudice and discrimination still exist in America. Islamophobia (prejudice toward or discrimination against Muslims due to their religion) remains strong among non-Muslims in America. In America, Jama'at-i-Islami takes advantage of this religious discrimination to influence Muslims, especially South Asian Muslims. They teach that this discrimination in American society is the influence of Christianity. In my recent interviews with South Asian Muslims, the majority of participants disagree with the view that discrimination is the result of Christian influence. This is shown in my data analysis later in this book, Chapter 5.

Although Jama'at-i-Islami is a minority group among South Asian Muslims, they are very strong and well organized in America. They strictly follow the teachings of Maududi about Christianity. Their perception of Christianity is essentially the same in America as in South Asia, which is a strongly negative perception, as they see Christianity as the enemy of Islam.

The Muslim Student Association (MSA). The Muslim Student Association was formed in the United States in 1963 by the initiative of South Asian Muslim students in Illinois, and soon became a nationwide organization in the United States.

Aminah Mohammad-Arif points out:

> From the early 1960s, South Asian Muslim students became involved in Islamic student groups. As these groups were not well organized, South Asian students, together with Muslims from other countries—Arabs, Turks, Iranians held a national conference at Urbana, Illinois, and founded, on 1 January 1963, the Muslim Student Association. (Mohammad-Arif 2002, 164)

The Muslim Student Association is very active among local and international Muslim students on different college campuses in America, such as MIT, Harvard, Boston University, Northeastern University, and Brandeis.

The Pluralism Project at Harvard University published an article entitled "Islam in America":

During the 1960s, Boston witnessed an influx of students from predominantly Muslim countries. The demographic shift coincided with the founding of the Muslim Student Association [MSA], the first nationwide Islamic organization, on the campus of the University of Illinois in 1963. Today there are active Islamic societies at Harvard, MIT, Boston University, Tufts, Northeastern, Wentworth Institute, and Suffolk. Some student groups, such as the MIT Muslim Student Association, are directly affiliated with the national MSA. Others, such as Harvard Islamic Society, are not. (Pluralism Project 2013, 2)

The Muslim Student Association works for the unity of Muslim students on college campuses, regardless of ethnicity, but at the same time they follow the ideology of Jama'at-i-Islami and the Muslim Brotherhood (both militant Islamic groups). For that reason, they should be classified as Islamist.

Jane I. Smith further points out:

The MSA was formed to strengthen national and international ties among Muslims of all national origins and ethnicities. Following the ideology of the Muslim Brotherhood of Egypt and the Jama'at-i-Islami of the Indian subcontinent, the group was created to provide a structure through which the Muslim student associations that had begun to appear on a number of American campuses could relate to one another. It soon developed into an agency with enormous influence in helping to redefine Islamic identity in America as something beyond national, ethnic, and linguistic allegiances. (Smith 2010, 169)

Promoting unity among Muslim students is one of the objectives of the Muslim Student Association. They have other objectives also, such as proselytizing non-Muslim students and seekers. This implies a perception of Christianity as a religion of those who are not true believers (infidels), in need of being converted to Islam.

Aminah Mohammad-Arif points out this aim of the Muslim Student Association: "to inform non-Muslims about Islam, so as to counteract prejudice, and to engage more or less directly into proselytizing activities." (Mohammad-Arif 2002, 164)

The Muslim Student Association promotes jihad (holy war) in its chapters on college campuses in America. This advocacy of jihad implies the perception that Christianity is an enemy of Islam, and therefore should be strongly opposed, and even attacked. There are numerous allegations from Christian organizations that the Muslim Student Association promotes extremist activities. Erick Stakelback, a CBN (Christian Broadcasting Network) news correspondent, reported in a broadcast on March 19, 2011, that "the group [MSA] has another track record that it doesn't advertise: several of [the] leaders have been convicted of terrorism, prompting some terrorist experts to call the MSA a recruiting tool of Jihad." (CBN News 2011, 1)

The goal of the Muslim Student Association is to establish Islamic shariah law worldwide, and all religious groups including Christians must be brought to comply with this law. Former FBI Special Agent John Guandolo told CBN News that, "the problem can be traced back to the group's roots in the Muslim Brotherhood—a jihadist movement that seeks to establish Islamic shariah law worldwide." He calls the Muslim Students Association the "focal point" for the Muslim Brotherhood in America. (CBN News 2011, 2) It should be remembered that many people in the United States consider the enforcement of shariah law as brutal and violent.

In conclusion, the Muslim Student Association is an effective organization in presenting Islam in a favorable light among non-Muslims in America. This organization has an active influence among young generation Muslims, especially Muslim students on college campuses in America. They generally embrace the conviction that Islam is the only true religion and therefore Christianity is perceived as the enemy of Islam. Furthermore, people outside the Islamic faith need to be converted to Islam. These perceptions are very strong among members of the Muslim Student Association in America.

The Islamic Circle of North America (ICNA). Most people consider the Islamic Circle of North America as a branch of Jama'at-i-Islami and an extension of the Muslim Student Association. It was founded in 1971, by the initiative taken by some former Jama'at-i-Islami leaders from Pakistan who immigrated to the United States. The majority of the members of this organization are originally from South Asia.

The main motive behind the creation of this organization was to spread the ideology of Jama'at-i-Islami, and to make this organization better known to Muslims from other countries. Aminah Mohammad-Arif states the objective of the Islamic Circle of North America:

> Ideologically also, the Islamic Circle of North America continues to defend the ideals defined by Mawdudi [the founder of Jama'at-i-Islami]. The leadership itself consists of members who were nearly all affiliated, among the South Asians at least, to the Jama'at-i-Islami before immigrating to the United States." (Mohammad-Arif 2002, 174)

Like Jama'at-i-Islami, the Islamic Circle of North America has the political ambition to establish Islamic states. They teach that Islam should regulate every aspect of life. Although they do not openly admit that they want to turn America into an Islamic country, nevertheless this is their hidden agenda. Their perception is that the United States is considered to be a Christian country; therefore if Christianity can be replaced by the true religion of Islam, the United States could become an Islamic country. This reveals their perception of Christianity as a false religion that should be replaced by the true religion of Islam.

Aminah Mohammad-Arif has conducted an extensive research regarding the hidden agenda of the Islamic Circle of North America. She states:

> Any political ambition to transform the State is very much on the back burner, or indeed written out of the ICNA objectives. To turn the United States into an Islamic state is not on the agenda, even though such an idea may not be completely absent from the thoughts of some activist members. The idea however is still emphasized that Islam should regulate every aspect of one's life, even in the secular society, and that only the defined law [shariah law] should rule the behaviour of Muslims. Since the ICNA advocates a return to [Muslim] Scripture and to a literal interpretation of the Qur'an and the Sunna [Sunnah], and insists on a rejection of Western

society, in this case American, it has as an organization, good fundamentalist credentials. (Mohammad-Arif 2002, 174–75)

All the literature of the Islamic Circle of North America clearly indicates that they hold Jesus Christ in high regard. They believe that Jesus is an Islamic prophet. Yet they flatly reject the teachings of Saint Paul about Christian doctrines. Quoting from the sayings of the Prophet Muhammad in the Hadith (collection of sayings of Muhammad) they often claim that Muhammad and Jesus had a close relationship with each other. Abu Huraira, who had been a close aide of Muhammad, later narrated the sayings of Muhammad, which were written as the Hadith some years later by *Sahih* (the authentic) Bukhari. One quotation about Jesus was:

> I heard Allah's Apostle [Muhammad] saying, I am the nearest of all the people to the son of Mary, and all the prophets are paternal brothers, and there has been no prophet between me and him [i.e., Jesus]. (Bukhari 1970, Volume 4, Book 55, Number 651)

The main objective of the Islamic Council of North America is to spread the ideology of Jama'at-i-Islami, the primary moving force behind this organization. They are strongly motivated by the political agenda of Jama'at-i-Islami, which is basically to work toward the goal of turning America into an Islamic state. If America were an Islamic state, this would mean other religions, including Christianity, would be marginalized or outlawed. Their correct perception is that most people in America are Christians, and thus this fact is the most serious obstacle to their goal of establishing Islam as the dominant religious influence in America. Therefore, in the perception of the Islamic Council of North America, Christians must be converted to Islam and brought to see how Islam is the only true religion. Since the philosophy of the Islamic Council of North America and Jama'at-i-Islami is basically the same, both groups clearly hold a negative perception of Christianity.

In conclusion, the growth of Islamist groups worldwide and the increase in the number of extremists expose South Asian Muslims in America to their influence. This is likely to affect the perceptions of

Christianity in a negative way and will doubtless recruit some adherents into the ranks of these extremist movements. These Islamists perceive Christianity as an enemy of Islam to be overcome and thwarted so Islam can expand in this country.

These Islamist groups advocate aggressive methods for spreading Islam in America, and only a minority of South Asian immigrants embrace their methodology. This is documented in the interviews with South Asian Muslims reported later in this book (Chapters 4 and 5).

In this section I have examined the most prominent theological influences that historically have formed and shaped perceptions of Christianity among South Asian Muslims worldwide. These are also reflected in the perceptions held by South Asian Muslims in America.

Since Islam came to South Asia, the perceptions of Christianity, both positive and negative, have been imparted and shaped by the reform movements, such as Deobandi, Barelwi, Tablighi Jama'at, and Ahmadiyya, as well as other sources including Sufism and Islamist groups.

The more positive perceptions of Christianity may be found in the influence of Sufism, including folk Islam; however, in more recent years the influence of Islamist groups has shaped many of these perceptions in a negative way. As a result, misperceptions of Christianity are increasing among South Asian Muslims in America. This is confirmed by the interviews presented later in this book.

Perceptions of Christianity naturally change over time, especially where Muslims are in the minority. Nevertheless, they want to retain their Muslim identity regardless of ethnicity. In their new cultural setting in America, South Asian Muslims are naturally more susceptible to the influences around them. Some come under the influence of Islamist groups and may become radicalized, and their perception of Christianity as an enemy of Islam intensifies, making them more hostile to Christianity in general and to Christians in particular. However, the majority of South Asian Muslims have not been radicalized, and these Muslims are more likely to become moderate and open and to embrace a more positive perception of Christianity.

In appendix A is a table summarizing the major theological influences that historically have shaped perceptions of Christianity discussed in this section.

PERCEPTIONS OF MAJOR CHRISTIAN DOCTRINES AMONG SOUTH ASIAN MUSLIMS IN AMERICA

In this section, I examine the perceptions of Christian doctrines held by South Asian Muslims in America. My aim is to ascertain both positive and negative perceptions of Christian doctrines embraced by these immigrants; however, my major interest is with the misperceptions because these present most of the barriers to communication and understanding. Most of these perceptions were formed over many years through the traditional Islamic teachings before these immigrants leave their native lands in South Asia. These are discussed in some detail in this section.

Most South Asian Muslim perceptions of Christian doctrines are erroneous or distorted in one way or another. However, there are a few perceptions that are basically accurate, yet may be strongly rejected by Muslims in general as well as South Asian Muslims in America.

In this section, I discuss three major classifications of Christian doctrines that include many incorrect perceptions among South Asian Muslims in America. One of these major classifications is the attributes of God. Another is the various perceptions of Jesus and the Christ (several Christological issues). The third is the revelation of God and the Bible.

It has been noted that there is a basic uniformity of perceptions held by Muslims in general around the world regarding these three major classifications of Christian doctrines. This is also true of South Asian Muslims, including those in America. It should be pointed out that Muslim perceptions in these three classifications of Christian doctrines, especially the attributes of God and several Christological issues, are based mainly on teachings in the Qur'an. In the Qur'an are both correct and incorrect perceptions in these three Christian doctrinal areas of concern. I agree with Hugh Goddard's statement:

> The Quran is, in a word, ambivalent about Jesus, Christians, and the Bible. It contains positive and affirmative statements but to them adds cautions and statements rejecting certain

things associated with Jesus and with Christians. So it is a sort of "yes ... but" situation. (Goddard 1996, 1)

Perceptions of Christian beliefs are usually formed within the culture of South Asia, strongly influenced by Islamic teachings and practice, and then Muslim immigrates bring these perceptions with them when they come to America. After they immigrate to their new country, despite the cultural influences in America, their basic perceptions of major Christian doctrines generally remain the same. But as time goes by, subsequent generations are more open to dialogue with their Christian classmates and neighbors about these Christian doctrinal issues. So misperceptions of major Christian doctrines can be corrected over time. This is discussed in more detail in this section.

ATTRIBUTES OF GOD

South Asian Muslims and Christians share many perceptions about the attributes of God. They agree that He is almighty, all powerful, all-knowing, and the Creator and Sustainer of the universe. Yet, there are certain areas in which South Asian Muslims have misperceptions about Christian beliefs of the attributes of God and His nature, which affect how they understand related Christian doctrines.

South Asian Muslims have serious misconceptions about three Christian doctrines regarding the attributes of God: God as a god of love, the fatherhood of God, and the triune nature of one God (Trinity).

The Biblical Idea: God Is Love. The most specific biblical reference to God states that God is love, found in 1 John 4:8: "He who does not love does not know God; for God is love." Throughout the New Testament there are numerous consistent references to God's love. (e.g., John 3:16; Rom 1:7; Rom 5:5; Rom 5:8; Rom 8:39; 2 Cor. 13:11; Eph. 2:4; 1 Thess. 1:4; 2 Thess. 2:16; Tit. 3:4; etc.)

On the other hand, South Asian Muslim perceptions of Allah in reference to love are based on certain Qur'anic teachings. Although all 114 chapters of the Qur'an (except Chapter 9) begin with "In the name of Allah, most benevolent, ever merciful," which may suggest a caring nature but does not specifically describe Allah as a god of love (someone can be benevolent and merciful but not loving), which can explain why the majority of Muslims in South Asia have a wrong perception about the biblical concept of God as a God of love, particularly 1 John 4:8 "God is love," which emphasizes His very nature as a loving God. This implies the possibility of a personal loving relationship with God, which many Muslims do not accept.

Of the two mainline Islamic branches (Sunni and Shi'a), Sunnis are the majority among Muslims in South Asia. Overlapping these two mainline Muslim branches, Sufism (Islamic mysticism) is popular, and Sufi philosophy has had a strong influence within Muslim society in the South Asian region as discussed in the previous section, particularly on the perceptions of Christianity. Whereas Sunni and Shi'a place little emphasis on the concept of Allah in personal loving relationship with humans, Sufi philosophy is closer to the biblical concept that God is love.

Except for Sufis, the majority of Muslims in South Asia insist that to love is to have an intimate relationship with a beloved one, and intimate relationships are only possible between human beings. Their logical argument is that since God is spirit, He cannot be said to have this type of intimate relationship; it is therefore impossible that God can love humans. Thus, the biblical idea of "God is love" (1 John 4:8) is incompatible with the way they perceive Allah.

The same misperception is found among South Asian Muslims in America, because most are also orthodox Sunni and Shi'a. To them it is too personal and intimate, disrespectful of a high and holy Allah, to suggest a relationship between human (unholy) and spirit (holy). In Islam, the dominant concept is that Allah is transcendent, not immanent, which rejects the Christian concept of God who is transcendent but also immanent and personal.

Of course, to the Christian, the ultimate expression of God's love is that He came to earth in human form (Jesus), to demonstrate His personal love for us: "For God so loved the world that he gave his one and only Son ..." (John 3:16)

Bruce A. McDowell and Anees Zaka point out:

Allah's love is what Christians would call common grace, in that He shows His mercy and care for His creation. But it is not personal or sustaining love. There is no redemptive love in Islam, unlike Christianity. (McDowell and Zaka 1999, 105)

The Fatherhood of God. Another biblical teaching about which South Asian Muslims have misperceptions is the concept of God as heavenly Father. The South Asian Muslim perception of the fatherhood of God is different from Christian belief. Christians believe God is their heavenly Father. When Christians call God "Father," Muslims think of it in terms of human relationships because fatherhood implies a familial relationship. Wendy Murray Zoba wrote an article, "How Muslims see Christianity," published in *Christianity Today*. He stated: "In Islam, God is all merciful, all knowing, all compassionate—Muslims have 99 names for what God is—but none conveys the intimacy of *Abba* whom we approach in reconciliation by virtue of his saving grace." (Zoba 2000, 1)

Jesus used *Abba* the Aramaic word for "father" in praying (Mark 14:36) and taught His disciples to pray in the same intimate terms (Luke 11:1–2), underscoring the intimate and personal relationship with God inherent in Christian teaching.

In contrast to the Muslim's view, in the Bible, Christ always addressed God as Father (e.g., John 14–17). He also taught His disciples in a model prayer to address God as Father (Matthew 6:9–13). Another example is when praying in the garden of Gethsemane, Jesus addressed God as Father (Mark 14:36, Luke 22:42).

Trent C. Butler in the *Holman Bible Dictionary* has noted that the "Aramaic word for father (was) used by Jesus to speak of His own intimate relationship with God, a relationship that others can enter through faith" (Butler 2003, 3).

Generally, Muslims misunderstand the biblical idea of God as Father, because they associate the idea of biological procreation with fatherhood. South Asian Muslims in America also misunderstand this teaching. They support their concept of Allah with the quote from the Qur'an: "He has begotten no one, and is begotten of none. There is no one comparable to Him" (Surah 112:3–4).

By addressing God as Father, Jesus amplified the concept of God as relational. This is a spiritual relationship, not a biological relationship between father and son, which is the South Asian Muslims misconception. Timothy C. Tennent explains it more clearly:

> It is essential to understand that fatherhood and procreation are two separate ideas. An adopted child may refer to his or her parents as "father" and "mother" even though there is absolutely no genetic, procreative link between them. It is an expression of relationship. This is because procreation and fatherhood are separate. In Christianity, the terms Father and Son refer to a spiritual, not a physical, relationship. The ideal father is related to his son through love, tenderness, and communion, and it is these relational qualities that the words convey. (Tennent 2002, 157)

The Unity of God and the Biblical Concept of the Trinity. The doctrine of the Trinity is one of the major disagreements between Christians and Muslims. Norman L. Geisler and Abdul Saleeb point out:

> In addition to misunderstanding the biblical data, Islamic scholars also offer philosophical objections to the doctrine of the Trinity. These too must be cleared away before they will be able to understand the biblical teaching about a plurality of persons within the unity of God." (Geisler and Saleeb 1993, 261)

Typically, Muslims, including South Asian Muslims, hold a misconception of this Christian doctrine, which is that Christians worship three gods. This perception of the Christian doctrine of the Trinity is that it is against the *tawhid* (the unity or oneness of God) in Islam.

However, in order to show the unity of God, some Muslim scholars will actually argue that the Islamic doctrine of tawhid is a common link between Christianity and Islam because both Islam and Christianity insist that God is one. Yet, to the Christian the concept of unity is three in one (triune), which is rejected by almost all Muslims as tritheism. One scholar is Sayyed Hossein Nasr, who emphasizes that "the doctrine of *tawhid,* or unity ... is ... central not only to Islam but also to Christianity, since the doctrine of the Trinity certainly *does not negate divine unity* in mainstream Christian theology" (Nasr 2009, 69). (Emphasis mine.)

Nasr's argument is correct. In Islam, Allah is a single being. Christianity does not deny the unity of God, believing in one God in three persons, who is tripersonal (three manifestations); a triune (three united in one) God, including Father, Son, and Holy Spirit. The Christian concept of the unity of God does not contradict the South Asian Muslims' concept of the unity of God.

In Islam the dominant thinking about the oneness of God is expressed in *"la ilaha illa Allah ..."* (there is no god but Allah), which is part of the Islamic creed. This implies the oneness of Allah. However, Christians also declare that God is one.

Timothy C. Tennent points out:

> To associate partners with Allah is to commit *shirk* [idolatry or setting other gods alongside Allah as partners] and is regarded by Muslims as an unpardonable sin [*kabirah*]. This prohibition clearly includes Christian Trinitarian Monotheism, because to identify Jesus Christ as God or as Son of God is, in the Islamic view, to commit *shirk*. (Tennent 2002, 146)

Among Muslims in South Asia as well as in America, the Christian doctrine of the Trinity is not only misunderstood but also misinterpreted as a tritheistic view of God. As Warren Chastain points out:

> The misunderstanding is deep: Impatient with the subtleties of the Trinity, the Muslim believes we have some kind of tritheism; and it will not do to answer his 1+1+1=3 logic with an evasive 1x1x1=1. The basic problem with the Muslim concept is that it is a mathematical oneness instead of the organic oneness of life; an abstract oneness instead of the composite oneness of personality; a cold, conceptual solitariness, instead of a vital, friendly, loving Father. (Chastain, 1981, 148)

I believe the origin of the Muslim misperception of the Christian doctrine of the Trinity can be historically traced back to the pre-Islamic

Arab world. Before Islam was introduced into Arabia, the pagan Arabian people believed in daughters of Allah, whom they worshipped along with Allah. Once Islam was introduced in Arabia, Muhammad rejected the notion of daughters of Allah, which he saw as polytheism. This would logically reject the idea of a son of God.

In rejecting the idea of daughters of Allah, the Qur'an mentions three names: "Have you considered *Lat*, *Uzza*, and *Manat*, the other third [of the pagan deities]? Are there sons for you, and daughters for Him [Allah]? This is certainly an unjust apportioning." (Surah 53:19–22)

Based on this Qur'anic passage, a famous Arab Christian theologian and evangelist, Fouad Masri, also added:

> Pre-Islamic Arabian paganism is partly to blame for this misconception [of the Trinity]. The problem is, the idea has endured and many Muslims understand the Christian Trinity to be a form of tritheism. Therefore, the Trinity is a form of blasphemy [*Al-Kufr*], for in this model others are associated as being equal with God [*Al-Shirk*]. (Masri 2014, 140)

Historically, as inheritors of Arabic Muslim traditions, typically South Asian Muslims consider the Christian doctrine of the Trinity a parallel to this pagan, Arabian pre-Islamic idea of daughters of Allah.

During my interviews with South Asian Muslims in America, all participants are asked this question: "Is the Christian doctrine of the Trinity polytheism (belief in multiple gods)?" Many of them have answered that they don't believe that the Christian doctrine of Trinity is polytheism. Their perception is not that Christians worship three gods. This indicates that their misperception has been corrected, either by dialogue with Christians who gave them the correct perception or acquiring proper knowledge through some other means. However, some participants have answered that they do believe that the Trinity is a polytheistic idea. This is shown in detail in the data analysis in Chapter 5. The interviews further reveal that many South Asian Muslims in America are confused about the Christian doctrine of the Trinity.

Misperceptions of Christian doctrines were already in their minds from the time they were still in their native lands. Confusion began historically in Muhammad's time, and even Muhammad heard the wrong interpretation of the Trinity from Christians with whom he had contact. So Christians in Arabia at the time of Muhammad are partly to be blamed for this misperception. This helps explain the misperceptions of the doctrine of the Trinity that have been passed along to South Asian Muslims.

Timothy C. Tennent states that Muhammad himself was confused by the way Christians described their God. He stated, "Muhammad's confusion is largely due to the fact that most Christians living in Arabia during his lifetime were Nestorians or Monophysites who themselves had deficient views of the Trinity." (Tennent 2002, 154)

Based on Qur'anic teaching, reflecting the misperception of Muhammad, most South Asian Muslims also falsely accuse Christians of believing in three gods (Surah 4:171; 5:73–75, 116). The charge of polytheism against Christians was the result of misinformation that consequently influenced perceptions of Christianity. Unfortunately, this denunciation of the Christian doctrine of the Trinity in the Qur'an seems to be based on a gross misunderstanding.

William Lane Craig points out, "But Muhammad evidently thought that Christians believed in the Trinity composed of God the Father, Mary, and their offspring, Jesus. It's no wonder that he regarded such a ridiculous doctrine as blasphemous!" (Lane 2013, 1)

This misinterpretation of the Christian doctrine of the Trinity, as consisting of Father, Mary, and Son as their progeny, is seen as blasphemy not only by Muslims but also by Christians. It is clearly against biblical teaching. The Bible says, "You were shown these things so that you might know that the Lord is God; besides him there is no other." (Deuteronomy 4:35); "Hear, O Israel: The Lord our God, the Lord is one." (Deuteronomy 6:4). Jesus also confirmed this Old Testament text about the oneness of God. "The most important one [command], answered Jesus, is this: 'Hear, O Israel, the Lord our God, the Lord is one'" (Mark 12:29).

Several scholars also comment on this misperception in the Qur'an. One example, Robert A. Morey wrote:

> The Bible proves this teaching from the Qur'an as interpreted by Muslim commentators to be false, although some obscure

Christian sects did at one time hold such a doctrine of the Trinity, the Trinity seen in the Quran is not the Trinity of the Apostles' Creed or of the Nicene Creed. (Morey 1992, 152–53)

Tor Andrae wrote about Muhammad's misunderstanding: "It is obvious that Muhammad sadly misunderstood the Christian teaching on the Trinity. To him Christians were made polytheistic by the worship of God, Jesus, and Mary." (Andrae 1960, 91)

Muhammad sought to reform polytheistic Arabian society into absolute monotheism. Abd al Masih points out:

> Muhammad, 1300 years after the prophet Isaiah, fought mercilessly against any form of polytheism. He could not tolerate other deities beside Allah. Through members of a Christian sect he obviously learned that the Christian Trinity consisted of Father, Mother, and Son (*Surah* 4:171; 5: 73, 116). He reasoned that Christians think that God slept with Mary and fathered Jesus biologically. (Masih 1996, 15)

In the Bible, the only true God reveals Himself as the Father, the Son, and the Holy Spirit, the three manifestations of one God. This never contradicts the unity of God. William J. Saal has noted that, "It is obvious that what most Muslims reject is not the biblical teaching about the Trinity, most have never heard the true Christian teaching stated, much less explained in a way they can understand" (Saal 1993, 105).

Norman L. Geisler and Abdul Saleeb comment on the Muslim failure to understand the Christian concept of the oneness of God in the Trinity:

> At the heart of Muslim inability to understand the Trinity is the Neo-Platonic concept of oneness ... In order to show the similarities between Muslim views and the views of Potinus, both writers further referred to the writings of Plotinus. " ...Plotinus ... viewed God [the Ultimate] as the One, an absolute unity in which is no multiplicity at all. ... For Plotinus, the One itself was beyond knowing, beyond consciousness, and even beyond being." (Geisler and Saleeb 1993, 262–63)

I agree with them that Muslims fail to understand the concept of Trinity. Here these two scholars point to the similarities between the Plotinian (Plotinus, the second century philosopher) and the Muslim views of God.

Clearly, from my interviews some South Asian Muslims in America see the Christian doctrine of the Trinity as tritheism. This perception reflects the erroneous concepts in both the Qur'an and in the teachings of Muhammad. As previously stated, these misperceptions about the Trinity were acquired from distorted views of some Christian sects in pre-Islamic Arabia.

Unfortunately, this confused misperception misses the concept of the triune God, which is unique to Christianity.

THE SONSHIP OF JESUS

To me the greatest controversy between Christianity and Islam arises from the Christian belief that Jesus is the "only Son of God" (John 3:16). The term "Son of God" creates a significant misperception about Jesus Christ for South Asian Muslims. Generally, Muslims have high regard for Jesus as a prophet, but not as deity or as progeny of God. Hammudah Abdalati wrote:

> It should be remembered here that acceptance of Jesus by Muslims is a fundamental article of faith in Islam, and that a Muslim can never think of Jesus in any derogatory terms. A Muslim is happily denied the liberty of defaming Jesus or any other prophet of God. (Abdalati 1975, 153)

In this section I discuss the biblical meaning of the term "the Son of God," what the Bible teaches about Jesus as the unique Son of God, and what the Qur'an says about the Christian doctrine of Jesus as the Son of God. I then examine the misperceptions about this doctrine held by South Asian Muslims in South Asia as well as in America.

The Biblical Meaning of the Term "The Son of God." Lack of understanding concerning the biblical meaning of the "Son of God" creates a problem and a wrong perception of this Christian doctrine in the minds of South Asian Muslims. First, it is important to examine the biblical meaning of the term "son." There are passages in the Bible where "son" simply refers to male offspring (biological descent). In other places, the term can refer to a close personal relationship, especially in reference to the expression "son of God" or "sons of God" (Exodus 4:22–23; Jeremiah 31:9,10; Hosea 11:1; Romans 8:14; 2 Corinthians 6:18; Galatians 3:126; Revelation 21:7) (Note: In all translations of the Bible, when Jesus is referred to as the Son of God, a capital S is used.). So the term "son" can have different meanings in the Bible. It can either mean biological descent or it can mean a special close personal relationship. South Asian Muslims misunderstand the term "son" when the term refers to Jesus as "the Son of God," because their misperception is that Christians believe Jesus is the biological offspring of God.

The Biblical Teaching: Jesus Is the Unique Son of God. For South Asian Muslims, John 3:16 is one of the most controversial verses in the Bible. There are two important concepts in this verse. In the King James Version (1611 AD), the original Greek phrase *"huion ton monogene"* is translated "the only begotten Son of God," which Muslims take to mean biological offspring.

In most modern versions, the more accurate translation of John 3:16 is "the only Son of God," or "the one and only Son of God," meaning unique in relationship and character, not biological (Revised Standard Version, English Standard Version, New International Version).

For a South Asian Muslim who knows Surah 112: "He is Allah, the One and Only; Allah, the Eternal, Absolute; He begetteth not, nor is He begotten; And there is none like unto Him" (Surah 112:1–4). The word *begotten* from the King James Version causes a problem for Muslims. Most South Asian Muslims take this in a literal, biological meaning, whereas the best translation is "unique Son of God."

In the Bible, before His birth the angel Gabriel told the Virgin Mary that her son would be called "the Son of God." "He will be great and will be called the Son of the Most High" (Luke 1:32, 35).

South Asian Muslims think that Christians call Jesus "the Son of God" because God biologically brought about his birth. Christians do not actually believe that. Neither the Bible nor the Qur'an supports this view. According to both the Bible and the Qur'an, the Holy Spirit played a major role in the birth of Jesus (Luke 1:34–35, Matthew 1:20, Surah 19:17). Any sexual implication is not compatible with the teaching of either the Bible or the Qur'an.

My interviews indicate that South Asian Muslims in America also have this misperception of the biblical teachings about Jesus as the Son of God. They think that Christians believe Jesus was the biological offspring of God. It is simply a misperception of the biblical teaching.

Part of the biblical teaching about Jesus as the Son of God includes the claims of Jesus himself, as well as His works. Norman Geisler and Abdul Saleeb point out:

> Before discussing Jesus' specific claims to be the Son of God, it is necessary to respond briefly to the Muslim misunderstanding of this claim. Many Muslims understand the phrase "Son of God" to imply that Jesus was the offspring of physical relations. (Geisler and Saleeb 1993, 243)

Because of His unique identity, Jesus claimed, "Anyone who has seen me has seen the Father" (John 14:9). When Jesus uses the term *Father*, as in this passage, He is referring to God, which clearly implies His claim to be the Son of God. Jesus further stated, "Do not believe me unless I do what my Father does. But if I do it, even though you do not believe me, believe the miracles that you may know and understand that the Father is in me, and I in the Father" (John 10:37–38). Thus, Jesus pointed to His works as evidence of the fact that He is the Son of God. In Matthew 16:17, when Peter said, "You are the Christ, the Son of the living God," Jesus commended him and indicated He would build His church based on this recognition.

In addition to the claims of Jesus and the evidence of the works of Jesus, there are other proofs in the Bible that He is the Son of God.

At Jesus's baptism, God's voice from heaven proclaimed: "This is my Son, whom I love" (Matthew 3:17). In His Transfiguration, God's voice once again proclaimed, "This is my Son, whom I love. Listen to Him!" (Mark 9:7).

The Qur'anic Interpretation of the Doctrine of the Son of God

For South Asian Muslims, Surah 112 referred to above, much confusion arises from the concept of "begotten" in this Surah. This Qur'anic passage refutes the notion that God produced offspring, a notion also found nowhere in the Bible. South Asian Muslims usually refer to this passage when refuting the doctrine of Jesus as the Son of God. They usually misunderstand the Christian reference to Jesus as the Son of God, to mean biological offspring of God.

There are two terms in Arabic for son, *walad* and *ibn*. Irfan A. Omar edited the book *A Muslim View of Christianity: Essays on Dialogue by Mahmoud Ayoub*. Omar quotes Ayoub:

> Two important Qur'anic terms: *ibn* and *walad*, both signifying a filial relationship. *Ibn* ["son"] which is used only once in the Qur'an in relation to Jesus, may be understood metaphorically to mean son through a relationship of love or adoption. The term *walad*, on the other hand, means "offspring," and this primarily signifies physical generation and sonship. It is the later term that is often used by Qur'an commentators to argue against the Christian concept of Christ's divine Sonship. The Qur'an, however, as we see when we study these two terms closely, does not use the *walad* specially to refer to Jesus. That is to say, the Qur'an nowhere accuses Christians of calling Jesus the *walad* offspring of God. (Omar 2007, 118)

The following Surah clearly argues against the idea that God has a son (offspring). "How could He have a son, when He has no mate?" (Surah 6: 101–102) In this verse the word used is *walad*, meaning offspring; furthermore this Surah rejects the notion of God having offspring. The Qur'an never uses the term of "son (*walad*) of God (Allah)" in referring to Jesus. This explains why there is an enduring and emphatic misperception concerning the Christian concept of Jesus as the "Son of God." This reveals that the Muslim rejection of the concept of Jesus as the Son of God is not being true to the Qur'an. In fact, a Christian may agree with these Qur'anic verses in Surah 112 and Surah 6, because Christianity never claims that God has a son in the biological sense.

It is clear that the Arabic word *Ibn* (son) is used in the Qur'an to signify special relationship, not offspring (walad). Biblical scholars uniformly agree that the Bible also intends a special relationship when referring to Jesus as the Son of God.

Irfan A. Omar quotes Mahmoud Ayoub:

> The language of the two scriptures [Bible and Qur'an] is highly symbolic and allegorical. The language of this verse [Luke 1:35 about the birth of Jesus] is clearly circumspect. It implies no sexual union or divine generation of any kind. Furthermore, while Luke's description agrees both in form and spirit with the Qur'anic idea of the conception of Christ, the language of the Qur'an is far more graphic and open to interpretation. (Omar 2007, 118,119)

Hugh Goddard also states:

> Initially this Quranic rejection (Surah 112:1–3) of sonship was almost certainly a rejection of polytheistic Meccan ideas, rather than Christian ones, and the problem is thus that even if subsequently statements like this have been taken to refer to Christianity, this may not have been their primarily intention or thrust. (Goddard 1996, 12)

I agree with Goddard's opinion regarding the concept of sonship.

There is another interesting Surah in the Qur'an related to the concept of son of God (Allah) from the Muslim perspective. The Qur'an mistakenly claims that "Jews say Ezra was a son of Allah" (Surah 9:30). This Surah uses the term *ibn* (close relationship), not *walad* (offspring). Ezra was a postexilic Jewish priest who revived the Mosaic Law (c. Fifth Century BC). There is no biblical or historical evidence that the Jews ever referred to Ezra as a son of God.

This Surah goes on to say: "And the Christians call Christ the son of Allah. That is a saying from their mouth; [in this] they but imitate what the unbelievers of old used to say. Allah's curse be on them: how they are deluded away from the Truth!" (Surah 9:30). Here, the Qur'an also uses the Arabic word *ibn* (close relationship), not biological offspring. Yet, here the Qur'an emphatically rejects the Christian doctrine that

Christ is the Son of God (Allah); however, the Bible just as emphatically declares Christ is the Son of God.

None of the biblical references to Jesus say "a son of God" but always "the Son of God," always with "the" and always with uppercase S. Jesus also clearly makes the claim: "I am the Son of God" (John 10:30–36).

There are some passages in the Bible where Jesus refers to the concept of sonship in His teaching, but never in the sense of biological offspring. "Blessed are the peacemakers, for they shall be called the sons of God" (Matthew 5:9), and, "Love your enemies and pray for those who persecute you, that you may be sons of your Father who is in heaven" (Matthew 5:44–45). These references always use a lowercase s, and clearly intend the idea of a close relationship, not biological.

In conclusion, Jesus is revered by Muslims as a sinless prophet. The Qur'an honors him as a prophet and acknowledges his miracles as authentic.

Unfortunately, confusion over the term *begotten* has led most Muslims to a perception that Christians believe in Jesus as the biological offspring of God, which is emphatically untrue.

When referring to Jesus, the Qur'an never uses the Arabic word *walad*, meaning biological offspring, but rather the word *ibn*, which implies a close personal relationship with God.

The Qur'an also mistakenly refers to Ezra as a son of God, which further adds to the confusion. Yet, the Qur'an also rejects the Christian idea of Jesus as the Son (ibn) of God (Surah 9:30). Nowhere in the Bible is there any suggestion of Ezra as a son of God.

The Bible consistently uses the phrase "the Son of God" when referring to Jesus, implying unity with God and a unique relationship between Jesus Christ and God.

THE TWO NATURES OF JESUS CHRIST (HUMAN AND DIVINE)

The Christian doctrine of the two natures of Jesus Christ is another of the major theological conflicts between Muslims and Christians. Muslims in general accept only one nature of Christ, which is human, because Christ was born as a human, but reject the divinity of Christ. South Asian Muslims in America also share these perceptions brought with them when they immigrate.

True Christians have always believed that Christ was fully divine and fully human. However, in the first century some confusion arose about this doctrine. In this section, I examine some of the historical confusion among early Christians concerning Christ's two natures, as well as how this confusion was resolved.

I further also examine the teachings of the Qur'an regarding the dual nature of Christ and investigate the sources of misperceptions of this Christian doctrine among South Asian Muslims in America.

According to biblical teaching, Jesus had two natures. He was fully God and fully man. (Colossians 2:9; John 10:30; Isaiah 9:6; Revelation 1:5–8; John 20:26–29; John 1:1–3, 14) The Christian church debated this Christological issue for many centuries before the birth of Islam. Based on correct biblical interpretation, the Council of Chalcedon in 451 AD adopted the creedal statement: "We, then, following the holy Fathers, all with one consent, teach men to confess one and the same Son, our Lord Jesus Christ, the same perfect in Godhead and also perfect in manhood; truly God and truly man" (Schaff 1910, 744–45).

Among Christians there were groups like Nestorians, Monophysites, and Arianists (followers of Arianism), who denied the belief that Christ had two natures. Muhammad's earlier encounter with Christianity was with groups such as these, and he thus received an incorrect teaching about Christ. Timothy C. Tennent stated:

> A different view based on similar theological grounds was known as Arianism named after Arius, the presbyter from Alexandria who vigorously promoted this view. Arians, like Muslims today, were deeply committed to protecting the oneness and immutability of God. They insisted that God can not share his essence with anyone else, for that would make him divisible and subject to change. (Tennent 2002, 181)

The question arises how Muhammad acquired the idea denying the two natures of Jesus Christ. Muhammad may have been influenced by the teachings of the Nestorians because they were in Arabia at the time of Muhammad. In any case, the view that Muhammad denied the two natures of Christ is reflected in the Qur'an.

J. W. Sweetman points out: "It can be shown conclusively that Arabia came into contact with all three major sections of the church i.e., the Byzantine, Nestorian and Jacobite-Monophysite churches." (Sweetman 1954, 2)

Islamic scholars were also later influenced by these teachings and rejected the idea that Christ had a dual nature, both human and divine. They influenced Muslim society and religious belief through their interpretations and teachings. Among them al-Baqillani, a famous scholar and theologian in the tenth century, was typical.

Yvonne Yazbeck Haddad and Wadi Z. Haddad point out:

> Al-Baqillani categorically rejected any notion of incarnation, or indwelling of the divine, or any of the attributes of the divine present in a human form [like Jesus] or in any created physical form. He perceived that any contiguity of the divine with the temporal created world serves to render the divine temporal, and therefore is liable to change, decay, and death—an impossible ascription to the self-subsistent and eternal God." (Haddad and Haddad 1995, 86)

South Asian Muslims misunderstand Christ's divine nature that he was fully God, although the Qur'an does declare that Jesus was sinless. "He [Jesus] replied: 'I am only a messenger from your Lord [sent] to bestow a good [pure, holy] son on you'" (Surah19:19). Here the word *He* refers to Jesus. Some translations say "good," others say "pure," and others say "holy." In this verse the Arabic word for "good" or "pure" or "holy" is "*zakiyan.*" Raouf Ghattas and Carol B. Ghattas have stated that in the Qur'an, "The word *zakiyan,* which is a title of Jesus, is interpreted by commentators as meaning 'pure'" (Ghatas and Ghattas 2009, 174). The terms holy and pure clearly indicate sinless.

Since both the Qur'an and the Bible claim that Jesus is sinless, therefore He must be divine, because no human being is sinless. Both the Bible and Qur'an believe there are no sinless adult humans. In the Qur'an no prophets (including Muhammad) claimed to be sinless or holy. Yet, there is a prevalent perception among some South Asian Muslims that prophets (including Muhammad) were sinless. It should be noted that in the Bible, Jesus himself claimed to be sinless (John 8:46).

Unlike all human beings and all other prophets, including Muhammad, Jesus had no biological father. Muslims believe that Jesus was specially created by God, like Adam. Yvonne Yazbeck and Wadi Z. Haddad point out: "For Islamic faith, Jesus, like Adam, is a special creation of God, but unlike Adam, he is free from sin" (Haddad and Haddad 1995, 65).

Although the nativity story in the Qur'an is somewhat different from that in the Bible, the main elements of the story are essentially the same. The basic teaching in the Qur'an affirms the virgin birth of Jesus through Mary, conceived by the Holy Spirit of God (Surah 19:16–29). Mary's conception by the Holy Spirit confirms the divinity of Jesus Christ; however, this doctrine is rejected by Islam. South Asian Muslims also believe in the virgin birth of Jesus but also reject His divinity.

The Bible says that Adam was created, but Jesus was born of a human, Mary; yet he was conceived of the Holy Spirit. The Qur'an also admits that Jesus was conceived of the Holy Spirit (Surah 19:19–21).

In the Bible, Jesus always talked in the first person, even as God talked in the Old Testament (Exodus3:14; John 11:25, 8:58). His miracle of raising the dead back to life (John 11:43–44) (and His own Resurrection) is proof that Jesus had power over death. Although South Asian Muslims believe his miracles, they argue that Jesus did all his miracles by the power of God like Moses and other Old Testament prophets.

Based on Islamic teaching, South Asian Muslims perceive that Jesus had divine power and used that divine power to perform miracles, yet they claim He was not divine. In my interviews with South Asian Muslims, I asked this question to all participants, and their answers are presented and analyzed later in this book.

Islam teaches that all prophets, including Jesus, were God's messengers, and they were all human, and further teaches that Jesus was created by God in a special way as a human, yet in Islamic theology He was not divine. Bible-believing Christians cannot deny that Jesus was fully a man (1 John 4:2–3), but at the same time Christians also believe that Jesus was fully God (John 10:30–39). Jesus was fully God indicated by His sinless life and unique character, which cannot be matched by anyone. He was hungry and thirsty (Luke 2:16, 41–52, 8:23; John 4:6–7, 11:35).

Like other Muslim groups, South Asian Muslims, including those in America, see only the human side of Jesus Christ, and they disagree with the true biblical teaching of His divinity, so to the Christian, the Muslim perception of Jesus Christ fails at this extremely important doctrine.

The Bible clearly teaches that no human being is sinless because all humans are sinful from birth due to inheriting Adam's sinful nature. On the other hand, the Qur'an teaches that at birth humans do not inherit Adam's sinful nature (Surah 53:39) rather all humans become sinful as they grow up, making personal choices that determine their eternal destiny. According to Qur'anic teaching, Adam disobeyed God and repented, receiving God's forgiveness (Surah 20:22; 115). Even though the Qur'an clearly states that all adult humans (including Muhammad) commit sin, yet the Qur'an acknowledges that Jesus was sinless, due to His special creation by God (Surah 19:19). This is a contradiction in the Qur'an.

The Qur'an also acknowledges the miracles of Jesus as authentic, as well as the fact that He is in heaven with Allah and will return to earth on Judgment Day. The Qur'an has no explicitly clear teaching about the subject of Christ's Second Coming; however, support for this doctrine is found in the Qur'an: "And [Jesus] shall be a Sign [for the coming of] the Hour [of Judgment]: therefore have no doubt about the [Hour] but follow ye Me: this is a Straight Way" (Surah 43.61). Yusuf Ali, a well-known translator of the Qur'an into English, comments on this verse:

> This is understood to refer to the second coming of Jesus in the Last Days just before the Resurrection when he will destroy the false doctrines that pass under his name, and prepare the way for the universal acceptance of Islam, the Gospel of Unity and Peace, the Straight Way of the Quran. (Ali 1987, 1337)

It is puzzling how the Qur'an can acknowledge all these characteristics of Jesus yet deny His divinity.

A large proportion of South Asian Muslims, including those in America, believe that all prophets, including Muhammad, are sinless, even though this is not supported by the Qur'an. Even Muhammad was required to confess his sin. (Surah 47:19) John Azumah stated:

> Although Muhammad's life serves as an eternal model for Muslims [Surah 33:21], he was a mortal like all other prophets [Surah 48:29]. As a mortal, he sinned and requires forgiveness [Surah 40:55, 47:19]. Muslims, unlike Christians who worship Christ, will always say that they do not worship Muhammad. But while Qur'anic and Islamic orthodoxy insist that Muhammad is a mere mortal, Muslim devotion and traditions have made extravagant claims on his behalf. (Azumah 2008, 21–22)

Thus, the Qur'an clearly attests to Muhammad as a sinner who required God's forgiveness, yet also clearly acknowledges Jesus Christ as sinless, yet does not recognize His divinity.

Muslim misperceptions regarding the two natures of Christ come from three sources. One source is the teaching of the Qur'an, and a second source is the influence of Christian heretical groups Muhammad encountered, discussed above. A third source is the Muslim scholars and clerics who interpret and teach Islamic doctrine. Orthodox Muslims consider the Qur'an as the "Mother of the Book (*Umm al Kitab*)," and the Qur'an is eternal. Muslims believe the Qur'an is contained on a tablet, kept eternally in heaven. For Christians, Jesus is the One who is eternal (John 1:1–17). So in His incarnation into human form, Jesus did not depart from His divine nature. Abdiyah Akbar Abdul-Haqq stated:

> Whatever arguments the Muslims use to prove the eternity of the Word of God embodied in the Koran [Qur'an] will apply, by and large, to the divinity of the Word of God incarnate [Jesus] through the Virgin Mary. The humanity of Jesus Christ was not divine by nature just as the Arabic language and material used in the production of copies of

the Koran [Qur'an] cannot easily be called divine even by Muslim orthodoxy. The Muslims hold a sort of two-nature theory about the Koran [Qur'an] as do Christians about Jesus Christ. It may be asked, is the Koran [Qur'an] read in material books of the same nature as its heavenly original—Mother of the Book? (Abdul-Haqq 1980, 69–70)

On the one hand, the Qur'an acknowledges that Christ was sinless; on the other hand, the Qur'an also acknowledges that no adult human being is sinless. It is self-contradictory. So the misperception of the two natures of Jesus Christ among South Asian Muslims is based on contradictory Islamic teaching.

THE CRUCIFIXION, RESURRECTION, AND ASCENSION OF JESUS

The most fundamental belief of Christians, clearly taught in the Bible, is the Crucifixion and Resurrection of Jesus Christ, yet South Asian Muslims deny both the Crucifixion and the Resurrection of Jesus Christ. This is one of the most important theological disagreements between Muslims and Christians all over the world, including South Asian Muslims in America. Another important doctrine discussed in this section is the Ascension of Jesus Christ, even though in Islamic terminology they do not use the term ascension, rather they state that Allah lifted (or raised) Jesus up.

In this section, I discuss the Qur'anic view of the Crucifixion, Resurrection, and Ascension: the contradictions, theories, and interpretations held by different Islamic sects among South Asian Muslims. Islamic teachings based on the Qur'an and related to these Christological issues are examined in light of the misperceptions that arise, not only among Muslims in South Asia, but also among those who immigrate to America. I further examine the Christian concept of the suffering Messiah, and how this Christian doctrine is misunderstood by South Asian Muslims in general, and specifically in America.

The Qur'anic Views and Some Contradictions. Based on the following Qur'anic verses, Muslims deny that Jesus died on the cross:

They said [in boast], "We killed Christ Jesus, the son of
Mary, the Messenger of Allah;" but they killed him not,
nor crucified him, but so it was made to appear to them,
and those who differ therein are full of doubts, with no
[certain] knowledge, but only conjecture to follow, for of
a surety they killed him not: Nay, Allah raised him up
unto Himself; and Allah is Exalted in Power, Wise. (Surah
4:157–58)

In this Qur'anic passage, "we" refers to the Jews. It may be inferred
from the passage where the Jews cried out to Pilate at Jesus's trial,
demanding His Crucifixion, "His blood be on us and on our children!"
(Matthew 27:25). In contrast to this, the passage in the Qur'an clearly
claims:

- ➤ Jesus was not killed or crucified by the Jews, even though it
  appeared to be so to them.
- ➤ Rather than Jesus being killed or crucified, "Allah raised him
  up unto Himself." This is usually taken to mean that Allah took
  Jesus Christ out of the world into heaven with Himself.

Benjamin T. Lawson observed on these verses:

This is the only verse in the Qur'an that mentions the
Crucifixion of Jesus. It has largely been understood both by
Muslims and, in some ways more interestingly, by Christians,
as a denial of the historical and, to many, irrefutable fact of
the Crucifixion of Jesus. (Lawson 2009, 1)

Under Roman law, only the Roman governor or a representative
of Rome had authority to order an execution. This is why the Jewish
people brought Jesus before Pilate, the Roman governor of Judea. In
Surah 4:157 the words "but so it was made to appear to them" creates a
confusion. If it only *appeared* to the Jews that Jesus was crucified, this
could mean on the one hand the idea of an apparition (Docetism), or
on the other hand that it was someone else who was crucified in place
of Jesus Christ (substitution theory).

There are many disagreements among scholars about the exegesis of these Qur'anic verses. Some scholars believe an influence of the docetic ideas was brought over into Islam. Docetism, a Christian heresy, taught that Jesus only *appeared* to die on the cross, and this teaching influenced some Christian churches in the first century but was soon declared a heresy. The Docetists believed that Jesus's physical body was an illusion, as was the Crucifixion of Jesus Christ. Because Jesus was divine, they think He could only *appear to* be human, hence the term "docetic" which means ghostly or an apparition.

Since Islam began in the seventh century, while Docetism existed in the first century, the question arises how could it be possible for Docetism to influence Islam after almost seven hundred years, especially in light of the doctrine being declared heretical in the first century by mainline Christian churches.

During Muhammad's time, a Christian community existed in the city of Najran, in the southwestern part of modern Saudi Arabia near the border of Yemen. Some scholars think that there might have been a docetic influence among these Christians in Najran. Ismail Acar has an opinion about the presence of a Christian community in Najran and Muhammad's encounter with them. He states:

> No doubt the most important interaction between the Christians and the Prophet was the visit of the Najran delegation to Madina. Makka and Madina had a very small Christian population [Waraqa ibn Nawfal was one of them]. The majority of Christian residents lived in Najran. The Prophet's first important encounter with Christian clergies was in the 9th year of Hijra (migration) (AD 631), one or two years before his death. (Acar 2005, 1)

Michael Hayek argues that since Najran was in Arabia, Muhammad might have encountered this Christian heretical group there, and that:

> This opinion may be related to a Christian heresy which had many supporters in Najran just before the rise of Islam. This was the heresy of the Docetics who denied the sufferings of Christ. Some of them claimed that Simon the Cyrene was the man who bore the likeness of Christ and died in his stead. (Hayek 1961, 21)

But nobody is sure whether Muhammad met this group. Tarif Khalidi, who edited and translated the book *The Muslim Jesus: Sayings and Stories in Islamic Literature,* speculated that Muhammad encountered some docetic form of Christianity:

> There is first of all the question of his Crucifixion, which Saint Paul described as being to the Jews an obstacle that they cannot get over, to the pagans' madness [1 Corinthians 1:23]. In denying the Crucifixion, did the Qur'an encounter the same difficulties? Did it simply believe some Docetic form of Christianity? This would be an attractive solution, especially since Docetism [from Latin *doceo,* to appear] is the exact equivalent of the Arabic in the Qur'anic verse *Wa lakin Shubbiha lahum* ["but so it was made to appear to them." (4:157)], the phrase with which the Qur'an denies the reality of the Crucifixion. Most scholars today would argue that while Docetic imagery is possible, Jesus of the Qur'an is unlike the Docetic Jesus in all other respects: the Qur'anic Jesus is very much flesh and blood, while in Docetism he is mere shadow. In denying the Crucifixion, the Qur'an is in fact denying that the Jews killed him, and elevates him to God as part of his vindication as a prophet, thus reconciling him to the general typology of Qur'anic prophecy. It is the Ascension rather than the Crucifixion which marks the high point of his life in the Qur'an and in the Muslim tradition as a whole. (Khalidi 2001, 12–13)

This passage (Surah 4:157) in the Qur'an clearly denies the reality of the Crucifixion of Jesus and denies that Jesus died on the cross. In denying the death of Jesus on the cross, a question arises: Did the Qur'an encounter the same difficulties mentioned by Khalidi? Does the Qur'an imply some docetic form of Christ Jesus that was crucified?

Most scholars today would argue that while docetic influence is possible, Jesus as portrayed in the Qur'an is unlike the docetic Jesus in all other respects. The Qur'anic Jesus is human, with physical flesh and blood, while in Docetism, He is mere shadow. In denying the Crucifixion of Jesus, the Qur'an is, in fact, denying that He died on the cross; rather

Allah lifted Jesus up to Himself. Instead of referring to this as ascension, Muslims simply say that Allah lifted Jesus up unto Himself.

The most prominent theory about the Crucifixion is called the substitution theory and was developed by Muslim scholars based on Surah 4:157–58, mentioned above. According to this Surah, especially the part which claims "but so it was made to appear to them," is taken to suggest the possibility that somebody died on the cross in place of Jesus Christ, someone who had a similar appearance or even was changed into the likeness (image) of Jesus. Referring to Al-Tabari, a ninth century Islamic scholar, Hugh Goddard stated:

> Al-Tabari gives a number of his explanations on these verses, [Surah 4:157–58] each of which is traced back to a different source. The first explanation is that all the disciples were changed into the image of Jesus, and so when those who wanted to kill Jesus came to look for him, one of his disciples went out to them and was then killed in the belief that he was Jesus. The second is that when one of Jesus' disciples pointed to Jesus in order to betray him, after the rest of the disciples had scattered, a likeness was shown to them [with no further explanation], and when they reached the wood [the cross] on which they wished to crucify Jesus, God raised him up to Himself and they crucified "what was made to appear to them." A third account contains ten different versions of one person who was made to look like Jesus: the sixth version is that it was a volunteer from among Jesus' disciples, by the name of Sergius, and another version is that it was Judas Iscariot who was crucified. Tabari's conclusion is simply: "God knows which of these was the truth." (Goddard 1996, 24–25)

Goddard further mentioned a thirteenth century Islamic scholar and commentator, al-Baidawi (d. 1286), also clearly affirmed the substitution theory, but in his commentary, the identity of the person who was made to look like Jesus was not clear. Goddard also included that another Islamic scholar, Al-Razzi (d. 1209), searched for the identity of a person who may have appeared in the likeness of Jesus, according to this substitution theory, and he concluded that there was someone who did take the place of Jesus on the cross, but he remained uncertain about who that may have been (Goddard 1996, 25–26).

Concerning the Crucifixion, these Qur'anic verses (Surah 4:157–58) create much confusion, and misperceptions about the death of Jesus Christ, and because of this confusion, several differing explanations have been developed by Muslim scholars. Some argue that there was no crucifixion at all; some argue that there was a crucifixion, but Jesus did not die and only passed out (swooned) and later revived; and yet another theory was the substitution theory that holds that another person who looked like Jesus was killed on the cross. This substitution theory has gained quite a following in numerous Muslim groups.

In my interviews among South Asian Muslims in America, I asked the participants about this Qur'anic passage. Everyone interviewed answered that they only know that Jesus was taken up to heaven before the Crucifixion took place. Most of them were unfamiliar with the substitution theory.

Many historical evidences of the Crucifixion of Jesus exist. Not only the biblical account, but other historic sources as well, clearly recorded the Crucifixion of Jesus. Iskander Jadeed has noted:

> History also recorded Christ's death. Historians recorded this event, devoting lengthy passages to it in their accounts. Some of these historians were: Tacitus, the heathen historian, in the year 55 A.D.; Lucian, the Greek, writing in 100 A.D.; Josephus, the Jew, who lived a few years after the Crucifixion. All the writings agree with the gospel account in regard to the birth, teachings, Crucifixion, and Resurrection of Christ. (Jadeed 1990, 20)

The vast majority of Muslims reject the Crucifixion of Jesus Christ; this includes the South Asian Muslims in America. Sulaiman Shahid Mufasir points out that "Muslims believe that Jesus was not crucified. It was the intention of his enemies to put him to death on the cross, but God saved him from their plot" (Mufasir 1980, 5). Mufasir's comment is supported by the Qur'anic verse:

> Who could prevail against God [Allah] if He had chosen to destroy Messiah, son of Mary, and his mother, and the rest

of mankind? For God's is the Kingdom of the heavens and earth and whatsoever lies between them. He creates what He pleases, for God has the power over all things. (Surah 5:17)

Norman Geisler and Abdul Saleeb give two theological concepts related to Muslim rejection of the Crucifixion of Jesus:

> The reason for Islamic disbelief in the Crucifixion of Jesus centers on two theological concepts: sovereignty and depravity. More precisely, it is based on the unique Islamic concept of sovereignty of God and their rejection of the Christian belief in the depravity of man. (Geisler and Saleeb 1993, 275)

Results of the interviews presented in this book confirm the perception of South Asian Muslims in America who typically reject the Crucifixion of Jesus Christ.

A Christian doctrine closely related to the Crucifixion is the Resurrection. Since Muslims reject the Crucifixion of Jesus Christ, for them, there could not be a Resurrection of Jesus Christ.

Another Christian doctrine is the Ascension of Jesus Christ into heaven. Christians believe that forty days after the Resurrection of Jesus, He ascended into heaven. However, based on Surah 4:157–58, Muslims believe that Allah "raised him up unto Himself" into heaven just before His Crucifixion could be carried out.

Many Muslims believe the substitution theory, that Allah transformed another person to appear exactly like Jesus, who was crucified instead of Jesus. Because of the Qur'anic phrase in Surah 4:158, "but so it was made to appear to them," the substitution theory was developed. This same phrase gave rise to the other theory, which claims that it was not Jesus on the cross, rather an apparition of Jesus (similar to docetic belief).

Interpretations by Some Islamic Sects and Scholars. In this section I discuss the different views of some Islamic sects related to the Crucifixion of Jesus Christ. I discuss different interpretations among the Muslim scholars regarding the exegesis of the Qur'anic passage concerning the Crucifixion of Jesus Christ. I further discuss the interpretations of scholars from the following sects: Sunni,

Shi'a, Ahmadiyya, and the two main branches of Shi'a, Ismaili and Zaydi.

Surah 4:157–58 is the only passage in the Qur'an where there is any mention of the Crucifixion of Jesus Christ. Regarding the exegesis of this Qur'anic passage, scholars have different views.

Almost all scholars from the two mainline Islamic sects, Sunni and Shi'a, agree that Allah saved Jesus from being crucified by lifting Him up unto Himself. However, a group in South Asia called Ahmadiyya disagrees with this view with an entirely different theory, called the swoon theory.

Mirza Ghulam Ahmad started a movement in India near the end of the nineteenth century. His group was named "Ahmadiyya," after his name. Ahmadiyyas believe that Jesus was crucified on the cross but did not die, rather swooned and was later revived. In Islamic circles this "swoon theory" is only believed by the Ahmadiyya. Jocelyne Cesari has stated: "These claims also further undermined Christian doctrine, a move further exemplified in Ghulam Ahmad's assertion that Jesus died some time later in Srinagar, India, rather than on the cross" (Cesari 2007, 28).

This swoon theory is opposed by the mainline Islamic sects (Sunni and Shi'a) in South Asia. As previously mentioned, in some Muslim countries, such as Pakistan, Ahmadiyya is not even recognized as a legitimate Muslim group by mainline Islamic sects, or even by governmental law.

The two main divisions of Shi'a are Zaydi and Ismaili. Each Shi'a branch has its own exegesis and commentary (*tafsir*) of the Qur'an. Most Zaydi scholars believe there was no crucifixion of Jesus Christ; however, some Zaydi in Yemen believe Jesus was crucified. In his examination of the Zaydi group in Yemen, Todd Lawson states the position taken by the founder of this group:

> The influential scholar and jurist al-Qasim ibn Ibrahim al Rassi ..., founder of the Yemeni Zaydi legal *madhhab* [school of thought], *upheld the historicity of the Crucifixion of Jesus.* The precise details of his teaching on this topic are as yet unclear. But there seems to be no compelling reason to doubt that he understood the Qur'an as *not denying* that the historical Jesus

was actually put on the cross and crucified. In one passage he explains and justifies the Crucifixion of Jesus as a ransom to God. (Lawson 2009, 77) (Emphasis mine.)

It is difficult to understand al-Rassi's argument. The Qur'an says, "they said [in boast], 'We killed Christ Jesus, the son of Mary, the Messenger of Allah;' but they killed him not, nor crucified him: Nay, Allah raised him up unto Himself" (Surah 4:157). Here the word *they* is understood to refer to the Jews. So it is saying that the Jews did not kill Christ or crucify him.

It seems al-Rassi interprets this passage in the Qur'an to say that the Jews did not kill Christ, but the Romans did crucify Christ. Thus, he holds the position that the Qur'an does not deny the historical Jesus was crucified on the cross.

However, this interpretation of al-Rassi affirming the Crucifixion of Jesus Christ, is in direct contradiction to the part of this passage that says, "of a surety they killed him not: Nay, Allah raised him up unto Himself." This part of the passage can only be logically understood in the context of the full passage as meaning that Allah raised Jesus Christ up unto Himself *in order to prevent His Crucifixion!*

With al-Rassi's interpretation in mind, another part of this passage where it says, "but so it was made to appear to them," could be explained to mean that it appeared to the Jews that they were successful in killing Jesus, even though it was the Romans who actually carried out His execution on the cross. To me al-Rassi's argument looks like twisted logic!

There are various disagreements among some Ismaili (another Shi'a group) scholars and commentators concerning the exegesis of the Qura'nic verse 4:157. Some of them agree with the historicity of the Crucifixion of Jesus; however, most of them do not.

In rejecting the Crucifixion of Jesus Christ, some Islamic scholars and preachers often cite the pseudogospels in defense of their teachings. The Gospel of Barnabas is the most popular of them. Many Muslims also cite the Gospel of Barnabas to refute the Crucifixion of Jesus Christ.

In the book *A Muslim View of Christianity: Essays on Dialogue by Mahmoud Ayoub*, the editor, Irfan A. Omar, quotes Ayoub, "*The Gospel of Barnabas* was discovered in 1709 in the Vatican library and was translated into Arabic in the early decades of the twentieth century" (Omar 2007, 226) No evidence has been found to authenticate this book and Christian scholars consider it apocryphal, because it is not part of the accepted canon of Christian scriptures. In 2004, Samuel Green wrote an article, "The Gospel of Barnabas," posted on Answering-Islam.org. In this article the writer gave the reason why the Gospel of Barnabas is not an authoritative source:

> The main topic of *The Gospel of Barnabas* is the life of Jesus. It retells most of the events of Jesus' life as recorded in the Biblical Gospels, but at some points there are changes and additions to these stories. These changes are not random; instead they follow a clear pattern. They are intentional changes to make the Biblical accounts conform to the teaching of the Qur'an. (Green 2004, unpaginated)

Green sounds like the Gospel of Barnabas was written after the Qur'an and with the purpose of making biblical accounts conform to the Qur'an.

Most Christian scholars agree that the Gospel of Barnabas was written in the late sixteenth century, not the first century as claimed by Muslin scholars. It is ludicrous to claim it was written in the first century because it repeatedly mentions the Prophet Muhammad's name, and he was not born until the sixth century. John Gilchrist points out:

> There were numerous apocryphal Gospels, Epistles and other forgeries ... one was titled *The Gospel of Barnabas*. No historical record whatsoever exists to show what sort of book it was or what it taught. ... There are many proofs that [*the Gospel of Barnabas*] is a 16th century forgery. It is not hard to prove to Muslims that this Gospel was first compiled many centuries after the times of both Jesus and Muhammad. (Gilchrist 1999, 138)

Iskandar Jadeed points out concerning the date of the original writing of the Gospel of Barnabas: "From an examination of the paper and ink used, it appears that it was written in the 15th or 16th century" (Jadeed 2010, 6).

John Gilchrist wrote that originally the Gospel of Barnabas was written in Spanish and Italian and later translated into Arabic (Gilchrist 1999, 135–36). The first century disciple named Barnabas, a coworker of the apostle Paul, was Greek-speaking, and would not know Spanish or Italian. The Gospel of Barnabas was named after this New Testament disciple, who was a fellow missionary and coworker with the apostle Paul on his first missionary journey (Acts 13:1–3).

Biblical Gospels were written by the person indicated in the title (e.g., the Gospel of Mark; the Gospel of Matthew, etc.). In contrast, Barnabas obviously could not have written the Gospel of Barnabas, because of references in the text and other evidences that indicate a much later writing.

In numerous interviews and discussions with South Asian Muslims in America, I have heard them cite the Gospel of Barnabas to refute the Crucifixion of Jesus.

In the Gospel of Barnabas, Jesus is described as a prophet but not the son of God. (p. 41, 58) This writing supports the Muslim claim that Jesus escaped crucifixion by being raised alive into heaven (p. 108). It further repeatedly states that Judas Iscariot, the betrayer of Jesus, was crucified in His place. (The Gospel of Barnabas 1998, 24–108)

Londsdale and Ragg write concerning the claim that Judas was the substitute for Christ on the cross:

> According to *The Gospel of Barnabas*, "Judas entered impetuously before all into the chamber whence Jesus had been taken up. And the disciples were sleeping. Whereupon the wonderful God acted wonderfully, insomuch that Judas was so changed in speech and in face to be like Jesus that we believed him to be Jesus. And he, having awakened us, was seeking where the Master was. Whereupon we marveled, and answered: 'You, Lord, are our master; have you now forgotten us?'" (Londsdale and Ragg 1907, 216)

The Gospel of Barnabas also narrates the Crucifixion of Jesus in this way:

> When the soldiers with Judas drew near to the place where Jesus was, Jesus heard the approach of many people,

wherefore in fear he withdrew into the house. And the eleven were sleeping. Then God, seeing the danger of his servant, commanded Gabriel, Michael, Rafael, and Uriel, his ministers, to take Jesus out of the world. The holy angels came and took Jesus out by the window that looketh toward the South. They bore him and placed him in the third heaven in the company of angels blessing God for evermore. ... Judas was so changed in speech and in face to be like Jesus that we believed him to be Jesus." (The Gospel of Barnabas 1998, 108)

The Gospel of Barnabas not only creates misunderstanding by providing erroneous information about the death of Jesus on the cross, but also contradicts the Qur'anic teaching that claims that Allah Himself lifted Jesus up, not angels.

It is thought that the main source of the confusion surrounding the Muslim controversy over the Crucifixion of Jesus Christ was the fact that, in Muhammad's time, no translation of the Arabic Bible was available. Local people had no access to authenticate writings in Arabic. Muhammad had to depend upon oral traditions, tales, and stories. Muhammad had contact with some Christians, but in most cases, these Christians provided him wrong information. So it turns out that many misperceptions held by Muslims in the present day are the result of misinformation and erroneous anecdotal material.

This misinformation about Christ's Crucifixion was later imparted to South Asian Muslims who brought the resultant misperceptions with them when they immigrated to America.

Because most Muslims do not believe in the death of Christ on the cross, they also do not believe in the Resurrection of Christ. Yet all Muslims believe there will be a general resurrection of the dead on the final judgment day. Their perception is that Christians have perverted the truth about the Crucifixion of Jesus Christ. This is because Muslims claim Allah saved Jesus from crucifixion by raising him up unto Himself.

In my personal observation, most Muslims in South Asia as well as in America are unfamiliar with the substitution theory. On the other hand, they are familiar with the swoon theory held by the Ahmadiyya.

Misperceptions of the Suffering Messiah. South Asian Muslims are familiar with the word *Messiah*. Apart from the Bible, the Qur'an is the only book where Jesus is called Messiah (*Al-Masseeh*). "When the angels said: 'O Mary, Allah gives you news of a thing from Him, for rejoicing, [news of one] whose name will be Messiah, Jesus, son of Mary, illustrious in this world and the next and one among the honored'" (Surah 3:45–46).

Based on these Qur'anic verses, most Muslims in South Asia as well as in America wrongly perceive that the term *Messiah* is a personal name, like "Jesus" in the Bible and "*Isa*" in the Qur'an. Unlike the Bible, the Qur'an does not understand that "Messiah" is the special title of Jesus, meaning "the Anointed One." This is taken to mean anointed by God.

However, South Asian Muslims misunderstand the Christian doctrine of the suffering Messiah. Jesus's disciples also were unclear about how the concept applied to Jesus, especially that He would be put to death on the cross. In the Gospels we find that Jesus frequently predicted his Crucifixion and Resurrection. These predictions are found in numerous references in the synoptic gospels of the New Testament (Mark 8:31, 9:31, 10:33–34; Matthew 20:17–19; Luke 18–31).

Todd Lawson points out:

> There are very good reasons to believe that Jesus did in fact anticipate his violent death and his triumph over death by his resurrection. Crucifixion is not a topic central to the Qur'an. It is, however, a topic central to Muslim-Christian relations over the centuries. (Lawson, 2009, 10)

Jesus's teachings and works pointed to the fulfillment of the Old Testament prophecy about His role as the suffering Messiah (Isaiah 53), particularly as it relates to His death on the cross. The Bible tells that He repeatedly reprimanded his disciples for failing to understand that, as the Messiah, He must suffer, die, and rise from the dead (Mark 10: 31–35). This is clearly and definitely a core teaching of Jesus Christ in the Bible.

South Asian Muslims do not understand the concept of the suffering Messiah because there is no such teaching in Islamic theology—that one can die for the sins of others. The biblical doctrine of the substitutionary atonement is a concept unfamiliar to them.

According to the Bible, Jesus suffered as the Messiah, fulfilling the prophecy of the prophet Isaiah (Isaiah 53) about the suffering Messiah. This prophecy came long before the birth of Jesus, in the eight century BC. Isaiah clearly described the suffering of the Messiah in Isaiah 53:4–5: "He was stricken, smitten …, afflicted …, wounded …, bruised …, by his stripes (whip marks) we are healed …, He was oppressed …, afflicted."

It is also difficult for a South Asian Muslim to accept the concept of the suffering Messiah. It is hard for them to imagine how a prophet of Allah could be humiliated in such a way and how the Almighty would tolerate it.

Part of the reason Muslims deny the Crucifixion is that they deny the possibility that Allah would allow His prophet to suffer. This would apply even more so to God's Messiah.

In summary, regarding the Crucifixion of Jesus, although there are various theories and interpretations among Muslim scholars, such as the apparition theory (Docetism), substitution theory, and swoon theory (Ahmadiyya), the overall prevailing Muslim perception is that Jesus Christ was not crucified. Christians believe that Jesus Christ sacrificed His life for the remission of sins for all who truly believe. Since Islam does not acknowledge that the sins of Adam are inherited by all humans, Islam finds the Christian teaching of the Crucifixion of Jesus Christ repugnant and rejects the doctrine of the propitiatory atonement of Jesus Christ—dying to pay the penalty for sin, for all who believe in Him.

In the Qur'an and in Muslim tradition, the high point of the life of Jesus Christ came when Allah raised Him up unto Himself in heaven, thus preventing His death on the cross. This is true because, according to the Qur'an, Jesus did not die on the cross but was raised up to heaven by Allah; therefore, the Crucifixion was prevented, and there was no Resurrection of Jesus from the dead. To the Muslims it would be a humiliation of God if He allowed Jesus to be killed in such a disgraceful way.

THE REVELATION OF GOD: THE BIBLE

Most Muslims perceive the Bible as a holy book. Christians and Jews are called "the people of the book" (*Ahl al-Kitab*) by Muslims. The Qur'an even affirms this (Surah 10:94; 29:46; 3:3, 4) Yet, Muslims also have the perception that the Qur'an supersedes all previous revelations from God. Furthermore, they believe the Bible has been altered in the course of history, especially through the process of translation, and thus accuse Christians of corrupting the Bible.

In this section, I first define and clarify the Christian doctrine of the Bible as the Word of God, the Holy Scripture, and the revelation of Himself and His will. A vital part of the doctrine of the Bible is its claim that Jesus Christ is the ultimate revelation of God. What we know of the life and teaching of Jesus Christ is in the Bible.

Second, I discuss the Qur'anic view of the Bible, as the basis for the Muslim perception of this doctrine of the Bible as the Word of God. Understanding what the Qur'an has to say about the Bible and how Muslims respond to Christian claims about the Bible and biblical teaching are essential to understanding the Muslim perception of Christianity.

Third, I then explore in detail the Muslim perception of the Bible and the specific core teachings and claims regarding the Bible. We look at what the Muslim perception and reaction is to this Christian doctrine. Muslims will naturally look at this in comparison to how they feel about their own holy scripture (i.e., the Qur'an). So understanding the Muslim views of their own scriptures becomes essential to an understanding of the Muslim perception of the Christian doctrine of the Holy Bible as God's revelation of Himself and His will.

Muslim perceptions related to the Bible are also typical of the majority of Muslims in South Asia as well as those in America.

The Christian Doctrine of the Bible. When Christians refer to the Bible, they use several terms, such as: the Holy Bible, the Holy Scriptures, the revelation of God, and the Word of God. A Christian belief closely related to the scriptures is that they must be fulfilled (Mark 14:49, Matthew 26:54–56, Luke 4:21). Because what is written in the scriptures is God's revelation, it is God's truth and must come to pass.

Among Christians are a variety of views about the origin and composition of the Bible. Most Christians say the Bible was inspired by God, and its writing was strongly guided by the Holy Spirit so as to be inerrant. Herschel Hobbs comments on the beliefs of most Christians about the Bible that "The Holy Bible was written by men divinely inspired and is the record of God's revelation of Himself to man. It has ... truth, without any mixture of error, for its matter" (Hobbs 1971, 18).

A small minority of Christians believe in a dictation theory of the origin of the Bible, suggesting that the specific words were divinely dictated to the writers of the Bible. Lawrence O. Richards states:

> Inspiration does not suggest dictation. Some have thought that dictation was required, and imagined that somehow the human writer's personality was blanked out: that God moved hands and minds without human involvement. But each writer of the Bible has his own literary style." (Richards 1982, 14–15)

Conservative Christians believe "the sole authority for faith and practice ... is the Scriptures ... (and) Jesus Christ, whose will is revealed in the Holy Scriptures" (Hobbs 1971, 3–4).

The Bible contains passages about its own authenticity and authority: "All Scripture is God-breathed [inspired by God] and is useful for teaching, rebuking, correcting, and training in righteousness, so that the man of God may be thoroughly equipped for every good work" (2 Timothy 3:16–17).

"Above all, you must understand that no prophecy of Scripture came about by the prophet's own interpretation. For prophecy never had its origin in the will of man, but men moved by the Holy Spirit spoke from God" (2 Peter 1:20–21).

Christianity emphasizes the meaning and the message of the Bible as inspired by God and guided by the Holy Spirit. It is the *message* that is inspired and important, not the specific original words. Words are just words, but when particular words are put together in a certain way, they convey a meaning—a message. For Christians, it is the message that is holy, inspired by God—not just the original words that are used to communicate that message.

> The Bible is more than a religious document to be preserved. And it is more than a classic of ... literature to be cherished and admired. It is a record of God's dealing with men, of

God's revelation of Himself and His will. It records the life
and work of Him in whom the Word of God became flesh
[became human] and dwelt among men. The Bible carries its
full message, not to those who regard it simply as a heritage
of the past or praise its literary style, but to those who read
it that they may discern and understand God's Word to
man. ... to understand and believe and obey His Word.
(Preface: *Harper Study Bible* 1962, vii)

One particularly important set of scripture passages relates to the
concept of the Messiah (the Anointed One). The Old Testament was
written in Hebrew, and *Messiah* is a Hebrew word. The New Testament,
which begins with a narrative about the birth of Jesus, is written in
Greek. The Old Testament word *Messiah* becomes Christ (*Christos*) in the
Greek New Testament. There was a prophecy in the Old Testament that
foretold that there would be the Anointed One (the Messiah, the Christ)
who would be sent by God and would be God's ultimate revelation of
Himself. Jesus would be known as the Christ (the Messiah).

No one has ever seen God; the only Son, who is at the
Father's side, He has made him known. (John 1:18)

Long ago, at many times and in many ways, God spoke to
our fathers by the prophets [in the Scriptures], but in these
last days he has spoken to us by his Son [Jesus Christ],
whom he appointed the heir of all things, through whom
also he created the world. He is the radiance of the glory of
God and the exact imprint of his nature, and he upholds the
universe by the word of his power. After making purification
for sins, he sat down at the right hand of the Majesty on high.
(Hebrews 1:1–3)

To the Christian, Jesus Christ is the ultimate revelation of God:

He [Jesus] is the image of the invisible God, the firstborn of
all creation. For by him all things were created, in heaven
and on earth, visible and invisible, whether thrones or
dominions or rulers or authorities—all things were created
through him and for him. And he is before all things, and in

him all things hold together. And he is the head of the body, the church. He is the beginning ... that in everything he might be preeminent. For in him all the fullness of God was pleased to dwell, and through him to reconcile to himself all things, whether on earth or in heaven, making peace by the blood of his cross. (Colossians 1:13–20)

The Bible claims that Jesus is the Son of God, that He was active with God in Creation, and that He is the only way to salvation from sin and the only way to heaven. He is the ultimate and complete revelation of God.

Human writers were inspired by God and wrote the sixty-six books of the Bible. In a few cases, God spoke directly to these writers (Exodus 17:14, Joshua 24:26). Different writers contributed to these texts, and all writers were inspired, chosen by God, and guided by the Holy Spirit, but the initiative was God's. All writers of the Bible were inspired by God's Spirit to write what God revealed to them (2 Peter 1:20–21, 2 Timothy 3:16–17).

About the formation and writings of the Bible, Lawrence O. Richards stated in *Illustrated Bible Handbook*:

Some have described the Bible as a "collection of religious writings." It is a collection. There are sixty-six books. They were written by forty different persons, over a span of some 1,500 years. The writers were fishermen, political leaders, and kings. A few were highly educated philosophers. One writer was a medical doctor. Three different languages were used in its writing: Hebrew, Aramaic and Greek. And yet the Bible is essentially one Book, and it tells a unified salvation story. (Richards 1982, 13)

Robert L. Plummer states:

The Bible is a collection of writings that Christians consider uniquely inspired and authoritative. While it is one unified book, the Bible is also a compilation of sixty-six smaller books, or literary works. These works, produced by men of various historical time periods, backgrounds, personalities, and cultures, claim the Holy Spirit as the ultimate authority and safeguard behind their writing. As 2 Timothy 3:16 asserts, "All Scripture is God breathed." (Plummer 2010, 17)

I agree with these writers that the Bible is one unified book and that God is the ultimate authority, initiative, and inspiration for the Bible.

Most Christians believe that the Bible was written by men inspired by God but free to express the truth of God in their own style, yet guided by God's Holy Spirit so as to prevent error.

The Qur'anic View of the Bible. Before examining the Qur'anic view of the Bible, it is important to clearly understand what Muslims believe about the Qur'an itself.

Muslims believe that the Qur'an was a series of revelations from God, dictated to Muhammad during his lifetime. According to Islamic history, the Qur'an was revealed by the angel Gabriel (*Jibril* in Arabic), verbally dictated to Muhammad gradually over a period of approximately twenty-three years (610–632 AD). It is unclear what language Gabriel used in dictating to Muhammad, but since Arabic was his native tongue, it is logical to assume it was in Arabic.

Muhammad, who evidently was illiterate, supposedly then memorized and orally recited these words to his close aides in Arabic, who wrote them down verbatim as the Qur'an, the holy book of the Muslims.

The word Qur'an in Arabic means "recitation" (spoken words). Concerning the word *Qur'an*, Richard Bell and William Montgomery Watt point out:

> It is possible that the root of this word [Qur'an] is the Syriac *Qeryana*, which carries with it the meaning of giving a scriptural reading or lesson in church. This word was adopted into Arabic as a title for the Muslim compilation of Scriptures. (Bell and Watt 1970, 136–37)

Muslims believe that the Qur'an is the *unchangeable* Words from Allah. "Those who believe and [constantly] guard against evil; For them are glad tidings, in the life of the present and in the Hereafter; *no change can there be in the words of Allah. This is indeed the supreme felicity.*" (Surah 10:63–64) (Emphasis mine.)

Fazlul Rahman comments regarding the importance of the words themselves:

> The voice from the depths of life spoke distinctly, unmistakably, and imperiously. Not only does the word Qur'an, meaning "recitation," clearly indicate this, but the text of the Qur'an itself states in several places that the Qur'an is verbally revealed and not merely in its "meaning and ideas." (Rahman 1966, 30–33)

Christians have a very different attitude toward the revelation of God in the Bible. The meaning and the message are of primary importance, not the exact words. However, as Rahman points out, Muslims revere the very words, because of the belief they were dictated by Gabriel directly to Muhammad.

So regarding the formation of the Qur'an, Muslims hold that the exact words as dictated by Gabriel, presumably in Arabic, are considered sacred. South Asian Muslims in America hold these same beliefs about the Qur'an.

In the Qur'anic view of the Bible, there are points of agreement and points of disagreement between Islam and Christianity. There is a wide range of teachings in the Qur'an regarding the Bible. For example, both the Qur'an and the Bible teach that God is One, God is Creator, and God is Almighty. On the other hand, the Qur'anic teaching disagrees with the Bible about the Incarnation of God in Jesus, the Crucifixion and Resurrection, and the divinity of Jesus Christ—even though it acknowledges that Jesus was sinless.

The Qur'an teaches that Muslims should accept and read certain Bible portions, such as the five books of Moses (Arabic *Tawrat,* Hebrew *Torah*) and the Gospels (Arabic *Injeel*) as authentic and authoritative revelation from God. In the Qur'an, Muslims are commanded to believe in these portions of the Bible, revealed to the Jews and Christians (Surah 4:163–65).

The Qur'an affirms and is in basic agreement with the Old Testament. It is understood by Muslims that the Qur'an teaches that the Torah was revealed to Moses (*Musa*), who is recognized as a prophet by Muslims, and is mentioned by name in numerous passages in the Qur'an (Surah 2:47–71; 7:103–37, 159–66; 20:9–97; 26:10–66; 28:2–46).

The Qur'an mentions the revelations given to the "People of the Book," (i.e., the Jews and the Christians), specifically mentioning the Law of Moses (Torah) and the Gospel of Jesus Christ, commending these biblical scriptures to the Muslims, thus authenticating them. According to the Qur'an, Allah even warned them not to question or dispute this revelation from God.

> It is He Who sent down to thee [step by step], in truth, the Book, confirming what went before it; and He sent down the Law [of Moses] and the Gospel [of Jesus] before this, as a guide to mankind, and He sent down the criterion [of judgment between right and wrong]. Then those who reject Faith in the Signs of Allah will suffer the severest penalty, and Allah is Exalted in Might, Lord of Retribution. (Surah 3:3–4)

John Gilchrist stated:

> As we have seen already, the Qur'an itself unambiguously confirms that the *Taurat* of the Jews (Torah) was the book regarded as such by them at the time of Muhammad and that the *Injil* (Gospels) likewise was the book in the possession of the Christians at that time which they themselves considered to be the word of God. At no time in history have Jews and Christians ever regarded any books as the sacred word of God other than those constituting the Old and New Testaments as we know them today. (Gilchrist 1988, 9)

The Qur'an also mentions the book of Psalms (*Zabur*), which the Qur'an says was revealed to David (*Dawud*) (Surah 4:163). The Qur'an authenticates all these Bible portions of the Jews and Christians mentioned above (Torah, Psalms, Gospels) (Surah 10:94).

There is no negative teaching in the Qur'an against these Bible portions: Psalms, Torah, and the Gospels. Yet there are obvious contradictions in the Qur'an with the content of the Gospels, especially the Christian doctrines contained therein. The Qur'anic teaching against certain doctrines in the Bible is where the problem lies.

The Qur'an affirms Christians and Jews who follow their scriptures, and accords to them a reward in the hereafter: "Those who believe [in the Qur'an], and those who follow the Jewish [Scriptures], and the Christians and the Sabeans—any who believe in Allah and the Last Day, and work righteousness, shall have their reward with their Lord; on them shall be no fear, nor shall they grieve" (Surah 2:62).

On the other hand, the Qur'an brings accusations against some "People of the Book" (i.e., Jews and Christians) who turn people away from the path of Truth (the Islamic way):

> Quite a number of the People of the Book wish they could Turn you [people] back to infidelity after ye have believed, from selfish envy, after the Truth hath become Manifest unto them: But forgive and overlook, Till Allah accomplish His purpose ... And they [Jews and Christians] say: "None shall enter Paradise unless he be a Jew or a Christian." ... Say: "Produce your proof if ye are truthful." Nay,—whoever submits His whole self to Allah and is a doer of good,—He will get his reward with his Lord; on such shall be no fear, nor shall they grieve. (Surah 2:109–112)

In the same Surah, the Qur'an comments on the "quarrel" (dispute) between Jews and Christians:

> The Jews say: "The Christians have naught [to stand] upon; and the Christians say: "The Jews have naught [to stand] upon." Yet they [profess to] study the [same] Book. Like unto their word is what those say who know not; but Allah will judge between them in their quarrel on the Day of Judgment. (Surah 2:113)

Obviously, Jews and Christians will have serious points of disagreement because Jews do not accept the divinity of Jesus Christ or that Jesus is the Messiah, or the Resurrection of Jesus, or that Jesus is the Son of God. And it is not the same Book—for the Jews restrict their allegiance to the Old Testament, and do not include the Gospels in their scriptures. The Qur'an does not understand that the Jews and Christians do not "study the same Book," because the Jews reject the Gospels.

Commenting on the Qur'an, Hugh Goddard stated:

> Jews and Christians have their scriptures, which were originally given to the prophets and to Jesus respectively. But, the Jews in particular, and also the Christians, have deviated from the teachings of their scriptures and so these ... have been, in some way, corrupted and distorted. These two statements together leave ample room for diverse and diverging subsequent interpretations and developments, both positive and negative. And so the ambivalence of the Qur'an is able to be the foundation of many different views of the Bible. (Goddard 1996, 11)

I agree with Goddard about the "diverse and diverging ... interpretations" of scripture and the "ambivalence of the Qur'an" regarding the Bible. But I disagree on the point that if Christians and Jews deviate from scriptural teachings, this somehow corrupts and distorts the scriptures. In fact, the Qur'an also does not agree that the scriptures themselves have been corrupted, and even declares: "No one can change the word of Allah" (Surah 10:64).

In the Qur'anic passage below, there is inclusion and affirmation of the Jews, but also condemnation ("we cursed them") for their breach of the Covenant with Allah:

> Allah did aforetime take a Covenant from the Children of Israel [the Jews] ... And Allah said: "I am with you: If ye [but] establish regular Prayers, practice regular Charity, believe in My apostles, honor and assist them, and loan to Allah a beautiful loan, verily I will wipe out from you your evils, and admit you to Gardens with rivers flowing beneath; but if any of you, after this, resisteth faith, he hath truly wandered from the path of rectitude." ... But because of their breach of their Covenant, *We cursed them*, and made their hearts grow hard ... (Surah 5:13–14). (Emphasis mine.)

While the Qur'an consistently affirms the scripture portions the Torah and the Gospels, there are many inconsistencies between the Qur'anic teaching and biblical doctrines. The Qur'an:

> ➢ Denies the triune God (Trinity)
> ➢ Denies the divinity of Jesus Christ
> ➢ Denies the incarnation of Jesus Christ
> ➢ Denies that Jesus Christ is the Son of God
> ➢ Denies the Crucifixion and Resurrection of Jesus Christ

Gabriel supposedly dictated the Qur'an to Muhammad, yet there are inconsistencies and internal contradictions. If Gabriel dictated the Qur'an—which authenticates the Gospels—then it should not make these denials of doctrines contained in the Gospels, which were available in Muhammad's time in the original Greek language. Thus, this inconsistency is clearly evident in the Qur'an.

The Bible declares in the Gospel of Luke that Gabriel spoke to Mary, telling her the child she would bear would be conceived by the Holy Spirit and would be the Son of the Most High and also would be called the Son of God (Luke 1:26–35).

Assuming the claim of the Qur'an, Gabriel—in his dictation to Muhammad—clearly authenticated and affirmed these Bible portions containing the declarations about the birth of Jesus. At the same time the Qur'an denies the doctrines affirmed in these Bible passages, thus revealing an internal inconsistency and contradiction in the Qur'an. This discrepancy also reveals a serious conflict between the teachings in the Qur'an and those in the Bible.

The fact that the Qur'an affirms the Gospels, while denying the content of the Gospels, even as clearly presented in the original language of the Greek text, represents a serious inconsistency and self-contradiction within the Qur'an itself.

Gabriel supposedly dictated the Qur'an to Muhammad, but Gabriel would also know the original message of the New Testament, which contradicts some of the teachings of the Qur'an.

Muslim Perceptions of the Bible. Muslims have several perceptions about the present-day Bible. Most Muslims consider the Bible as a holy book and an earlier revelation of God. However, many Muslims accuse Christians of corrupting the Bible. Based on interviews presented in Chapters 4 and 5, this includes most conservative and fundamentalist South Asian Muslims in America. This is also confirmed by a significant number of conversations I have had about this subject with South Asian Muslims in the Boston area.

Muslims accuse Christians of corrupting the Bible, because they believe any translation corrupts the words of the original texts. Regarding the accusations of corruption of the Bible, it is important to differentiate between two accusations: 1) that the Bible is corrupted when translated into a language different from the original text, and 2) that the original texts of the Bible themselves have been altered or changed, and thus corrupted. It is important to be clear about which of these accusations are being brought against the Bible.

In this section, I seek to maintain this distinction regarding the accusations of corruption that are brought against the Bible. When stating that the original text has been corrupted, I mean that some Muslims claim the literal words of the earliest manuscripts of the Bible have been corrupted through alteration, either accidental or intentional.

Muslims believe that when the original texts of the Bible are translated, this corrupts the Bible because the words are changed. This belief is widespread among Muslims today, including those in America. This common belief is primarily because they consider their own scriptures (the Qur'an) to have been dictated to Muhammad by the angel Gabriel, speaking directly for God, and therefore the exact words in Arabic are considered sacred, and if the words are translated into another language, the result is not considered authentic. Yet, they believe translations of the Bible are corruptions. This reveals an inconsistency in their thinking.

On the other hand, Christians place more emphasis on the meaning and message carried by the words, and do not consider the exact original words in the original language to be sacred, while mandating that they be carefully preserved. Rather the content—the message, the meaning carried by the words—is what is considered sacred and to be translated with great care. The preponderance of published Bibles available today is not in the original languages, although Bibles are also available in copies and scans of the original texts of Hebrew and Greek.

In this section, I discuss the accusation by Muslims of the corruption of the Bible, as well as sources of these criticisms and the reasoning behind them. I also explore the views of Muslim scholars regarding this accusation as well as the authenticity and reliability of the Bible. I further discuss the South Asian Muslim perception regarding the authenticity of present-day Bible translations.

Muslims also claim that their holy book, the Qur'an, supersedes the earlier biblical revelations of God (the Bible), even though the Qur'an itself does not make this claim. This means that many Muslim scholars claim all previous revelations from God are replaced and made obsolete by the Qur'an. South Asian Muslims generally also concur in this conviction. This implies not only that the Bible is superseded by the Qur'an, but this carries with it the implication that the Bible is outdated and not to be trusted as a reliable revelation from God, even though the Qur'an itself authenticates portions of the Bible. This further implies that any inconsistency or contradiction between the Bible and the Qur'an means the Qur'anic teaching takes precedence as the higher authority.

Muslims have an incorrect perception of the corruption of the Bible in use today by Christians. Muslims reject any translation into another language, regardless of the accuracy and reliability of the translation.

Muslims also do not consider any translation of the Qur'an from the original Arabic language as authentic. This is because they believe that the Qur'an was dictated verbatim to Muhammad, and therefore only the Arabic version is considered authentic, and corruptions of the authentic text. Therefore, it must be in the original language. This explains the main reason they reject any translations of the Bible.

The majority of South Asian Muslims in America today hold this same conviction. John Azumah stated:

> The Qur'an has to be recited in Arabic and cannot be translated into another language. Even though translations may be undertaken, the translated Qur'an will not be accorded the same spiritual and devotional status as the Arabic version. This version is highly venerated by Muslims, almost as if it possesses magical properties. (Azumah 2008, 46)

Passages from the Qur'an are often misused as references by Muslim preachers and clerics in their attempts to discredit the Bible and argue that ignorant Christians have falsified and corrupted the Bible, particularly the Torah, the Psalms, and the Gospels. Yet, the Qur'an clearly declares that nobody can change the words of Allah, (Surah 6:115, 5:44–46, 21:48, 3:3–4), and affirms that these Bible portions are authentic—the revealed word of Allah. This logic does not seem to hold up. If nobody can change the words of Allah, this literally would mean the words themselves cannot be changed, but Christians hold that it as the message and meaning of the words that are sacred and cannot be changed. This is a fundamental disagreement between Christian and Muslim.

The majority of Muslims in South Asia, as well as in America, are comprised of laypeople who rely on the interpretations and teachings of their clerics. The reason for this is that very few Muslim laypeople understand Arabic, and they are therefore unable to read the Qur'an for themselves and are taught that translations are not authentic and are unreliable.

In the region of South Asia, Muslim preachers and clerics often discourage their Muslim laypeople from owning or reading the Bible. Instead of being free to participate in a comparative study of the Bible and the Qur'an, they depend on the opinions and teachings of their clerics and preachers. Without seriously examining the comments of the Qur'an about the Bible for themselves, the majority of South Asian Muslims have the misperception that the Bible is corrupted and therefore must be avoided. Moreover, the influence of Muslim clerics and preachers is very strong among South Asians, including those in America.

Since most Muslims in South Asia do not understand Arabic, they will not understand the content and message of the Qur'an, except as taught by their clerics, who are not always well versed in Qur'anic teaching. This implies that the Arabic words, which they do not understand, are more important than the message, which they could understand if allowed to read the Qur'an in their own language.

Muslims are encouraged to read the Qur'an in Arabic from their childhood, and even to memorize it in Arabic; however, the average Muslim in South Asia does not understand Arabic and so is unable to study the Qur'an independently or even to know the meaning of what has been committed to memory, even though the Qur'an has quality translations in the major languages in South Asia today.

Translations of the Qur'an are not generally used at the mosques and Islamic schools (*madrasas*), including those in America. Also, it should be mentioned that if the meaning was of the same importance as the words, then logically one would expect the mandatory study of the Arabic language for all adherents. In contrast to this, the Christian emphasizes the meaning and message of the Word of God, and this creates a favorable attitude toward translations, which is contrary to Muslim teaching. So the different perceptions regarding the Word of God become evident.

South Asian Muslims in America see the variety of Bible translations available today, and they are reminded about their indoctrination that criticizes and rejects translations of the Qur'an, and this seems to reinforce their misperception that the Bible has been corrupted through translation and is therefore not to be trusted. Christians believe a proper translation does not corrupt the meaning; only the words are changed to capture the meaning in a different language, but the original text is left unchanged.

Many South Asian Muslims in America today are not aware of the numerous references in the Qur'an that commend and authenticate the holy books of the Jews and Christians: *Tawrat* (Torah), the *Zabur* (Psalms) and the *Injil* (Gospels), (cf. Surah 3:3–4; 10:94; 5:45–46; 35:31; 5:68; 3:3; 2:136; 4:163, 136). I have come to hold that opinion through interaction and dialogue with South Asian Muslims over many years.

Many Muslims today have the opinion that they no longer need the previous holy books since today they have the complete Qur'an. However, even the Qur'an directed Muhammad to consult with the people who read the previous holy books. "If you are in doubt of what we have sent down to you, then ask those who have been reading the Book for a long time before you" (Surah 10:94). "The Book" here clearly refers to the Bible portions (Torah, Psalms, and Gospels). Neither the Qur'an nor Muhammad himself ever suggested that these texts of the Bible are corrupted.

In saying "who have been reading the Book (for a long time) before you," clearly the angel Gabriel was referring to and commending the Jews and Christians (and their holy books) as he spoke to Muhammad. If the Bible was corrupted, surely the angel Gabriel would not direct

Muhammad to consult with the people who had been reading a corrupted book.

A significant number of other books in the Bible are not mentioned in the Qur'an, and Muslims today consider that these other books of the Bible were added by humans and are not part of God's revelation.

Most South Asian Muslims have the perception that the Torah, Psalms, and Gospels are not available in the original versions in the present day, which is clearly untrue. Furthermore, very reliable facsimiles and copies of these original texts are not only readily available but have been carefully authenticated by renowned historians and scholars, with many scholarly notations referring to rigorous study and careful preservation of the earliest manuscripts.

Through many discussions and conversations over many years of ministry, I have come to see that the perception of most South Asian Muslims is that the Bible has been corrupted, but they are unsure how or when or by whom it was corrupted. A prevalent opinion is that Jews and Christians altered the original texts of their Bible, even though they offer no evidence or claim as to how these changes in the original languages took place. This belief is clearly in opposition to the declarations of the Qur'an.

These are very serious charges denigrating the Bible and challenging its authenticity, because Christians base their beliefs and practice on the Bible and rely on the accuracy of the translations based on the preserved earliest manuscripts.

Examining the contrasts between Muslim perceptions of the Bible and Christian perceptions, Muslims feel that translations are corruptions, but Christians believe that they are essential to an effective communication of the meaning and message of the Word of God and to make these available to all people of every language. Christians can easily argue that translations are important because of the importance of the meaning and message expressed by the holy writings and of getting this message across to the maximum number of people, not just the exact words in the original language, which most people do not understand.

Translations are necessary to convey the message of God to everyone, and it is essential for translators to be very careful to adhere to the original content and message intended by the Holy Spirit who inspired the writers. The most reliable translators are extremely careful in trying to discern and communicate the message God intended in the original texts.

The following verse from the Qur'an supports my argument against the charge Muslims bring, that the Bible has been corrupted:

> It is He [Allah] Who sent down to thee [step by step], in truth, the Book, confirming what went before it; and He sent down the Law [of Moses] and the Gospel [of Jesus] before this, as a guide to mankind, and He sent down the criterion [of judgment between right and wrong]. (Surah 3:3)

This Surah claims that Allah Himself "sent down" the books of the Law (Torah) and the Gospels. Therefore, this is an authentication of these Bible portions. For them to be corrupted, some human would have to alter the original texts and distort their meaning. Of course, Christians do not agree with the Qur'anic teaching that the original scripture portions were "sent down" by God; however, Christians do agree that these scripture portions are authentic and reliable as the Word of God.

Raouf Ghattas and Carol B. Ghattas commented on this Qur'anic verse regarding the Muslim accusation of Bible corruption:

> God says to Muhammad that he gave to him a true book, agreeing with the two books he already had in his hand, the Tawrat and Injil, which were light for people before [the time of Muhammad] ... This means that Muhammad had these books in his hand at the time—if not literally, he still knew something about them. Muslim scholars, read this verse as saying that the Qur'an proves that Tawrat and Injil spoke about God sending Muhammad as a prophet. However, many Muslims, in searching for proof of this statement, have examined the Law and Gospels, finding it mentions nothing about Muhammad. From this the whole theory of corruption of the Tawrat and Injil takes place, though there is no linguistic basis for it. (Ghattas and Ghattas 2009, 41)

I agree with the point that these authors make concerning the supposed corruption of the Tawrat (Torah) and Injil (Gospels), that these are a false accusation, and I further agree that these scripture portions never mentioned the name of Muhammad, centuries before he was born.

If I only describe the Muslim perception of the Bible as corrupted, with no rebuttal or comment, then it might appear that I think there is no reasonable response to the accusation, but, of course, I strongly refute this accusation.

It is important to know how the Qur'an was compiled into the present-day book, because it is a logical comparison and parallel to the Muslim perception of the credibility of the Bible as relates to its formulation. The accusations they make against the authenticity of the Bible related to its composition can also be brought against the Qur'an.

Historically the Qur'an was not in book form during Muhammad's lifetime but would have been written onto parchment but not yet compiled into a single book, which is the form of the present-day Qur'an. This was also true of many early manuscripts of the Bible.

The process of compilation began after the death of Muhammad. From the time of the first Caliph (successor of Muhammad, the political and spiritual guide), Abu Bakr (632–634 AD) and ended up during the third Caliph Uthman (657 AD). A commission was set up, headed by Zayd Ibn Thabit, who had been one of the close associates of Muhammad and served as his scribe. Finally, one text of the Qur'an was officially adopted.

In his compilation, Zayd Ibn Thabit was instructed to follow the guidelines which required the text be according to the accent and dialect of Muhammad's own tribe, the Quraysh. Hammudah Abdalati tells about these guidelines:

> All the copies in use were collected and replaced by one standard copy which was to be used according to the accent and dialect of Quraysh [Muhammad's own tribe], the very same dialect and accent of Muhammad himself. (Abdalati 1975, 195)

The present-day book form of the Qur'an was officially compiled and adopted twenty-five years after the death of Muhammad. Timothy C. Tennent points out, "The Qur'an, which began as an oral recitation, was officially written down and codified in 657, twenty-five years after Muhammad's death" (Tennent 2002, 144).

Referring to the Bukhari Hadith (vol. 6, p. 479), John Gilchrist stated:

> During the reign of Uthman, the third successor [caliph] to Muhammad, word came to him that the Muslims in the various provinces were differing considerably in their reading of the Qur'an. Uthman decided to unite the people on a mushaf wahid [single text] and, after calling for Zaid's codex which was conveniently in Medina in Hafsah's possession where the caliph had his seat of government, he ordered Zaid with three others to transcribe his manuscript into seven exact replica copies and to send one copy to each province with *the order that all the other manuscripts of the Qur'an in existence be burnt.* (Gilchrist 1999, 22) (Emphasis mine.)

This burning of early manuscripts would be a significant loss, because of the Muslim's emphasis on original texts for credibility and authenticity, and the accusations brought against the Bible related to original texts.

Almost all the other texts were destroyed by the order of Caliph Uthman, but in some places, people refused to destroy their copies, especially in some parts of Iraq and Syria. Alford Welch stated:

> The dominant versions of this account then state that Uthman circulated copies of the result to the major metropolitan areas and ordered all other written Qur'anic material to be destroyed. When the Uthmanic text was made official, Ubayy destroyed his codex while Ibn Masud refused to do so. [This] may be examples of historical telescoping, meaning that the people of Syria (possibly over a period of many years) gave up their distinctive reading (i.e., that of Ubayy), while the people of Kufa refused to give up theirs (i.e., that of Ibn Masud). (Welch 1977, 183,199)

Many South Asian Muslims do not know this history of the compilation of the Qur'an or the order to destroy the earlier Qur'anic texts. So lack of knowledge about the background history of the Qur'an naturally raises serious questions about the reliability and authenticity of the Qur'an itself related to the original manuscripts and the copies in use today.

This also leaves Muslims open to the same accusations they bring against the Bible related to original manuscripts. What happened to the originals that were not burned? This leaves a logical assumption that what the Muslims are memorizing and reciting today is not true to the original documents.

It is important to know that accusations of the corruption of the Bible developed long after the death of Muhammad. Abdiyah Akbar Abdul-Haqq stated:

> Despite all evidence from the Koran [Qur'an] to the contrary, Muslims developed a strange doctrine of the corruption of the Judeo-Christian Scripture during the centuries after their prophet. It is easy to see that such a fanciful theory not only goes against the Qur'an but also violates common sense. (Abdul-Haqq 1980, 36)

In the eleventh century, Ibn-Khazem (or Ibn-Hazm) was the one who first brought the accusation of textual corruption (tahrif) of the Bible. Referring to Ibn-Khazem, Gerhard Nehls wrote the article "Why Do Muslims Believe the Text of the Bible Has Been Corrupted?" This article states:

> In 1064, Ibn-Khazem [Ibn-Hazm] lived among the circle of ruling hierarchy of the Umayyad government in Cordoba, Spain), first charged that the Bible had been corrupted and the Bible falsified. This charge was to defend Islam against Christianity because Ibn Khazem came upon differences and contradiction between the Bible and the Qur'an. Believing by faith that the Qur'an was true, the Bible must then be false. He said, "Since the Qur'an must be true it must be the conflicting Gospel texts that are false. But present texts must have been falsified by Christians after the time of Muhammad." (Nehls 1992, unpaginated)

I agree with Nehls that Ibn-Khazem had no historical evidence or support for his claims that the Bible has been corrupted but only his obviously biased efforts to discredit the Bible.

Many other Muslim scholars were confused by what Ibn-Khazem meant by the accusation of the corruption (tahrif) of the Bible. Was the corruption a result of translation, which does not alter the original text, or did he mean a corruption of the original text itself?

It is not clear what Ibn-Khazem intended. Writing over four hundred years after Muhammad, did he mean the original texts were corrupted or that translating the words of the text corrupted it? Since Muhammad himself, in the Qur'an, affirmed and validated the Bible portions known to him at that time, then whatever Ibn-Khazem meant by his accusations would be a direct contradiction.

Misinterpretation of the Bible by some Christian sects took place in Arabia in the time of Muhammad. They misinterpreted some Christian doctrines and communicated their beliefs to Muhammad. Misinterpretation does not mean the original texts were changed. They may have simply misunderstood certain biblical passages and teachings, or they may have developed some false doctrines that were not really based on scripture. Misinterpretations of the Bible can create misperceptions in the minds of Christians and also of Muslims. Historically some of these misperceptions were passed along to Muhammad, as in the case of the biblical doctrine of the Trinity, which led him to think Christians believed in polytheism. Surah 5:76 says: "They do blaspheme who say: Allah is one of three in a Trinity: For there is no god except One God. If they desist not from their word [of blasphemy], verily a grievous penalty will befall the blasphemers among them."

Hugh Goddard responded to the charge of Bible corruption brought by Ibn-Hazm (Ibn-Khazem):

> He [Ibn Hazm] does not simply reject the biblical text [and other religious texts] as having been corrupted, but ridicules certain parts: ... He also challenges the Bible because of its accounts of the sins of a number of prophets, such as David, accounts which Ibn Hazm rejects on the grounds that the *prophets were sinless* so the accounts must have been

made up ... Ibn Hazm's views and language were thus both extremely strong. (Goddard 1996, 36) (Emphasis mine.)

I agree with Goddard that Ibn-Khazem is clearly wrong about prophets being sinless, except for Jesus who alone was sinless according to both the Bible (cf. John 8:46) and the Qur'an. (cf. Surah 19:19) Neither the Qur'an nor Muhammad himself ever claimed the prophets to be sinless, except for Jesus. The Qur'an makes no claim of sinlessness for Muhammad or any other prophet, except Jesus.

The following Surah is proof that the Qur'an never claims that Muhammad was sinless. Muhammad had to ask forgiveness of his own sin and the sins of his followers: "Know then, therefore, there is no god but He, and ask forgiveness for your sins and those of believing men and women" (Surah 47:19).

Muhammad himself also never claimed that he was sinless. On the other hand, the Bible definitely claimed that Jesus was sinless. In John 8:46, when Jesus said, "Which of you convicts me of sin ..." Thus, He clearly implies His own claim to sinlessness. Also, in Luke 7:48–49, Jesus clearly said, "Your sins are forgiven." So how could Jesus forgive the sins of others unless He, Himself was sinless? In fact, those who accused Jesus said, "Who can forgive sins but God alone?" (Luke 7:49).

The Bible reinforces and affirms this claim:

> Since then we have a great high priest who has passed through the heavens, Jesus, the Son of God, let us hold fast our confession. For we do not have a high priest who is unable to sympathize with our weaknesses, but one who in every respect has been *tempted as we are, yet without sin.* (Hebrews 4:14–15) (Emphasis mine.)

As previously mentioned, the Qur'an also clearly acknowledges that Jesus was without sin. When the Angel Jibril (Gabriel) appeared to Mary to announce her conception of Jesus, he said: "Nay, I am only a messenger from thy Lord, [to announce] to thee the gift of a holy son" (Surah 19:16–19).

It is obvious that "holy son" means without sin. One Hadith (sayings of Muhammad) also records that Jesus was sinless, which clearly indicates that Muhammad himself believed that Jesus was sinless! This is recorded in *Sahih* (the authentic) *Muslim Hadith* (Vol. 4, p. 1261).

Thus, the claim of the Bible of Jesus being sinless is supported by the Qur'an and the Hadith.

Islamic writers in the fourteenth century criticized the Christians who misinterpreted the Bible; among them Ibn Taimiyya (d. 1328) and Ibn Khaldun (d. 1382) were prominent. Both concluded that it was not the original text of the Bible that had been corrupted but rather the interpretation of the Bible that was corrupted. In 2014, an article entitled "Tahrif," published by Billion Bibles, argued against Ibn-Khazem's charge of corruption (*tahrif*) against the biblical text:

> There are at least two problems with *tahrif*. Firstly, by the time Ibn-Khazem claimed *tahrif* against the Bible, the Bible had been around for a thousand years and hundreds of manuscripts of the Bible across the Middle East, Europe, and North Africa attested to its accuracy. Any claim of textual corruption needs to present evidence of the supposedly corrupted text before their supposed corruption. Neither Ibn-Khazem nor anyone since has produced any such evidence of *tahrif*. Secondly, *tahrif* of the Bible contradicts Muhammad and his Quran, which attest to the accuracy of the Bible. (Billion Bibles 2014, 1)

I agree with Billion Bibles' challenge to the claims of Ibn-Khazem that he provided no evidence of his claim of textual corruption and that his accusations contradicted both Muhammad and the Qur'an.

Following are some references related to the accusation of tahrif (corruption), and based on these references, I argue that the charge of corruption of the Bible text is serious and contradicts the teaching of both the Qur'an and Muhammad. Because Muhammad and the Qur'an clearly claim authenticity and authority for the portions of the Bible known to Muhammad (Torah, Psalms, and Gospels), which were the copies of the original Hebrew and Greek texts in the possession of Jews and Christians in the time of Muhammad in that region.

The Muslim apologist Alhaj A. D. Ajijola, in 1978, also brought accusations against the Bible in an attempt to discredit its authenticity:

> The first five books of the Old Testament do not constitute the original Torah, but parts of the Torah have been mingled up with other narratives written by human beings and the original guidance of the Lord is lost in that quagmire. Similarly, the four Gospels of Christ are not the original Gospels as they came from Prophet Jesus ... the original and the fictitious, the Divine and the human are so intermingled that the grain cannot be separated from the chaff. The fact is that the original Word of God is preserved neither with the Jews nor with the Christians; Qur'an, on the other hand, is fully preserved and not a *jot* or *tittle* has been changed or left out in it. (Ajijola 1978, 79)

This reveals a total misunderstanding of the Gospels, which did not come "from the Prophet Jesus," were not recited or written by Him, but under the inspiration of the Holy Spirit were clearly written by others about the life and teachings of Jesus. The Gospels of Christ were written by disciples of Jesus: Matthew, Mark, Luke, and John, and the Bible clearly specified the author in the title of each Gospel (e.g., in the original Greek text: *Kata Markon*: "According to Mark.")

Norman L. Geisler and Abdul Saleeb responded to the above accusations of Ajijola: "These charges bring us [Christians] once again to the Islamic doctrine of tahrif, or corruption of the Judeo-Christian Scriptures. ...Muslim theologians have generally formulated two different responses." (Geisler and Saleeb 1993, 209).

The two different responses mentioned by Geisler and Saleeb are: corruption of the *meaning* of the text, and the corruption of the *text itself*. The following statement by Michael Nazir-Ali explains these two different distinct types of accusations of corruption (tahrif) mentioned above: "The early Muslim commentators (e.g., Al-Tabari and Ar-Razi) believed that the alteration is *tahrif bi' al ma'ni*, a corruption of the *meaning of the text without tampering with the (original) text itself*. Gradually, the dominant view changed to *tahrif bi'al-lafz, corruption of the (original) text itself*" (Nazir-Ali 1987, 46). (Emphasis mine.)

This statement differentiates between corruption of the "meaning of the text without tampering with the original text," and "corruption of the original text itself." Christians would agree that both these types of change are corruptions and not to be tolerated. To the Christian also, changing the meaning of the text is a corruption, whether the original is changed or not, because understanding the meaning and the message are essential to understanding the Word of God. And, of course, any change of the original text is a corruption because the original must be carefully preserved and never altered.

Bukhari Hadith (sayings of Muhammad recorded by Bukhari) commented also mentioning the charge of tahrif (corruption) of the Bible:

> The word Tahrif signifies to change a thing from its original nature; and that there is no man who could corrupt a single word of what proceeded from God, so that the Jews and Christians could corrupt by misrepresenting the meaning of the words of God. (Bukhari 1970, Vol. 7, p. 1127)

This quotation clearly refers to corruption through misinterpreting, yet the original words are not changed. So according to the Bukhari Hadith, tahrif is the charge of misinterpretation, not alteration of God's words. However, whenever a South Asian Muslim and a Christian read the Bible and the Qur'an together, it is evident to both that vital differences exist between the content of these two books, even though there are many similarities as well. Many South Asian Muslims believe these differences are corruptions introduced by Christians and Jews into the Bible over time, even though it can be easily shown that the translations are consistent with the original Hebrew and Greek texts.

Referring to the view of Sayyid Ahmad Khan, a famous Muslim theologian from the Indian subcontinent, regarding the charge of corruption of the text of the Bible, Hugh Goddard points out, "Sayyid Ahmad Khan's view can therefore be summarized as being that the text of the Bible may have been wrongly interpreted by Christians, nevertheless the text as it stands is fundamentally reliable" (Goddard 1996, 53).

In response to the above comment by Goddard, again Christians would agree that the Bible text may be wrongly interpreted, either through misunderstanding of what the words are saying, or deliberately twisting the meaning of the message contained in the words of the Bible. This is a different kind of corruption, where the message of the original text, or the message of a correct translation, may be misinterpreted. This would corrupt the meaning, but the original message and the message of the translation remain accurate and reliable.

Many manuscripts in original languages are available today that dated long before the birth of Islam. Norman L. Geisler and William E. Nix have argued:

> The manuscript evidence does not support the accusation of textual corruption. With respect to the authenticity of the Old Testament, the Dead Sea Scrolls, which date from 1000 B.C., confirm in an astounding way the accuracy of the Masoretic manuscripts, which date from A.D. 900." (Geisler and Nix 1980, 405, 408)

Most South Asian Muslims mistakenly think that since human writers were involved in writing the Bible text (as Christians believe), it therefore cannot be the direct revelation of God, as they believe is the case with the Qur'an. Hence their perception is that the Bible is not an authoritative book or is a lesser authority than the Qur'an.

Because the Qur'an was supposedly dictated, while the writers of the Bible were inspired humans, guided by the Holy Spirit, the majority of Muslim preachers in South Asia, as well as in America, propagate their biased conviction that therefore the Qur'an is superior to the Bible.

Muslims believe that Islam is the continuation and extension of Judaism and Christianity and is an improvement and correction of these previously incomplete religions and their holy books (especially the Law, Psalms, and Gospels). This perception is in direct contradiction to the Qur'an itself and therefore to Muhammad.

Many Muslim scholars often quote Surah 5:48 in order to support their argument that the Qur'an supersedes all the previous revelations of God. "And to you We have revealed the Book containing the truth, confirming the earlier revelations, and preserving them [from change and corruption]" (Surah 5:48). This Surah does not say that the Qur'an is superior to all other previous books revealing God. To claim this is a misleading interpretation of the Qur'an.

Muslims do not admit any corruptions of the Qur'an. Like other Muslim groups, South Asian Muslims in America believe there are no corruptions in the original dictations by Gabriel to Muhammad and his recitations to his scribes. Thus, they conclude, the Qur'an corrects and supersedes the Bible of the Jews and Christians.

Bruce A. McDowell and Anees Zaka point out:

> Muslims hold to a dictation view of revelation, that the angel Gabriel dictated the very words of God from an eternal book in heaven. About three centuries after Muhammad's death, Muslim theologians asserted that the Qur'an was uncreated and coeternal with Allah. (McDowell and Zaka 1999, 74)

This development was a new doctrine invented by the imagination of some Islamic scholars many years after the Qur'an was written, which clearly implies that Allah did not create the Qur'an; rather, it was coeternal with Him. This development was clearly motivated by Muslims seeking to claim an elevated status and authority for the Qur'an and constitutes an attack on the reliability and authority of the Bible. These scholars developed the idea that the Qur'an was coeternal with God because of the biblical claim that Jesus was coeternal with God. So I believe Islamic scholars invented this parallel claim that the Qur'an is coeternal with Allah.

Still, there have been some controversies among Muslim scholars on the issue of whether the Qur'an is coeternal with God and therefore not created. In the tenth century, disagreement developed among Muslim scholars about whether the Qur'an was "created speech" or "uncreated speech." By "created speech" is meant Allah's words created or caused something to come into being. By "uncreated speech" is meant declarations by God, such as dictated words. Yvonne Yazbeck Haddad and Wadi Z. Haddad point out:

> God's revelation to Muhammad, embodied in the Qur'an, was understood by early Muslims to be the "very speech of

God" and has been accepted as such by all those who affirm God's attributes are eternal. The problem arose when the question was raised whether or not this meant that the Qur'an itself is eternal or noneternal. The ensuing controversy over this issue was sharp and severe. The *Asharites* [School], al-Baqillani among them, held to the position that the Qur'an is God's uncreated speech. Members of the opposing *Mutazilite* School, on the other hand, believed the Qur'an to be God's speech, but created." (Haddad and Haddad 1995, 86)

For those portions of the Bible that contradict the Qur'an, Muslims, including South Asian Muslims in America, bring the charge of corruption against the Bible. Their accusations are not based on any archeological evidence or historical facts but only to justify their personal faith and their desire to discredit the Bible in order to elevate the Qur'an.

The Qur'an claims that no one can change the word of God (Surah 6:34; 10:34). There is also a strict warning in the Bible. "If anyone adds anything to them, God will add to him the plagues described in the book. If anyone takes words away from this book of prophecy, God will take away from him his share in the tree of life and in the holy city, which are described in this book" (Revelation 22:18–19). No Christian will dare to make any change to the Bible if this warning is heeded. Yet, South Asian Muslims misunderstand and accuse Christians of corrupting their own holy book (the Bible).

Muslims claim the Qur'an was dictated by Gabriel to Muhammad and further claim that it was descended (*nazil*) from heaven upon the Prophet Muhammad. The only way both these ideas can avoid contradiction is that Gabriel's verbal dictation to Muhammad has the same meaning as descended upon Muhammad.

Misunderstanding about the Bible arises in Muslim minds because of their personal convictions about the superiority of the Qur'an. William J. Saal points out:

Thus, Muslims often speak of the Qur'an as having descended upon the prophet Muhammad. This notion is clearly reflected by the division of the Qur'an into *Suras* (i.e., series, revelations). In no sense was Muhammad's personality or understanding involved in the Qur'an; it was dictated to him. (Saal 1991, 29)

While I agree with Saal that Muslims hold both the descended theory and also the dictation theory, it seems to me these ideas are logically compatible if they mean that descended upon Muhammad is by means of Gabriel's dictation.

Some three centuries after Muhammad, there arose yet another belief that the Qur'an was coeternal with God and "uncreated speech," which disallows the idea of dictation, which implies created by speech. These ideas seem to logically conflict with each another. How can a document be dictated, coeternal, and uncreated, and also be descended upon Muhammad? Of course, Muslims themselves do not speak with one voice on these conflicting theories.

Based on another Qur'anic passage, Muslims also hold yet another traditional belief related to the Qur'an that it was preserved on a tablet: "This is indeed the glorious Qur'an [Preserved] on the guarded tablet" (Surah 85:21–22). This passage is not explicitly clear about specifically where or when the Qur'an was preserved. Some say this means the original Qur'an is preserved on a tablet in heaven.

Thus, it is clear that there are numerous, often conflicting theories related to the origin of the Qur'an and its preservation, and debates continue among various Muslim groups. The controversies are multiple, conflicting, and ongoing. This reveals various Muslim opinions about their own holy book and their various opinions about the Bible, which relate to their misperceptions about the Christian doctrine of the Bible as God's inspired word of revelation.

At the beginning of the eighth century when the Islamic invaders from Arabia came into South Asia, some South Asians converted to Islam. The majority of Muslims in South Asia today are the descendants of those converts to Islam many generations ago, as well as the South Asian Muslim population in America.

In order to preserve the supremacy of the Arabian culture, traditions, and the Arabic language, from the very beginning Arab invaders and preachers imposed their Islamic religion, ideas, and philosophy on the new converts, as they gained control and influence. The Arabic language was a major emphasis, because it was interwoven with the religion of Islam, especially because the original text of the Qur'an is in the Arabic language, and the Arabic words are considered sacred. Consequently, South Asian Muslims today also share in the Islamic bias against any translations of the Qur'an.

Also, because of this attitude, Muslims do not accept translations of the Bible. Although human writers were engaged in writing the Bible, they were not writing their own ideas but were recording a message from God inspired by the Holy Spirit. The Bible itself testifies that no one wrote their own interpretation of the scriptures. "Above all, you must understand that no prophecy of Scripture came about by the prophet's own interpretation. For prophecy never had its origin in the will of man, but men spoke from God as they were carried along by the Holy Spirit" (2 Peter 1:20–21).

To summarize, some theological perceptions of major Christian doctrines among the majority of Muslims are negative. Historically, many misperceptions about Christian doctrines arose from misinterpretations of the scriptures possessed by Christians and Jews on the Arabian Peninsula during the time of Muhammad. Many of these misperceptions became incorporated in the Qur'an.

These misperceptions were passed along to South Asian Muslims when Islam came into the South Asian region from Arabia in the early eighth century. Today, these same misperceptions were brought by South Asian Muslims when they immigrated to their new home in America.

Misperceptions of major Christian doctrines are so well established in the minds of South Asian Muslims in America that they are very difficult to correct, even in the second and third generation of descendants of immigrants.

For these misperceptions to be corrected, Muslims must be exposed to the true Christian doctrines. Yet, it should be kept in mind that some of the Muslim perceptions are correct. For example, they are correct when they say that Christians believe Jesus is the Son of God; however, part of that perception is that by son we mean offspring, which is not correct. If then, Christians correct the Muslim perception so they understand Christians do not believe Jesus was a biological offspring of God, they may still reject the divinity of Jesus. So there can be a correct perception but still no agreement between Muslim and Christian.

However, many have little interest in learning about Christianity and are discouraged from interacting with Christians by the Muslim influences within their subculture. Furthermore, their misperceptions of Christian doctrines are usually reinforced by what they hear in their mosques and from their Muslim teachers.

As new generations emerge—sons and daughters of these Muslim immigrants—in their new cultural environment in America, and as these new generations become more integrated into mainline American society, they will form new impressions and meet true Christians in the classrooms and workplaces, so their misperceptions become more subject to correction.

Thus, many of their biases against Christianity can be reduced, and they can become more open to dialogue and to discovering the truth about Christianity and Christian doctrines.

To summarize, in this chapter I explored theological perceptions of Christianity with two main focuses.

First, I explored theological influences that historically shaped perceptions of Christianity among South Asian Muslims. This included the influence of some Islamic reform, revivalist, and radical movements in the region of South Asia. Over time these movements shaped the Muslim perceptions of Christianity, and these perceptions are prominent today among South Asian Muslims in America.

Second, I discussed the Muslim misperceptions of major Christian doctrines and how these misperceptions are found among Muslims in South Asia as well as among South Asian Muslims in America today.

In this chapter, I also showed how Islamic reform movements such as Deobandi, Barelwi, Tablighi Jama'at, and Ahmadiyya significantly contributed to the theological perceptions of Christianity held today among South Asian Muslims. I further discussed how revivalist movements like Sufism, folk Islam, as well as radical Islamic movements like Jama't-i-Islami and similar groups, have influenced perceptions of Christianity.

I then showed how these movements not only have influenced the development of theological perceptions of Christianity among South Asian Muslims, but also are prominent today among South Asian Muslims in America.

The majority of South Asian Muslims in America maintain close ties with their country of origin, so influences from that region that generate and reinforce perceptions of Christianity are still in effect.

The majority of Muslim perceptions of major Christian doctrines are based on the teachings of the Qur'an and Hadith. Yet, there are also some Muslim perceptions of Christian doctrines that were developed by Muslim scholars long after the time of Muhammad.

In this chapter, contrasting doctrines of Christianity and Islam, such as those concerning the death of Jesus Christ on the cross and His bodily Resurrection, were presented. I further presented details about various Muslim theories related to the Crucifixion of Jesus. These theories include the "swoon theory," which was first introduced by the Ahmadiyya movement and is unique to South Asia. This teaching has created a variety of misperceptions among South Asian Muslims. These theories: the swoon theory, the various substitution theories, and the docetic apparition theory all go against the teaching of the Bible and often contradict the teaching of the Qur'an.

I anticipate that knowledge of theological perceptions of Christianity among South Asian Muslims in America can generate an interest that can open the door for dialogue and interaction between Christian and Muslim. This in turn can help to build relationships and correct many misperceptions, which can provide opportunity for an effective communication of the true gospel of Jesus Christ.

Perceptions of Christianity among South Asian Muslims in America are not only shaped by their theological understanding of major Christian doctrines but are also shaped by some sociocultural influences in American society that are discussed in the following chapter.

CHAPTER 2

SOCIOCULTURAL INFLUENCES

ON PERCEPTIONS OF CHRISTIANITY AMONG SOUTH ASIAN MUSLIMS IN AMERICA

South Asian Muslims who immigrate to America bring with them predetermined perceptions of Christianity that were developed by sociocultural emphases and practices in their native lands. After their resettlement in America, they encounter sociocultural emphases and practices very different from their culture of origin, which influences their perceptions of Christianity, either to reinforce them or modify them. This is partly because they closely associate what they see in their new sociocultural environment with Christianity. These sociocultural emphases and practices influence their adaptation to their new culture.

This chapter explores these sociocultural emphases and practices in American society and the effect these have on the perceptions of Christianity held by South Asian Muslims in America. It also includes a discussion of the responses of South Asian Muslims in America to their new sociocultural milieu, as these relate to their perceptions of Christianity. It further explores the challenges of adaptation, acculturation, and integration to their new sociocultural environment faced by South Asian Muslim immigrants.

In this book I am using the term *sociocultural* to describe the sociological and cultural milieu characteristic of the South Asian Muslim subculture in America and to some extent the milieu characteristic of the regions of origin for the South Asian Muslim immigrants to America.

Merriam-Webster Dictionary defines sociology:

1. The science of society, social institutions, and social relationships; *specifically*: the systematic study of the development, structure, interaction, and collective behavior of organized groups of human beings.
2. The scientific analysis of a social institution as a functioning whole and as it relates to the rest of society. (Merriam-Webster Dictionary.com, 2017)

Luzbetak and Hesselgrave provide definitions of culture that form the basis for the way I will use the term *culture* in this book.

Louis J. Luzbetak describes culture: "Culture is a design for living. It is a plan according to which society adapts itself to its physical, social and ideational environment" (Luzbetak 1963, 60–61). Then Hesselgrave provides further clarification concerning the characteristics of culture:

➢ Culture is *learned*—it is not biologically determined or restricted by race.
➢ Culture is a *shared* system, and therefore it is held in common by a society.
➢ Culture is an *integrated* whole, all the parts of which function in such a way as to affect each other and contribute to the totality.
➢ Culture constantly *changes* as a result of innovations, internal pressures, and cross-cultural borrowing. (Hesselgrave 1991, 100) (Emphasis his.)

In this book the working definition of culture I am using is the sum of attitudes, customs, and beliefs that distinguishes one group of people from another. Culture is transmitted through language, rituals, institutions, and art.

So as I use the term *sociocultural* in this book, it includes concepts of education, language, law and politics, religious beliefs, social organizations, values, and attitudes.

SOCIOCULTURAL EMPHASES

In this section, I compare and contrast some sociocultural emphases prevalent in South Asia and in America. The immigrants' perceptions of Christianity are shaped by their responses to sociocultural influences. I also include how these Muslims experience attitudes of American people toward Muslims and how their responses to these attitudes shape their perceptions of Christianity.

The vast majority of Muslim immigrants to America from South Asia come from countries where Islam is the dominant religion. The sociocultural emphases in their native lands are very different from those found in American culture, because as previously mentioned, Islam exerts a strong influence in every sphere of life where it is the dominant religion. Islam is not only influential in establishing beliefs and practices of Muslims but also strongly influences culture, customs, traditions, economics, and politics. John Azumah states:

> For Muslims, Islam is a complete way of life and there can be no separation between private and public, spiritual and temporal, religion and politics. They therefore make every effort to lay claim to the public space from which Christians tend to retreat. (Azumah 2008, 12)

I do not agree that Christians retreat from the public arena. In America, it is not possible for Christianity to control the society; it can only influence it, because the United States constitution separates church and state. On the other hand, I do agree with him that Islam is thoroughly integrated into all facets of Muslim society. In their new country, the sociocultural environment is entirely different, because Christianity cannot dominate every sphere of people's lives as Islam does in South Asian Muslim countries where it is the dominant religion.

In contrast, a secular and democratic sociocultural environment persists in America.

Most South Asian Muslim immigrants fail to differentiate between American culture and Christian values and influences. What they observe in the new sociocultural environment, they assume is either the result of Christian influence or is condoned or tolerated by Christianity. They closely associate the sociocultural milieu in America with Christianity and Christian values and teachings. This is what most of them expect because of the dominating influence of Islam in the countries from which they come.

In American society, Muslim immigrants frequently observe behaviors of which they strongly disapprove and often do not realize that most Christians would also disapprove of many of these behaviors. Many South Asian Muslims come to the United States with the perception that America is a Christian country in the same way they see their own native lands as Islamic countries. In their perception, all American sociocultural emphases and practices have been introduced or approved by Christianity. In my interviews (see Chapters 4 and 5) many participants have shared this opinion.

It is true that many Christian values were embraced in American society in the past, but this has diminished drastically over time. In present-day American society, many cultural practices do not reflect Christian values. In 2009, a *Newsweek* article, "Culture: The End of Christian America," written by Jon Meacham, quoted R. Albert Mohler Jr., president of the Southern Baptist Theological Seminary:

> A remarkable cultural-shift has taken place around us. The most basic contours of American culture have been radically altered. The so-called Judeo-Christian consensus of the last millennium has given way to a post-modern, post-Christian, post-Western cultural crisis which threatens the very heart of our culture. (Jon Meacham 2009)

I agree with Mohler that this country is going in a direction contrary to its Judeo-Christian foundational principles. Muslims from South Asia come to America with the expectation that the Unites States of America is a Christian nation, and they often find some customs and practices they observe in their new homeland repulsive to them. This is offensive to them because the customs and traditions are very different from what they have come to embrace in their homelands. They believe these offensive practices are either established or condoned by Christianity, which reveals a major misperception of Christianity.

In their homelands, the majority of South Asian Muslims identify Christianity with Western culture. One of the main reasons behind this is the fact that Christianity was originally preached in South Asian countries by Western missionaries. Often missionaries failed to contextualize their approach and presentation of the gospel to the local sociocultural environment. Paul G. Hiebert points out: "Consequently, the gospel was seen by the people as a foreign gospel. To become Christian, one had to accept not only Christianity but also Western cultural ways" (Hiebert 1994, 76). I agree with Hiebert that this contributed to the prevailing perception associating Christianity with Western culture. This perception became established in the minds of South Asian Muslims and was brought by South Asian Muslim immigrants to America.

I have identified a representative sample of some important sociocultural emphases in American society, which include individualism, sociocultural prejudices, and women's rights.

INDIVIDUALISM

In this section I present the working definition of individualism, explore individualism as one of the predominant emphases in American society, and explain how individualism contrasts with communalism (collectivism), which is more characteristic of South Asian Muslim society. I further explore how these contrasts affect the perceptions of Christianity among South Asian Muslims in America.

Individualism is a moral, political, or social outlook that stresses human independence and the importance of individual self-reliance and liberty. The *Merriam-Webster Dictionary* defines individualism as "the conception that all values, rights, and duties originate in individuals" (Merriam-Webster.com 2017).

Edward Younkins provides a more detailed definition:

> Individualism is the view that each person has moral significance and certain rights that are either of divine origin or inherent in human nature. Each individual exists, perceives, experiences, thinks, and acts in and through his own body and therefore from unique points in time and space. It is the individual who has the capacity for original and creative rationality. (Younkins 1998, unpaginated)

Individualism as a mark of identity contrasts with corporate or communal identity, where an individual's identity is determined by his or her place within a group, as is true in societal structures such as those usually found in South Asia. Individualism contrasts with communal living, also called communalism or collectivism, which is allegiance to one's own ethnic group rather than to the wider society or to society as a whole. The term collectivism is frequently seen in contemporary sociological writings; however, it is basically synonymous with the definition of communalism (*Power Thesaurus* 2017).

In 2015, Kazi Anwarul Masud wrote "Communalism and India," an article that analyzes the structure of social groups in India. He quoted from a noted Indian historian, Bipin Chandra, with a definition of communalism: "The belief that because a group of people follow a particular religion, they have, as a result, common social, political, and economic interests" (Masud 2015, unpaginated). Having grown up in South Asia, I know that communal living is more typical of the societal structure in South Asia.

In contrast to the communal living norms in South Asian society, the situation is very different in American society. Individualism is seen in many areas of American society: economics, politics, and culture. It is a characteristic most Americans are proud to own, like being proud of one's independence or self-sufficiency. It has had an enormous and far-reaching effect in shaping the character and reputation of the American people. In an article about individualism, posted on *Britannica.com*, Steven M. Lukes wrote:

> Individualism is a political and social philosophy that emphasizes the moral worth of the individual. ... in the

United States, individualism became part of the core
American ideology by the 19th century, incorporating the
influences of New England Puritanism, Jeffersonianism, and
the philosophy of natural rights. (Lukes 1971)

In American society, a great deal of emphasis is placed on individual
choice. Even within a family, there are individual choices. From
childhood individualism is taught as a value even within the family,
encouraging personal individual preferences.

Cathy Douglass, in the article "Examining America's Sociocultural
Values: Individualism," wrote:

From the earliest age in America, children are encouraged to
develop their sense of individual identity, achievement, and
responsibility. Many Americans give their new born babies
their own room and crib [cot] from the first day they come
home from hospital. As the baby grows, every individual
achievement is celebrated and encouraged at the youngest
possible age, such as feeding himself, dressing himself,
walking to a neighbor's house, talking on the phone politely
etc. (Douglass 2000–2012, 4–5)

In contrast to individualism, communalism (collectivism) is more
characteristic of most societies in South Asia, including Muslim societies.
The group is what is important, rather than the individual. In many
places in South Asia, communalism (collectivism) is closely associated
with sectarianism, which is also prevalent in South Asia. Sectarianism is
defined as having a "sectarian spirit or tendencies; excessive devotion to a
particular sect, especially in religion" (Dictionary.com). Another definition:
"Sectarianism is strong support for the religious or political group you belong
to, and often involves conflict with other groups" (CollinsDictionary.com).

A consequence of this sectarianism is often violence between
different religious sects. In 2013, Zafarul Islam Khan wrote "Sectarianism
and Its Local and Regional Complexities—A South Asian Perspective,"
published in *Milli Gazette*. Khan stated:

Sectarianism, which is called "communalism" in South
Asia, especially means to belong to a social, religious, or

political group but in practice it denotes a biased attitude in favor of one's own group and against other group(s) which are perceived as a threat to a particular group's economic, religious, or political interests. (Khan 2013, 1)

I disagree with Khan that sectarianism is the same as communalism, because sectarianism requires extreme devotion to a particular sect. The same feelings of sectarianism are present among some South Asian radical Muslims and Islamist groups in America, which is also seen in their attitudes toward Christianity. In numerous conversations and interfaith dialogues with South Asian Muslims, sectarianism is of major concern to some South Asian Muslim participants; however, they represent only a small percentage of the South Asian Muslim population in America.

From the interviews I conducted as research for this book, it is clear that South Asian Muslims often view individualism as selfishness and rebelliousness. These interviews also reveal that they associate individualism not only with American society but also with Christianity.

The perception of South Asian Muslims in America is that individualism can create injustice, inequality, and pride, as well as disregard for the interests of the group and others in the society. Imad-ad-Dean Ahmad points out: "Individualism has a bad name in much of the world, only because it has been tainted with concepts like materialism, hedonism, and lack of concern for the rights of others, concepts that are really not inherent in it" (Ahmad 2005, 1–2). I agree that individualism has a bad name, at least in South Asia where I grew up. On the other hand, Ahmad argues that materialism and hedonism are not inherent in individualism, but I believe to some extent they are.

There are some positive aspects of individualism. Individualism can create self-esteem, independence, and self-sufficiency. On the other hand, communality (a feeling of group solidarity), or communalism (collectivism), can create an atmosphere of love, cooperation, a sense of belonging, and interdependency, but at the same time it can tend toward aloofness, isolationism, and a sense of superiority. Both individualism and communalism have positive and negative attributes; neither is all good or all bad.

South Asian Muslims in America have an erroneous perception that Christianity only emphasizes individualism. In fact, Christianity does emphasize the individual but also emphasizes interdependence, cooperation, and collaboration, Christianity teaches that the individual who truly believes in Jesus and commits to follow Him is acceptable to God and has eternal life, regardless of the society of which he is a part. Thus, the individual can receive salvation regardless of the fate of the corporate group of which he may be a part. This emphasizes the value of the individual in the eyes of God. However, Christian identity is also related to conformity to the values and ideals of the church and the Christian subculture.

As I previously mentioned, South Asian Muslims come to America with the perception that America is a Christian nation. In early 2015, I interviewed several South Asian Muslims in Greater Boston. They had some positive comments about American cultural practices, but regarding the American characteristic of individualism, all of them stated their emphatic impression that individualism is a direct result of the influence of Christianity. These conversations are typical of many I have had with South Asian Muslims, who uniformly associate individualism as a characteristic emphasis of Christianity. While it is correct that individualism is a characteristic emphasis within Christianity in American society, individualism in American society is not the result of Christian influence.

Dennis N. Voskuil points out:

> If Christianity appears popular in America today, this is so, at least in part, because it has embraced rather than resisted individualism in American culture. Individualism lies at the very heart of the American character. Our family structures, our political institutions, and our economic systems have been shaped by the pervasive power of individualism. (Voskuil 1987, 22)

South Asian Muslim immigrants in America become very much aware of the differences of sociocultural emphases in their new country compared to their native lands. This is a part of their experience of culture shock. Because of their predetermined perception that America is a Christian country, whatever they observe in American culture, they associate with Christianity. Individualism and communalism (collectivism) both have positive and negative characteristics.

It is unfortunate that the majority of South Asian Muslims in America associate Christianity with practices in American culture that are offensive to them. Most of these practices that are offensive to them are not the product or emphasis of Christianity, and many of them are also offensive to Christians.

SOCIOCULTURAL PREJUDICES

In this section I examine prejudices from the sociocultural perspective as they relate to South Asian Muslims in America and how this affects their perception of Christianity. I discuss how prejudice against Islam is prevalent in American society and explore some of the primary causes of this prejudice. I also discuss certain prejudices South Asian Muslims typically acquire before they immigrate to America.

Prejudice is a universal, complex issue with far-reaching implications. The fourth edition of the *American Heritage College Dictionary* defines the term prejudice: "An adverse judgment or opinion formed beforehand or without knowledge or examination of the facts to irrational suspicion or hatred of a particular group, race or religion." (*American Heritage College Dictionary* 1993)

Uzma Mazhar also provides a definition of prejudice in the article "Theology: Prejudice—Islamic Perspective" published by the Muslim Women's Coalition in 2000. Mazhar stated:

> Prejudice is premature judgment—a negative attitude towards a person or group of people which is not based on objective facts. These assumptions are usually based on stereotypes which are oversimplified and over-generalized views of groups or types of people. The root of all prejudice is fear and ignorance. (Mazhar 2000, 1)

I agree with Uzma Mazhar that people are often prejudiced when they form opinions without knowing the facts, but I disagree with her that "the root of all prejudice is fear and ignorance." Not all prejudice comes from ignorance; even well-educated people have prejudices.

In the United States, sociocultural and religious prejudice still exists in every area of society. Prejudice results in discrimination toward certain groups and individuals within the society. Discrimination is not just negative feelings but also includes behavior and actions against a target group. Even today, racial prejudice against African Americans is still prevalent in American society. In a recent nationwide poll conducted by Cable News Network (CNN) and the Kaiser Family Foundation (KFF), "roughly half of Americans–49%–say racism is a big problem in society today." A majority of those interviewed across racial divisions said "tensions between racial and ethnic groups in the United States have increased in the past 10 years. Roughly a quarter said tensions have stayed the same." (CNN and KFF November 25, 2015)

In 1965, an immigration act was passed by the United States Congress making it much easier for Muslims from many nations to come to the United States. Since that time the population of Muslim immigrants has greatly increased.

Most South Asian Muslims have the perception that the majority of Americans, regardless of their own heritage, hold religious prejudices against Islam. Many of these immigrants in America also hold the perception that anti-Muslim sentiment is primarily the result of the influence of Christianity especially fundamentalist Christians. The interviews presented in Chapters 4 and 5 document these perceptions.

The majority of South Asian Muslim immigrants perceive that most Americans have some Islamophobia (prejudice against Islam), and today this term is frequently heard in the news media in the United States. Islamophobia (literally fear of Islam) is a religious prejudice.

The *Oxford English Dictionary* defines the term *Islamophobia* as "intense dislike or fear of Islam, especially as a political force; hostility or prejudice towards Muslims" (Oxford English Dictionary 2010).

In 2015, the Bridge Initiative Research Project of Georgetown University conducted research on Islamophobia and gave their definition of Islamophobia. They stated:

> Islamophobia is prejudice towards or discrimination against Muslims due to their religion, or perceived religious, national, or ethnic identity associated with Islam. Like anti-Semitism, racism, and homophobia, Islamophobia describes mentalities and actions that demean an entire class of people. Jews, African-Americans, and other populations throughout history have faced prejudice and discrimination. Islamophobia is simply another reincarnation of this unfortunate trend of bigotry. (Bridge Initiative Research Project 2015)

The Center for Race and Gender at the University of California, Berkeley, quoted a 1991 Runnymede Trust Report that listed a number of beliefs that characterize Islamophobia:

> ➤ Islam is monolithic and cannot adapt to new realities.
> ➤ Islam does not share common values with other major faiths.
> ➤ Islam … is archaic, barbaric, and irrational.
> ➤ Islam is a religion of violence and supports terrorism.
> ➤ Islam is a violent political ideology. (Center for Race and Gender 2016)

Many South Asian Muslims in America perceive that a majority of Americans hold Islamophobic views about Islam. Most of these immigrants have the perception that Islamophobia in American society is the root cause of discrimination against them. They also see this as an influence of Christianity, because to them Christian influence is closely associated with American society.

South Asian Muslims also have some sociocultural prejudices of their own which they bring with them when they immigrate to America. Within the Muslim society in South Asia, there are some prejudices related to indigenous social status classifications. These classifications are commonly referred to as the caste system, yet Muslims in South Asia prefer the term "social stratification."

This caste system, prevalent in many parts of South Asia, predisposes Muslim immigrants from that area toward certain sociocultural expectations in their new homeland. This affects what is anticipated from the societal structure in terms of identity, behavior, attitude, and a person's role in society.

In many cases, some of the attitudes and mind-set of the caste system were adopted by societies where Islam is dominant, although Islamic teaching theoretically rejects the caste system. In some sense, Islamic leaders adopted and taught attitudes and perspectives that are characteristic of the caste system (e.g., the belief that Islam is the superior religion in comparison with all other religions). This attitude clearly implies that other religions, including Christianity, are inferior in comparison with Islam. Thus, for whatever reason, Muslims are indoctrinated to look down on Christianity—and this establishes perceptions of Christianity as an inferior or even heretical religion and to be rejected.

Perceptions of Christianity held by South Asian Muslims therefore are fraught with error, false teachings, and strong prejudices against Christians and their religion.

Also, there is a strong emphasis on the corporate structure of society both in the countries where the caste system is practiced and in societies where Islam is dominant. Individualism and independent action are typically discouraged.

Islam theoretically does not support the caste system, yet in some parts of South Asia, in actual practice the Muslim society tolerates it and even participates in it. Despite its theoretically egalitarian principles, Islam in South Asia historically has been unable to avoid class and caste inequities. Caste-like societal structures (social stratifications) are still prevalent in the Muslim-majority countries of South Asia. According to the *World Heritage Encyclopedia*:

> Contrary to the Qur'anic worldview, there is a system of social stratification among some Muslim communities that has similarity to the caste systems ... Religious, historical, and sociocultural factors have helped define the bounds of endogamous [similar social unit] groups for Muslims in South Asia ... The social stratification among Muslims in the "Swat" area of North Pakistan has been meaningfully compared to the caste system in India. The society is rigidly divided into subgroups where each Qaum [lineage, clan] is

assigned a profession. Different Qaums are not permitted to intermarry or live in the same community. (World Heritage Encyclopedia 2016)

Based on this information, whether referred to as "social stratification" or "the caste system," in actual practice it is the same thing.

There are three main groups among South Asian Muslims: Ashraf, Ajlaf, and Arzal. Ashrafs claim a superior status derived from their foreign ancestry. This perspective is very similar to the caste system, where one group is considered superior on the basis of heritage or ancestry.

Ajlafs are assumed to be converts from Hinduism and are therefore drawn from the indigenous population. To many, this implies a lesser caste or status within the social structure. These in turn are divided into various occupational castes.

In addition to the Ashraf and Ajlaf, there is also the Arzal caste. Arzals are regarded by anticaste activists as the equivalent of untouchables in the Hindu society, hence the attitudes of the caste system toward the lowest class are simulated in this societal structure. Other Muslims don't associate with this group. The Arzals are relegated to menial professions such as scavenging and carrying night soil.

In 2013, I interviewed some South Asian Muslim intellectuals in Greater Boston. While asking their family names, many of them proudly told that their ancestors originally came from Arabia or other Middle Eastern countries and Persia. They were quick to brag about their heritage from superior classes such as Ashraf. They declared their foreign ancestry outside of India and made it clear that they are not from an ancestral line converted from an indigenous Hindu background, which would fall into the lower Ajlaf or Arzal castes.

Peter McNee, referring to the lower Arzal caste, stated: "They are forbidden to enter the mosque or use the public burial ground" (McNee 1976, 4).

McNee in his research on *Crucial Issues in Bangladesh* further commented regarding the practice of the caste system among Muslims in Bangladesh. In his observation, the Ashraf are considered a superior class among the Muslims and are further identified by family names or high-status titles such as: *Saiad* (*Saiyed*), *Sheik* (*Sheikh*), *Pathan* and *Mughals* (McNee 1976, 2–3).

McNee further pointed out:

> The true *Saiad* holds the first place in the Muslim social system just as the *Brahman* amongst the Hindu. He traces his descendants directly to Ali, Muhammad's son-in-law by his wife Fatima. They are divided into *Hasani* and *Husani* as they claim descent from one or other of these famous martyrs. By sect they are usually *Shiahs* [Shi'a]. (McNee, 1976, 2–3)

Many Muslim scholars have declared the caste-like features in South Asian Muslim society as a flagrant violation of the Qur'anic worldview. However, sections of the *Ulema* (scholars of Islamic jurisprudence) advocate religious legitimacy and tried to reconcile and resolve the disjunction between Qur'anic egalitarianism and Indian Muslim social organization through a twisted interpretation of the Qur'an and shariah law to justify the caste system within Muslim society.

In 2000, Yogindar Sikand, in his article "Islam and Caste Inequality Among Indian Muslims," stated:

> Scholarly writings on caste among Indian Muslims generally note the division that is often made between the so-called "noble" castes or *ashraf* and those labeled as inferior, or *razil*, *kamin* or *ajlaf*. The *ashraf-ajlaf* division is not the invention of modern social scientists, for it is repeatedly mentioned in medieval works of *ashraf* scholars themselves. To these writers, Muslims of Arab, Central Asian, Iranian and Afghan extraction were superior in social status than local converts. This owed not just to racial differences, with local converts generally being dark-skinned and the *ashraf* lighter complexioned, but also to the fact that the *ashraf* belonged to the dominant political elites, while the bulk of the *ajlaf* remained associated with ancestral professions as artisans and peasants which were looked down upon as inferior and demeaning. (Sikand 2000, unpaginated)

Prejudice within the non-Muslim surrounding community in America towards Islam as well as anti-Muslim sentiment, shape the South Asian Muslim perception of Christianity. These Muslims associate Christianity with the prejudices and discrimination they experience as Muslims and as immigrants, so their reaction of resentment is often directed toward Christianity.

However, they also have prejudices among themselves toward each other. As elsewhere in the world, including South Asia, there is Sunni against Shi'a, and animosity against other Islamic sects. These prejudicial attitudes toward fellow Muslims are also found among the South Asian Muslims in Boston.

WOMEN'S RIGHTS

In this section I explore the issue of the rights of women in American society and contrast this American sociocultural emphasis with that found in Muslim society in South Asia as well as among the South Asian immigrants in America. I discuss how these differences in emphasis related to women's rights affect perceptions of Christianity held by South Asian Muslims in Boston.

Unlike women from Muslim-dominated countries in South Asia, women in America enjoy more rights. Historically the establishment of rights for women in American society required much struggle over a long period of time. Kenneth J. Bechtel has provided a brief history of the establishment of women's rights in America. Bechtel stated:

> The rights of women in the United States have been a source of debate since the country's inception. As early as 1789 Abigail Adams urged her husband, John Adams, to "remember the ladies" at the Constitutional Convention in Philadelphia. In 1848, a meeting in Seneca Falls, New York marked the official beginning of a recognized women's movement. Out of that meeting came the Declaration of Sentiments that ended with the phrase "all men and women

are created equal." However, it would take another 72 years before women were even given the right to vote. (Bechtel undated, unpaginated)

The role of women in American society has changed dramatically over time. Socioculturally and politically the role of women has grown to be very strong in America. During the last several decades, American women have held an increasing number of public offices in federal, state, and local government. Also, a woman's individual identity is more recognized in America, especially as compared to South Asian Muslim societies. In 2011, Arshi Saleem Hashmi, in the article "Issues of Women's Rights in South Asia," stated:

A woman's individual identity is often questioned and compromised in South Asia. Family law in this region which ought to encompass areas women's rights also accommodates gender discrimination. The center of society is the family unit, yet woman, the main character, is often ignored in getting acknowledgement socially as well as legally. Family law here has provided ground for debate for feminists in search of laws with respect to gender. (Hashmi 2011, 1)

Male authority in the home is predominant in most South Asian countries. Traditionally Muslim culture in general supports this practice and it is even advocated in the Qur'an:

Men are the support of women as God gives some more means than others, and because they spend of their wealth [to provide for them]. So women who are virtuous are obedient to God and guard the hidden as God has guarded it. As for women you feel are averse, talk to them persuasively; then leave them alone in bed [without molesting them] and go to bed with them [when they are willing]. If they open out to you, do not seek an excuse for blaming them. (Surah 4:34)

In pluralistic, postmodern American society, women are more assertive and outspoken than ever before. In America, women enjoy much more freedom compared to the women in Islamic society in South

Asia. In South Asian, Islamic society is conservative and governed by religious obligations and rules. In American society, the situation is quite different, and religious influence is much less interwoven with the mores of the society.

Coming from a society where religion is so rigidly determinative of what is customary and acceptable, South Asian Muslim immigrants to America are surprised to see the freedoms allowed women in America. In some cases, they are astonished to see how some women in American society exercise their independence, and many of these immigrants have expressed their opinion that in America women's rights go too far.

Many people in America say that when women take advantage of women's rights, it is the influence of liberal feminism. Liberal feminism advocates gender equality in every sphere of life. *Webster's New Universal Unabridged Dictionary* defines liberal to mean "favoring reforms tending toward personal freedom for the individual," and feminism to mean "the theory that women should have political, economic, and social rights for women equal to those of men." This suggests a movement striving to achieve political, economic, and social rights for women equal to those of men (Webster's New Universal Unabridged Dictionary 1979).

The revised version of the article "Liberal Feminism" was published in *Stanford Encyclopedia of Philosophy* in 2013. This article also provides a definition of liberal feminism:

> Liberal Feminism conceives of freedom as personal autonomy—living a life of one's own choosing—and political autonomy—being co-author of the conditions under which one lives. Liberal feminists hold that the exercise of personal autonomy depends on certain enabling conditions that are insufficiently present in women's lives, or that social arrangements often fail to respect women's personal autonomy and other elements of women's flourishing. They hold also that women's needs and interests are insufficiently reflected in the basic conditions under which they live, and that those conditions lack legitimacy because women are inadequately represented in the processes of democratic self-determination. (*Stanford Encyclopedia of Philosophy* 2013, 1)

According to this definition, the autonomy of women in every sphere of life, even in private life, is more pronounced in American culture, so South Asian Muslim immigrants must make some significant attitudinal adjustments in America. This situation affects the perception of Christianity among many South Asian Muslims in America because of the strongly held idea that American society is greatly influenced by Christianity. Most South Asian Muslims feel this give a bad reputation to Christianity, because they believe religion should demonstrate against attitudes and behavior in society that they deem inappropriate or even immoral.

Regarding this facet of American culture related to women's rights, strong opinions held by South Asian Muslims associate women's rights in America as a Christian endorsement. This creates negative perceptions of Christianity among South Asian Muslims in America. They generally believe that some women's rights are a good thing, but if women are too aggressive in exercising their rights then many Muslims object. Muslims typically object to women having any form of dominance or authority over men.

However, over time, the second and third generation offspring of South Asian Muslim immigrants in America become more integrated into American society and adopt some ideas different from their elders. As a result, different perceptions toward Christianity develop within the second and third generations. The interviews presented in this book included second- and third-generation descendants of immigrants and support these observations.

Most young women who are second- and third-generation offspring of South Asian Muslim immigrants in America tend to be more assertive in their attitudes yet usually retain their Muslim identity. Interviews and dialogues with a sampling of these young women suggest to me that they anticipate a life where they will be afforded more rights than their mothers. Some of these young Muslim women do not like the controls imposed by Islamic traditions and the Muslim clerics. This tends to erode their submission to Islamic authority and often is reflected in more favorable perceptions of Christianity.

In interviews with South Asian Muslims in America (Chapters 4 and 5) a diverse perception is revealed among participants in answering questions on the issue of women's rights in America influenced by Christianity. These interviews also bring to light a varied perception concerning the role of Christianity as it relates to women's rights.

In 2009, in the *Journal of International Women's Study*, Mercia Hermansen and Mahruq F. Khan wrote:

> In America, many South Asian Muslim girls actively participate in activities that affirm the importance of "Islamic knowledge" as powerful ... This pursuit of Islamic knowledge could be seen as contributing to identity maintenance at a challenging time during the life cycle while it also reflects a global trend of Muslim females appropriating authority. (Hermansen and Khan 2009)

This quotation indicates that many South Asian Muslim girls are strong advocates in favor of Islam, and participate in activities that demonstrate this and declare that Islam favors women's rights, in spite of the fact that the Qur'an clearly defines a subordinate role for women in respect to men.

Some Muslim clerics and fundamentalist Muslims perceive that Christianity is the cause of the rise of liberal feminism; however, this is an erroneous perception. Christianity does not speak with one voice about women's rights. Those who call themselves Christian speak with many voices on this issue, ranging from one extreme to the other. Consequently, there are multifaceted perceptions among South Asian Muslims in America regarding the position of Christianity on the issue of women's rights.

SOCIOCULTURAL PRACTICES

In this section I explore the differences of sociocultural practices between South Asia and America and how these differences reflect perceptions of Christianity among South Asian Muslims in America. I also discuss some sociocultural practices in American society and responses of South Asian Muslims to these practices. I further discuss how these responses reflect perceptions of Christianity among South Asian Muslims in America.

The sociocultural practices of South Asian Muslims in their native lands are different than in America, because religion plays a much more extensive and dominant role in Muslim society, especially in countries where Islam is the dominant religion. Although many intellectuals and political leaders in Muslim-dominated countries in South Asia often say that the practice of religion is personal and private, in actual practice Islamic influence is much more pervasive in these areas. Islam strongly influences culture, customs, and traditions in Muslim society in South Asia. Even though there are many nonpracticing Muslims in the region of South Asia, religious identity is still an imperative expectation within that culture, and Islamic influence and control are pervasive in the culture.

When Muslims from South Asia in America observe sociocultural practices in American society that are not in accord with their own traditional sociocultural practices, obviously some emotional reactions result that will express their attitudes and perceptions of the sociocultural norms.

Most Muslims from South Asia come to their new sociocultural environment in America with the predetermined idea that in America every sociocultural practice is influenced by Christianity. Their perception is that every custom is either caused by, condoned by, or tolerated by Christianity, because they see Christianity as the dominant religion and therefore directly related to sociocultural practices. They expect that Christianity as the dominant religion should function in the culture as Islam functions in their homelands. In the interviews I conducted among South Asian Muslims in America, a number of participants shared their views and opinions affirming this perception. This is explored in more detail in Chapters 4 and 5.

I discuss some important sociocultural practices in American society including public display of affection, racism, and marriage and divorce.

Public Display of Affection

Public display of affection is a common practice in some cultures in the world. However, the level to which this is acceptable can vary dramatically from culture to culture, depending on the specific mores of the culture. This section identifies the norms that exist in American culture, how these differ from South Asian Muslim culture, and how most Muslim immigrants from South Asia typically respond to these norms in their new sociocultural environment in America.

Farlex Dictionary of Idioms defines public display of affection as: "A physical act of intimacy between a romantic couple done in the view of others. Often shortened to the abbreviation PDA." (*Farlex Dictionary of Idioms* 2015)

Typically, South Asian Muslim immigrants are not accustomed to seeing men and women holding hands, or even touching, as they walk down a street in any public arena, as this is considered inappropriate in Muslim-dominated countries in South Asia. Although the situation is gradually changing in many South Asian countries, still public display of affection between male and female is usually socially unacceptable.

In some South Asian countries, while public display of affection is forbidden by the societal norms, nevertheless gender mixing (male and female meeting together) is becoming more common in the workplace, schools, and public parks. In these meetings, male and female spend time together, but societal censure remains strict, especially regarding touching or embracing.

Valentine's Day in recent years has become quite popular in many urban societies in South Asia. Only in cities, especially at university campuses, on Valentine's Day and during other cultural festivals, young boys and girls meet together, but still public display of affection is not common and is typically disapproved in the society. Even shaking hands between genders is restricted in many Muslim societies in South Asia.

When South Asian Muslim immigrants first arrive in America, typically they are surprised to see young men and women hugging and kissing each other in public. Because such practices are taboo in the cultures from which they come, this becomes part of their culture shock in their new homeland.

As previously mentioned, South Asian Muslims have the predetermined idea that Western culture is strongly influenced by Christianity. Consequently, many Muslim immigrants in America have the perception that public display of affection is approved by the Christian church, and this obviously affects their perception of Christianity in a negative way.

Although this practice is not uniform among the churches in America, nevertheless this lends itself to the impression among Muslims that sexual promiscuity is prominent in Christian churches in America. To some extent this is a correct perception, because public display of affection is often condoned or at least tolerated by many churches in America. This practice is frequently evident even during the worship services. This is so foreign to the societal norms to which Muslim immigrants are accustomed that it often creates a strong revulsion among them.

This issue was raised by a number of participants during my interviews with South Asian Muslims in Greater Boston. Among participants there are diverse perceptions regarding the influence of Christianity on the practice of public displays of affection. These are shown in Chapters 4 and 5 of this book.

RACIAL DISCRIMINATION

Racism is a typical prejudice of the human race. It varies from person to person and culture to culture, but it is common to all nations. Racial discrimination is one of the typical sociocultural practices in American society. In this book, "racial discrimination" refers to discrimination based on ethnicity, language, skin color, religion, etc.

In this section, I explore the extent of racial discrimination in present-day American society. Contrasting American and South Asian Muslim society I further explore some of the specific discriminations against Muslims in America and some of their typical responses to this, particularly how it affects their perception of Christianity.

Throughout America's history, racial discrimination has been a major concern. Even after the successes of the civil rights movement in the 1960s, racism remains prevalent in American society and continues to affect the harmonious relationships among cultural, ethnic, and religious groups. This includes Muslims in America, who encounter prejudices based on their ethnic identity as well as their religious identity.

A powerful stimulus toward anti-Muslim racism was the attacks of September 11, 2001, because they was perpetrated by Muslims, and the event was publicly celebrated by the populous of numerous Muslim countries. This spurred a significant resurgence of fear and repulsion of all Muslims worldwide, including those in the United States.

After this event, anti-Muslim sentiment significantly escalated and even more so after recent Islamic radical militant movements in Muslim countries and terrorist attacks on American soil and on American people. This type of Muslim aggression and violence has generated strong negative abhorrence against Muslims and has stimulated prejudice against Islam and Muslims worldwide, including South Asian Muslims in America. This has resulted in a marked increase in discrimination in America against Muslims.

While tolerance is a major emphasis in the areas of education, media, politics, religion, etc., especially as relates to racial attitudes, because America is a multiracial and religiously diverse nation, there will always be racial tensions. In 2010, the Southern Poverty Law Center published the article "Ten Ways to Fight Hate: A Community Response Guide:"

> Race and religion inspire most hate crimes, but hate today wears many faces. Bias incidents [eruptions of hate where no crime is committed] also tear communities apart—and threaten to escalate into actual crimes. In recent years, the FBI has reported between 7,000 and 8,000 hate crime incidents per year in the United States. *The good news is ...* All over the country people are fighting hate, standing up to promote tolerance and inclusion. More often than not, when hate flares up, good people rise up against it—often in greater numbers and with stronger voices. (Southern Poverty Law Center 2010) (Emphasis theirs.)

Seven years later, in 2017, the rate of hate crimes, especially those based on religion, are much higher. In November 15, 2016, Cable News Network (CNN) presented the latest FBI report on annual hate crime and attacks against Muslims in the United States:

> The latest FBI annual hate crime report shows a sharp spike in the number of hate crimes nationwide, with attacks against Muslims increasing the most sharply. In one year, anti-Muslim hate crimes in the United States rose 67%, from 154 incidents in 2014 to 257 incidents in 2015. (Cable News Network 2017)

It is true that established public policy decries and officially forbids discrimination in the United States Constitution and in the Supreme Court; however, in practice, America is still in some respects a racially divided society. This is not just a religious issue; it is a sociocultural issue as well.

The intensity of racial discrimination is still high. According to the survey conducted by Pew Research Center in 2013:

> ... 48% of whites said a lot of progress has been made compared with 32% of blacks just before the 50th anniversary of Martin Luther King's March on Washington. The divide widens further when the question is: how much more needs to be done in order to achieve racial equality? About eight-in-ten (79%) black say "a lot" compared with just 44% of whites. (Pew Research Center 2013)

Many South Asian Muslims experienced sociocultural discrimination while still in their native lands. As previously stated, historically many Muslim societies in South Asia continue the legacy of the caste system (social stratification) from their Hindu background. But the nature of this discrimination is different in many respects from the racial discrimination prevalent in American society.

Today the discrimination that exists in South Asian Muslim society is based on religious identity, socioeconomic status, and heritage. In Muslim-dominated countries in South Asia, because of Islamic influence in the society, there is much discrimination and even violence against minority communities, as well as against non-Muslims. Hatred and violence occur also between the two mainline branches of Islam (Sunni and Shi'a), and in many areas, it has become routine. In contrast to that, in America the discrimination is not usually expressed with the same degree of intensity and violence.

Historically, in America there has been some anti-Muslim sentiment not only because of religious differences of belief and practice between Christianity and Islam, but also because of radical Muslim acts of violence not just in America but worldwide. Most scholars agree that anti-Muslim sentiment is not new. Aminah Mohammad-Arif points out: "Western anti-Muslim sentiment is very ancient." (Mohammad-Arif 2000, 234).

In 2012, Michigan University published an article, "Attitudes Toward Muslim Americans Post - 9/11" written by Mussarat Khan and Kathryn Ecklund in the *Journal of Muslim Mental Health*. Referring to the American-Arab Anti-Discrimination Committee and the Council of American Relations, Khan and Ecklund pointed out:

> During the process of adjusting to the aftermath of September 11, Muslim Americans faced an upsurge in negative stereotypes expressed by the larger society, and Muslim immigrants, more than any other immigrant group, were met with negative attitudes. (Khan and Ecklund 2012, 1)

Many South Asian Muslims in America have a predetermined idea that Christian churches in America accept racial discrimination. This misunderstanding naturally affects their perception of Christianity. To some extent this is a correct perception, in that in some churches racial discrimination is tacitly practiced. This helps to create a perception among Muslim immigrants that Christianity approves discrimination, which is not correct, since Christian teaching rejects and the Bible denounces discrimination (e.g., Acts 6:1–9).

Most South Asian Muslims come to America to enjoy freedom and a better life. Since many of them have the predetermined idea that Christianity approves discrimination, when they observe discrimination in American society, this confirms their preconception. So this negative perception of Christianity becomes reinforced.

In my interviews with South Asian Muslims in America, nearly half the total number of participants shared their perception that they had experienced some form of racial discrimination because of their ethnicity. This perception may or may not be true. Many of them complained that they were discriminated against in their workplace. Some complained that they were refused a bank loan to start an entrepreneurial enterprise, which they felt was simply because of their identification as Muslim. Obviously, this may or may not be true but reveals their perception. This is shown in more detail in Chapters 4 and 5 of this book.

This kind of treatment creates an erroneous perception of Christianity among South Asian Muslims in America, because they closely associate what they observe in the sociocultural environment with Christian influence or acceptance.

Among South Asian Muslims, racial discrimination is associated with Christianity, and because of their preconceptions and the way they interpret their experiences in America, these preconceptions are often reinforced in their minds.

FAMILY PRACTICES

Family is the basic relational structure of the human race. Family is a word with many different meanings. It is important to clarify the definition of family as it relates to this book. In this book, we are only concerned with definitions of family related to human units of relationship. *Merriam-Webster Dictionary* defines the family as follows:

- ➤ a group of individuals living under one roof and under one head
- ➤ a group of persons who come from the same ancestor
- ➤ a social group composed of one or two parents and their children
- ➤ a social group different from but considered equal to the traditional family (Merriam-Webster Dictionary.com 2017)

My goal is to explore the typical family structure in America and how family values are practiced in American society contrasted to those typical in South Asian Muslim society. These are further compared to those typical in the subculture of South Asian Muslims in America. I further explore the way family values as practiced in America affect the perception of Christianity among South Asian Muslims.

Family structure in American society is changing rapidly. Family structure includes the following considerations:

> The number of household members
> The birth rate of children in an average nonimmigrant American family
> The ways parenthood is conducted
> The primary wage-earner(s) of the family
> Divorce and remarriage
> Configuration of family units [parent-offspring construct]

My research has revealed some of the main reasons for recent changes in family structure in American society. In 2015, the Pew Research Center reported:

> Family life is changing. Two-parent households are on the decline in the United States as divorce, remarriage, and cohabitation are on the rise. And families are smaller now, both due to the growth of single-parent households and the drop in fertility. Not only are Americans having fewer children, but the circumstances surrounding parenthood have changed, today fully four-in-ten births occur to women who are single or living with a non-married partner.

While family structures have transformed, so has the role of mothers in the workplace—and in the home. As more norms have entered the labor force, more have become breadwinners—in many cases, primary breadwinners—in their families.

As a result of these changes, there is no longer one dominant family form in the United States. Parents today are raising their children against a backdrop of increasingly diverse and, for many, constantly evolving family forms. By 1980, 61 percent of children were living in one dominant family form, and today less than half (46 percent) are (Pew Research Center 2015).

Based on this report, if this trend continues, the average American family will become smaller.

In 2010, American sociologist and mental health professional Michelle Blessing, in her blog, "Meaning of Family," mentioned that family structure has changed dramatically over the last fifty years. She mentioned six specific types of family structures identified by society today:

> ➢ The traditional nuclear family structure, (one-male, one-female parent and children)
> ➢ Single parent family (one parent raising one or more children on their own)
> ➢ Extended family (consists of two or more adults who are related, either by blood or marriage living in the same home)
> ➢ Childless family (couples who either cannot or choose not to have children)
> ➢ Stepfamily (children from two separate families melding into one new unit for the remarriage of their mother or father after divorce)
> ➢ Grandparents family (children raised by grandparents for a variety of reasons). (Blessing 2010, unpaginated)

The nuclear family structure is still prominent today in the American sociocultural environment, but gradually this construct is diminishing. Unfortunately, the stepfamily structure is growing because of the increase of divorce and remarriage today in America. In my interviews (cf. Chapters 4 and 5) with South Asian Muslims in Greater Boston, many participants shared their disapproval of these changes in American socioculture related to family structures.

It is important to note some differences between the sociocultural family structures found in South Asian Islamic countries and those in America. In South Asia where Islam is dominant, there is a close correlation between what children are taught in the mosques and schools and what parents and grandparents teach them at home. The dominant values of Islam are reinforced with a high degree of consistency. In the South Asian Muslim subculture in the United States, there is also a close correlation between what the children are taught at mosque-schools (*madrasas*) and what they are taught at home. This is at variance with what is found in the typical American home, where differing values are taught at home in comparison with what the child may be taught at school or at church or by watching television programs.

In contrast to typical family structures in America, most South Asian Muslim families, both in South Asia and in America, hold to the nuclear family structure, and whenever possible also the extended-family structure. The extended-family structure can include parents, children, grandparents, uncles, aunts, nieces, and cousins living together in one household. In many areas of the South Asian region, extended-family members frequently live at one household in a joint-family structure, or they may live nearby and maintain close ties.

Predominant family values include close ties, frequent contact, respecting elders, and caring for elderly parents and grandparents. These practices reflect the family values typical in the South Asian region. However, these typical traditional family structures are diminishing slowly in recent years, especially in urban areas and where the single-parent family structure is practiced. Even in those situations, close family ties are usually maintained. In large urban areas, in some families the traditional close family ties may become loosened, because work responsibilities may demand long-distance travel, difficult work schedules, etc.; however, these situations remain a small minority.

Most South Asian Muslim families in America typically maintain the traditional family values practiced in their native lands. In Muslim families, children are taught the core values and emphases of their religion, culture, and traditions by their parents and grandparents, as well as by extended family members. Parental authority is maintained in most Muslim immigrant families. South Asian Muslim parents living in an American multicultural society such as that found in America perceive a serious challenge to maintaining the traditional values brought from their homelands. This is clearly evident to me through my frequent contact and observation of South Asian Muslim homes.

As previously mentioned, first generation South Asian Muslim immigrants come to America with a predetermined idea that the sociocultural environment in America is strongly influenced by Christianity. When they immigrate to their new country, they associate all sociocultural practices in American society either directly or indirectly with the influence of Christianity. This is evident from the interviews presented later in this book. Of course, this is an erroneous perception that reveals a lack of understanding of the separation of church and state that is operative in American democracy.

When they become aware of the departure from the traditional nuclear family structure in modern-day American society and how alternative family structures are rapidly increasing, they assume that this change is either caused or approved or tolerated by Christianity. This becomes part of their perception of Christianity.

South Asian Muslims have the perception that Christianity has authority to change the society like Islam exerts control in every aspect of life in their motherlands. In the democratic structure of American society, churches have no direct authority or control over society. Churches can only exert influence in the society through their collective voice and teachings and through the influence of Christian adherents, and this influence is still evident to some extent today. However, this influence is less extensive today in our post-Christian era as secularism expands. In 2015, Pew Research Center in an extensive new survey reported in the article "Religion and Public Life":

> The Christian share of the U.S. population is declining, while the number of U.S. adults who do not identify with any organized religion is growing ... Moreover, these changes are taking place across the religious landscape, affecting all regions of the country and many demographic groups ... the percentage of adults (ages 18 and older) who describe themselves as Christians has dropped by nearly eight percentage points in just seven years, from 78.4% in an equally massive Pew Research survey in 2007 to 70.6% in 2014 ... Over the same period the percentage of who are religiously unaffiliated—describing themselves as atheist, agnostic, or "nothing in particular"—has jumped more than six points, from 16.1% to 22.8%. (Pew Research Center 2015)

South Asian Muslims in America have the perception that individualism in American society and demands for personal privacy in family and private life are associated with Christian teaching and influence. This also is an incorrect perception. This is also supported by the interviews later in this book.

To summarize this section, the family structures and family values practiced in present-day American society are closely related to the perceptions of Christianity among South Asian Muslims in America.

SOCIOCULTURAL ACCULTURATION

South Asian Muslim immigrants in America acculturate into their new culture to varying degrees and in a variety of ways. This is in response to what they experience of the sociocultural emphases and practices in American society. Each immigrant has a unique response, deciding which parts of the new culture he or she will embrace and to what extent.

In this work, sociocultural acculturation is the process of integrating into the receiving culture. Acculturation is essentially the same as integration, and integration is a continuum, ranging from adaptation as a minimum adjustment necessary to dwell in the new cultural environment to assimilation as a maximum of integration. Below is an image of what is called the "human curve" representing the percentage of acculturation or integration within the population of Muslim immigrants.

Adaptation

Usual Assimilation

0% PERCENT ACCULTURATION / INTEGRATION 100%

The height of the curve represents the number of the population who acculturate to that percent, or to that extent. Adaptation is an extreme strategy that strongly resists acculturation, while assimilation is the other extreme of those who try to fully acculturate into the host culture, adopting the characteristics of that culture.

These concepts specifically relate to immigrants adjusting to their new American culture, and in this book to the sociocultural environment in America.

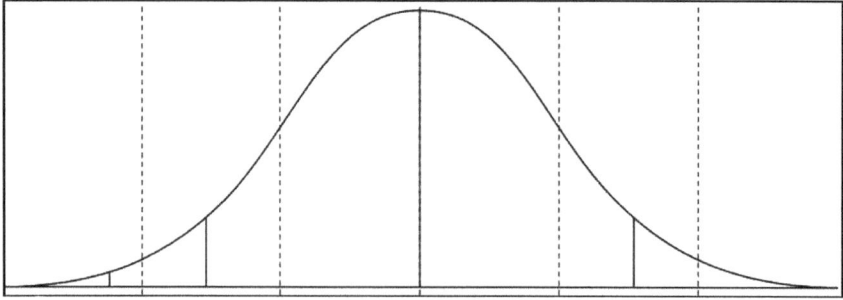

Each immigrant to America will become situated in a somewhat unique sociocultural environment. *Merriam-Webster Dictionary* defines acculturation: "Cultural modification of an individual group or people by ... borrowing traits from another culture." (Merriam-Webster Dictionary.com 2017) So according to Webster, when people acculturate they adopt traits from the receiving (or host) culture.

In this section, I explore the extent to which South Asian Muslim immigrants acculturate or integrate into American society in America. I examine the levels of integration, from adaptation to assimilation. I further explore the identity crisis many second-generation children of immigrants face in response to influences they encounter in their homes, in the mosques and South Asian Muslim subculture, and in the larger context of the American sociocultural environment. I specifically examine how these adaptations are related to perceptions of Christianity among South Asian Muslims.

Acculturation by integration is discussed in detail in the following section.

LEVELS OF ACCULTURATION INTO AMERICAN CULTURE

When we talk about acculturation, integrating into a culture, we refer to more than one culture since there is a culture from which the individual comes (culture of origin) and the culture into which the individual is adjusting (receiving or host culture).

Acculturation is the process of integrating into the new culture. In 2016, Khan Ali wrote in his blog "How is Cultural Integration Defined?":

> Cultural integration is a form of cultural exchange in which one group assumes the beliefs, practices, and rituals of another group without sacrificing the characteristics of its own culture. Cultural integration is generally looked upon as positive because nothing is lost. (Ali 2016, unpaginated)

This seems a good working definition; however, I do not agree with his assumption that the two cultures are necessarily fully compatible. Also, by integration I include attitudes and customs that are part of the receiving culture. Sociocultural acculturation or integration further refers to the principles by which individuals interrelate with one another in a society.

I see integration as a continuum of various levels of acculturation. The most minimal level of acculturation is adaptation where an individual makes the least possible adjustment to the receiving culture. A higher level, for example an estimated level of perhaps 10 percent integration on the continuum up to perhaps 80 percent, might be considered a more typical level. Above 80 percent, the other extreme of integration is assimilation, where an individual intentionally attempts to give up his culture of origin, which I personally believe is rarely possible.

An article from PubMed Central refers to an article by John W. Berry, who provides a refinement of the definition of cultural integration: When an individual "adopts the receiving culture and retains the heritage culture" (Schwartz, Unger, Zamboanga, Szapocznik 2013). This suggests that sociocultural integration includes significant parts of both the culture of origin (heritage culture) and the receiving (host) culture. Of course, this assumes that elements of both cultures are compatible.

One major advantage of cultural integration is that to some extent an individual can retain his own cultural identity while acculturating into the receiving culture.

I have had many discussions over many years with Muslim immigrants, and they typically struggle with the decision of what extent to acculturate while still retaining their personal identities. Even with the advantages of cultural integration there is still considerable struggle in the process of acculturating into the new culture. It takes time to adjust and to decide what parts of the new culture to embrace and what parts of the culture of origin to retain. Ideally there comes a time when the new immigrant becomes comfortable and relaxed with the chosen level of integration within the new social environment.

Cultural integration includes acclimating and accommodating to a new lifestyle, making new friends who belong to the American culture, and finding acceptance as part of this new culture. It also implies some clear understanding of the American culture and governmental system and understanding the rights of privileges of citizens of this society as well as the responsibilities of citizens. This naturally includes South Asian Muslims in the American area who aspire to become true citizens of their new country.

A first-generation immigrant might decide to adapt to the receiving culture with minimal acculturation and resist adopting traits of the new culture. A person can adapt to the culture while remaining aloof and isolationist or even hostile. So such a person could adapt to the new culture while acculturating to a very limited extent.

In many discussions I have had with South Asian Muslims, I found that they frequently talk about some of the concerns that come to mind upon arrival in their new homeland

They frequently mention the struggle to discern which parts of American culture conflict with Islamic traditions and values. Such expressed concerns are more typical among the more devout first-generation Muslim immigrants, who comprise the majority of South Asian immigrants.

From interviews with South Asian Muslims in America (cf. Chapters 4 and 5) I have observed three categories of participants. One group is religiously devout Muslims, usually first-generation immigrants. They want to follow strict religious principles especially related to food restrictions and preparation (*halal*, meaning approved according to Islamic law, like *kosher* food for strict Jews), abstention from drinking alcohol, and conforming to dress codes (wearing veil-like *hijab, burqa,* and *dupatta*, traditional garments which cover women's head, face, and body). For that reason, they tend to avoid socializing with mainstream Americans, most of whom drink alcoholic beverages. Thus, they are often reluctant to socially integrate into mainstream American society. They prefer to socialize mostly within their own cultural group, preferably other Muslims who share the same heritage culture. Aminah Mohammad-Arif points out:

> The first generation—noticeable especially amongst women who wear the veil—seem also to come to a more intellectual understanding of their religion in the land of migration, and to leave behind them the more mechanical ways of practising Islam that they knew in their home country. (Mohammad-Arif 2002, 104)

The religiously devout are generally more likely to integrate to a limited degree in their adaptation to the receiving culture.

A second group is religiously moderate and is more open to socializing with non-Muslim neighbors. These are mainly second-generation South Asian Muslims who are born or brought up here in the United States. In social gatherings, they can have their choice of food; however, they still avoid meat products unless properly prepared (halal) and avoid any pork products. Some of them choose to wear the veil (hijab) even with blue jeans. There are several reasons for adopting traditional prescribed Muslim attire (such as the hijab, burqa, and dupatta). In her interviews with South Asian Muslim young girls, Aminah Mohammad-Arif shares her observation by giving two reasons:

> By doing so, they firstly reassure parents that they are protected from the nefarious emancipation they might otherwise be led to in American society. Secondly, they do it for themselves: under the "protection" of the veil, these girls, who are often highly educated, feel they can enter professional areas which were traditionally the preserve for men, without fear of offending Islamic law. (Mohammad-Arif 2002, 104)

The religiously moderate tend to integrate to a greater extent than the religiously devout. These would not usually be described as adapting to a minimal extent, nor as those who attempt to assimilate into the host culture.

The third group includes nonpracticing Muslims (nominal Muslims), who are more liberal in their practice of Islam. They don't bother about food restrictions of Islam and are not concerned about distinct apparel (such as the hijab, burqa, and dupatta for the women). This third group is a minority among Muslim immigrants. This group is more open and flexible to cultural integration.

Some nonpracticing Muslims might even aspire to assimilate into the American culture; however, this high level of acculturation is very rare, especially among first-generation immigrants.

So the extent to which South Asian Muslim immigrants integrate into mainstream American society varies from person to person, but because of their Muslim identity, religious ideology and practice are important considerations related to the question of integration.

Out of these three categories of South Asian Muslims in America, the religiously devout group has the most negative perceptions of Christianity because they so closely associate Christianity with all sociocultural emphases and practices in American society, many of which they believe are not compatible with Islam. It is true that in the past, many Christian values were practiced in American culture, but Christian influence has diminished significantly over time.

In present-day American society, many cultural practices do not reflect Christian values. Religiously devout Muslims, especially many of the older generation, fail to understand this, and many erroneous perceptions of Christianity develop in their minds. Because of their perception that Christianity is closely associated with American culture, they are strongly disinclined to integrate into American culture.

The moderate and liberal groups both have a combination of positive and negative perceptions of Christianity.

One positive perception of Christianity is that not all sociocultural emphases and practices in American society are bad, even though they also assume these reflect the values and influence of Christianity. The relative social freedom they enjoy in America facilitates interaction with Christians, and these interactions tend of modify their preconceived perceptions of Christianity.

Another perception of Christianity held by South Asian Muslims is that Christian churches in America could have a much greater influence against certain sociocultural emphases and practices in America that are not compatible with either Christianity or Islam. To some extent this perception is true, because Christianity could have a stronger voice in opposition to some practices that society accepts. However, Christianity does not speak with one voice, because Christianity includes a wide range of adherents from fundamentalist to liberal. Some sociocultural practices and emphases are denounced by some Christian groups and endorsed by others.

Some South Asian Muslims think Christianity tolerates or lends silent support to some emphases and practices they see as incompatible with Islam. Many who were interviewed (cf. Chapters 4 and 5) held the view that Christianity could be more influential in setting values in American society. However, they also tend to think that Christianity, as the dominant religion in America, has much more power in government and value-setting than is possible in this democratic societal structure. This shows their misunderstanding of American democracy as well as their misperception of Christianity in America.

Nonpracticing and moderate South Asian Muslim immigrants have a much more positive perception of Christianity and consequently are much more likely to acculturate to a higher extent. As discussed above, by moderate Muslim I mean those less strict in their religious practices and convictions and more open to other religious groups. Their perception of Christianity is in contrast with what they were taught about Christianity in the society of their country of origin. After immigrating, many of these Muslims discover that there are many good practices in American culture and society which resulted from the direct influence of Christianity. Aminah Mohammad-Arif shared some positive perceptions of many South Asian Muslim immigrants about American society. She stated:

> They [South Asian Muslims] identified the following things that they particularly valued: the freedom; the ordered society; honesty; the value placed on intimacy and privacy; efficient system; punctuality; people's dedication to work; cleanliness; the broad-mindedness of Americans. (Mohammad-Arif 2002, 231)

To summarize this section, adaptation to a different culture is possible with very limited acculturation into that culture. Immigrants use various strategies to acculturate into their new cultural environment. Adaptation is the minimum of acculturation required to live peaceably in the different culture. Another typical strategy for acculturation involves a higher level of integration, where the immigrant retains parts of the original culture while adopting parts of the receiving culture. The extent of integration varies widely from Muslim to Muslim, to some extent related to their religious convictions and their perception of Christianity as the dominant religion in America.

I see cultural integration as a continuum with the ratio of the receiving culture to the culture of origin varying from person to person. For example, one immigrant may retain 70 percent of her original culture compared to 30 percent of her receiving culture, while another may retain 30 percent of his original culture compared to 70 percent of his receiving culture. The former example would reside in the receiving country, but would strongly retain the values, customs, and traditions of her original culture. The latter would integrate very well and might even approach assimilation into the receiving culture.

There seems to me to be a correlation between the extent of integration and the perception of Christianity. Those with stronger negative perceptions of Christianity, based on their predetermined ideas as well as their observations of sociocultural practices in American society, are more disinclined toward integration into the American culture. On the other hand, immigrants with stronger positive perceptions of Christianity are more inclined to fuller integration.

Up to this point I have had little to say about the extreme case of acculturation called assimilation, because this is so very rare and difficult to achieve, even when the motivation and desire are present, which is also rare.

However, because assimilation is theoretically possible, especially among the second- and third-generation offspring of immigrants, I will include a description and discussion of this very high level of integration.

In 2016, a blog was posted by Matthew O'Brian on immigrationreform. com contrasting assimilation and integration:

> *Assimilation* is generally defined as adopting the ways of another culture and fully becoming part of a different society. Whereas *integration* is typically defined as incorporating individuals from different groups into a society as equals. The difference is subtle but significant. (O' Brian 2017, unpaginated) (Emphasis mine.)

In this work assimilation is extreme integration at the very high end of the spectrum of integration.

Merriam-Webster Dictionary provides a definition: "Assimilation refers to the process through which individuals and groups of differing heritages acquire the basic habits, attitudes, and mode of life of an embracing culture" (Merriam-Webster Dictionary.com 2017). More perspective was provided in 1974, when the American Anthropological Association published the article "Acculturation and Assimilation: A Clarification," in which they quoted a definition of assimilation by Park E. Robert and Ernest W. Burgess:

> It [assimilation] is a process in which persons and groups acquire memories, sentiments, and attitudes of other persons or groups; and by sharing in their experience and history, are incorporated with them in a common cultural life. (American Anthropological Association 1974, 351–67)

Thus, assimilation suggests incorporation with the people of the receiving culture into a common cultural community. In this work assimilation means an individual intentionally embraces the receiving culture and attempts to become an integral part of it, while letting go of his or her heritage cultural identity. Assimilation refers to the process by which individuals and groups of differing heritages acquire the basic habits, attitudes, values, and mode of life of a receiving culture.

Full assimilation is very rare and is the extreme of cultural integration, which retains parts of the heritage cultural identity and characteristics. Assimilation is a gradual process by which a person or group belonging to one culture adopts the practices, identity, and characteristics of another, thereby becoming an accepted member of that culture. This suggests full acculturation.

Various factors come into play in considering the degree to which South Asian Muslims in America work at assimilating into their surrounding subculture in America. Opposing pressures from their friends and neighbors and colleagues in the Muslim community dissuade and discourage them from assimilating, and they must go against those social pressures if they are to assimilate.

Unlike many other nations, America is known as a multiethnic and multinational "melting pot" with immigrants from many different ethnic and national origins who are considered American. America has a much broader definition of national identity than many other nations. With such wide variety in nationality and ethnicity among those who comprise this country, an immigrant might wonder what it means to be American in cultural identity.

In numerous interviews with South Asian Muslims, I have discovered that most of them resist assimilation. I have observed four main reasons I believe this resistance to assimilation is true:

> They are reluctant to completely identify with American culture and give up their ethnic identity related to their culture of origin.
> They closely associate Christianity with American culture.
> They have the conviction that Christianity is antithetical to Islam.
> Assimilation is extreme or radical integration.

Based on these interviews with South Asian Muslims immigrants, fewer than half desire to integrate into American culture; however, very few who do desire to integrate have any interest in assimilation.

To summarize this section on sociocultural acculturation: The basic strategy for acculturation, or cultural integration, includes adaptation that is the minimum required, followed by a wide range of integration in varying degrees into the receiving culture, and ending with the maximum possible integration being assimilation. In order to assimilate, a person gives up his or her own cultural heritage and totally adopts the receiving culture as one's own, which is extremely difficult and very rare.

Most South Asian Muslim immigrants have the perception that in order to acculturate they must embrace some Christian values that they see as antithetical to Islam.

ACCULTURATION OF CHILDREN
OF MUSLIM IMMIGRANTS

In this section, I discuss acculturation of children of South Asian Muslim immigrants in America. I include children who are born outside of America who immigrate with their parents as well as children who are born in America, including second- and third-generation offspring. I further discuss how these children of South Asian Muslim immigrants face challenges to their acculturation into American culture and how their perceptions of Christianity are related to their acculturation.

In 2010, the American Psychological Association, in its Journal, *American Psychologist,* published a research paper—"Rethinking of the Concept of Acculturation: Implication for Theory and Research"—written by Seth J. Schwartz, Jenifer B. Unger, Byron L. Zamboanga, and Jose Szapocznik. These writers cited M. Gibson's definition: "Broadly as applied to individuals, acculturation refers to changes that take place as a result of contact with culturally dissimilar people, groups, and social influences" (Schwartz, Unger, Zamboanga, Szapocznik 2010).

Based on this comment by Gibson, acculturation also includes the children of immigrants because being raised in the home of immigrants means to some extent they are in "contact with culturally dissimilar people."

Children of Muslim immigrants also must deal with the challenges of acculturation, but to a significantly lesser extent than their immigrant parents. I am convinced from many discussions with children of immigrants that children are generally more adaptable than their parents.

In numerous visits and conversation with South Asian Muslim parents and their children at the high school level, I have observed that children apparently have less stress in acculturating than their parents.

I further have observed a slight difference in the acculturation process between American-born children and children who immigrate with their parents. Of course, older children born abroad will naturally have more difficulty acculturating than children born in the United States.

From interviews and numerous visits to Pakistani families in the Boston area, I observed that in most Pakistani families, the children are taught that socially acceptable behavior for Pakistanis is different from that of typical American children and that Muslims do not drink alcohol and should be strict about Islamic food restrictions (halal). They are also taught the Pakistani traditions related to dating and selecting life partners, which are also quite different from those typical in America.

Many Pakistani children are taught Urdu (the official language of Pakistan) and taken to Pakistan for vacations so as to reinforce their cultural heritage and identity, and sometimes this reinforcement is more at the hands of grandparents who cling to the home culture and prejudices more strongly than the immigrant parents, who are seeking ways to acculturate while still avoiding assimilation.

Children of South Asian Muslim immigrants note the contrast between the family values in their own homes and those in typical American homes, as they interact with American children in the context of schools and other social settings. This underscores for them the reality of differences that exist between the heritage culture and the receiving culture in America. Pakistani writer Zeenat Anwar, in her article "But we are Americans Now! Our youth, Our Families and Our Future," stated:

> They [Pakistani children] mingle with children who are not of their complexion and whose social behaviors are different: American children are free, Pakistani children are wary. American children are independent, Pakistani youngsters are directed by their parents. American kids have no inhibitions with the opposite sex. Our [Pakistani] kids are more held back. Any attempt to change results in confusion and guilt complex. (Anwar 1995, 252)

South Asian Muslims in America, especially second- and third-generation young people, usually (or typically) think that their religious convictions can fit comfortably into the rapidly changing culture and shifting values in America.

South Asian Muslim parents place a high priority on teaching their children their religion and family values, which they think are even more important for their children living in the multicultural and pluralistic society in America. Many parents try to impart to their children their conviction of the superiority of Islam as well as their negative perceptions of Christianity. Aminah Mohammad-Arif points out:

> Parents see the practice of Islam as the most effective way of transmitting traditional values and limiting Westernization of their children. Religion is tasked with inculcating not only values but also bearings [cultural identity] so as to avoid the "disintegration" within American society. (Mohammad-Arif 2002, 98)

This suggests that to the Muslim parent it is not only important to teach their children Islamic values but also the Muslim cultural identity. Numerous discussions I have had with children of South Asian Muslim immigrants reveal that many feel estranged from mainstream American society.

The following comments are derived from these discussions and observations. These children welcome opportunities to interact with their classmates and friends, some of whom come from conservative Christian families, where Christian values are taught and practiced. Over time, many misperceptions and much misinformation about Christianity held by these children of Muslim immigrants become diminished.

Aminah Mohammad-Arif points out:

> Young people will want to know about religion [Islam], but not necessarily in the way their parents taught them. There are also some young South Asians who are drawn by the spiritual rather than the dogmatic side of religion and they merely observe on a minimal level. (Mohammad-Arif 2001, 100)

Mohammad-Arif's statement indicates that the rejection of the "dogmatic side of religion" [Islam] by the children of South Asian

Muslim immigrants, which was taught by their parents and Muslim leaders, will make them more open to other religious groups as well as Christianity.

It seems to me the children of South Asian Muslim immigrants who are born in the United States naturally have a better understanding of American customs and Christian values than recent Muslim immigrants. From my personal observation with the children and their parents, they seem more aware that not all Christian values are reflected in American customs and practices. I also believe these children generally have a more positive perception of Christianity than their parents.

Yet, I also am convinced many of these children will face challenges from their parents and surrounding Muslim community as they integrate into American culture and adopt some personal values that are closer to Christian values than those held by their parents.

Parental authority is still strong in most South Asian Muslim immigrant families in America, and parents seek to impart their own values and religious views. Aminah Mohammad-Arif states:

> However, if we consider the level of conservatism of the parents, the propensity of the children to rebel remains relatively low … This low propensity for rebellion, which shows up in analysis of the relationship between the generations in a diasporic situation, shows that young South Asians accept [parental authority] without much [negative] reaction. (Mohammad-Arif 2001, 93–94)

Children of South Asian Muslim immigrants experience various pressures from their parents and the surrounding Muslim community to conform to the values and views of their parents. These pressures all affect their perception of Christianity in both positive and negative ways. There is pressure from parents and the home environment to adopt the ideas and ideals of their parents because the parents often believe their ideas and ideals are superior, including their Muslim convictions, and fear their children will deviate from Islamic teaching and influence.

They are also regularly exposed to the efforts of the mosque leaders (those in authority) who attempt to indoctrinate them with Islamic values and views. On the other hand, they also feel pressure to fit into the surrounding larger American culture, conveyed to them through the media, experiences and influences at public school, through interaction with their new American friends, and the attractiveness of the freedoms inherent in American culture.

Many of them are also attracted to Christianity, Christian values, and the examples of Christian love they experience and observe as they interact with and observe Christians within the larger sociocultural environment.

For all South Asian Muslim immigrants in America there is always a gap between the traditions and convictions of the older generation (first generation) and those of the children and grandchildren of those immigrants. On the part of the older generation there is always a concern about the extent to which the subsequent generations adopt the receiving culture. Aminah Mohammad-Arif states:

> Members of the second generation ... have quickly absorbed American ways of thinking [even if they have not done so to the exclusion of other identities] and do not perceive themselves as foreigners in American society. (Mohammad-Arif 2002, 233)

This is also true for children (second and third generation) of South Asian Muslim immigrants in America.

The main theme of this chapter is sociocultural influences on perceptions of Christianity among South Asian Muslims in America. In this chapter, I explored these sociocultural influences in three main areas.

First, I explored the contrast between sociocultural emphases in American society and those in Muslim society in South Asia. These emphases affect perceptions of Christianity among Muslim from South Asia, which are also found among those in America.

Second, I discussed some sociocultural practices in American society. I focused particularly on the practices disapproved by South Asian Muslims and how these practices create or reinforce misperceptions in Muslims minds, which in turn affect the perceptions of Christianity held by South Asian Muslims in America.

Third, I discussed sociocultural adaptation—the way South Asian

Muslim immigrants in America respond to sociocultural emphases and sociocultural practices in American culture and the extent to which they choose to integrate into the American culture. I also included a discussion of the adaptation to the American culture by children of South Asian Muslim immigrants who receive shaping influences from their parents as well as from the surrounding cultural environment, which consists of the Muslim subculture and the larger US culture and society.

Many sociocultural emphases and practices in American society create or reinforce perceptions of Christianity among South Asian Muslims who come from diverse cultural backgrounds. South Asian Muslim immigrants also come with the presupposition that all sociocultural emphases and practices in American society are influenced by Christianity and that Christian churches in America accept or tolerate these emphases and practices in society—the good as well as the bad. This presupposition affects perceptions of Christianity among South Asian Muslims in America.

In this chapter I discussed a representative sampling of sociocultural emphases and practices prevalent in American society. In light of this study, I am convinced that understanding the South Asian Muslim adaptation to American culture is important to help Christian workers build relationships with Muslims from South Asia and open doors for effective communication of the gospel.

The sociocultural emphases and practices in American society discussed in this chapter clearly affect perceptions of Christianity among South Asian Muslims, yet there are various ethical and moral issues and practices that also influence perceptions of Christianity, discussed in the following chapter.

CHAPTER 3

INFLUENCES OF ETHICAL (MORAL) ISSUES

ON PERCEPTIONS OF CHRISTIANITY AMONG SOUTH ASIAN MUSLIMS IN AMERICA

Ethical (moral) issues in American society influence the perceptions of Christianity among South Asian Muslims. Both ethics and morals relate to right and wrong conduct and beliefs. While these two words are sometimes used interchangeably, they are different.

Ethics refers to rules provided by an external source, for example codes of conduct in workplaces or religious principles or guiding principles that help an individual or group decide what is right or wrong.

Morals and/or morality refer to an individual's own principles regarding right and wrong—what an individual or group believes is right or wrong.

There are many ethical and moral issues in postmodern American society. But in this book, I only discuss a representative sample of controversial ethical issues, especially those foremost in the minds of South Asian Muslims and most likely to affect perceptions of Christianity for these Muslims in America.

I have identified three main ethical issues that are controversial to South Asian Muslims. The three ethical issues to be discussed in this chapter include:

> ➢ Homosexuality and same-sex marriage
> ➢ Unmarried couples living together
> ➢ Abortion

For each ethical issue discussed, I also include typical responses of South Asian Muslims in America, and how this can affect their perceptions of Christianity.

In this chapter, I explore predetermined ideas of Christianity among South Asian Muslims in America related to those ethical issues in American society that are controversial for many Muslims in this area. I compare the opinions and views of these Muslims with those held by most conservative Christians in America. I further explore how and to what extent the convictions and responses of South Asian Muslims influence their perceptions of Christianity.

HOMOSEXUALITY AND SAME-SEX MARRIAGE

Homosexuality is a common term in the Western world. *The American Heritage Dictionary of the English Language* defines homosexuality: "Sexual desire for others of one's own sex. Sexual activity with another of the same sex." (Morris 1978, 631).

Homosexual people are typically called gay in American vernacular. Many female homosexuals prefer to be referred to as lesbians. A frequent term used to describe people who strongly disapprove of homosexual practice is "homophobic." Another frequently used acronym is LGBT, referring to lesbian, gay, bisexual, and transgender.

Quoting from F. Beach (1950), Randall L. Sell defines homosexuality "as sexual behavior, including sexual congress, between individuals of the same sex, especially past puberty. Homosexuality refers exclusively to overt behavior between individuals of the same sex" (Sell 1997, 359).

This practice is very controversial to Muslims mainly from a religious perspective. Homosexuality is condemned by the religion of Islam and in all Muslim societies. In some Muslim societies there is severe public punishment for those caught in homosexual activity. Several Qur'anic verses denounce this practice. "Why do you go for males unlike all other creatures? Leaving the consorts your Lord has made for you? But you are people who exceed the bounds" (Surah 26:165–66). "Remember Lot, when he said to his people: Why do you indulge in obscenities when you know it is evil? You lust after men in place of women. You are indeed a stolid people" (Surah 27:54–55). "And We [Allah] sent Lot, who said to his people: Why do you commit this lecherous act which none in the world has committed before? In preference to women you satisfy your lust with men. Indeed, you are a people who are guilty of excess" (Surah 7:80–81). These verses of the Qur'an clearly denounce homosexuality as forbidden, and this practice is considered to be sinful in Islam.

Regarding the Qur'anic verses Surah 7:80–81 (see above), Raouf Ghattas and Carol B. Ghattas point out:

> We read in this passage the story of Lot [also mentioned in the Bible] in a very condensed form. He was sent as a prophet to his people to call them to leave their sinful practices of homosexuality, but they rejected his message. (Ghattas and Ghattas 2009, 101)

The Bible also clearly denounces homosexuality as sin. For example, in the Old Testament, in Genesis 19:1–23, we see the story of Sodom and Gomorrah, where Lot entreated the people in his town not to act wickedly and to leave his male guests alone. The story goes on to describe the persistence of people in these towns indulging in homosexuality and describes the subsequent annihilation of the two communities at the hand of God.

Other Old Testament passages clearly also prohibit homosexuality: "You shall not lie with a male as with a woman; it is an abomination" (Leviticus 20:13). "If a man lies with a male as with a woman, both of them have committed an abomination; they shall be put to death; their blood is upon them" (Leviticus 20:13). This passage calls for the death penalty—the same as adultery. In the New Testament, we can see similar proscriptions in 1Corithians 6:9: "Do you not know that the wicked will not inherit the kingdom of God? Do not be deceived: Neither the sexually immoral nor idolaters nor adulterers nor male prostitutes nor homosexual offenders." Other passages in the New

Testament, such as Romans 1:26–27 and 1 Timothy 1:10 emphatically condemn homosexuality.

Regarding the condemnation of homosexuality in the Old Testament, *Baker's Evangelical Dictionary of Biblical Theology* states:

> Condemnations of sexual sin in the Old Testament focus on heterosexual acts, but it is important to note that all sexual sin, including homosexuality, is prohibited in relation to the positive model of marriage presented in Genesis. Thus, while the Old Testament describes homosexual activity as intrinsically unjust or impure, these condemnations do not differ qualitatively from condemnations of heterosexual deviations from the marriage model. (Baker's Evangelical Dictionary of Biblical Theology.com 1996)

Because of their close association of Christianity with cultural practices in America, South Asian Muslims in America are not aware that many conservative Christians in this area strongly oppose homosexuality as against their convictions and faith.

Most South Asian Muslims in America have the perception that Christian churches in this area are too weak in their opposition and public denunciation of homosexuality. Since few churches in this area demonstrate publicly against homosexuality, to most Muslims this implies Christianity sympathizes with and silently supports homosexuality and gay marriage. In interviews with South Asian Muslims in Greater Boston, most of the participants confirmed this impression (cf. Chapters 4 and 5).

Homosexuality is legally approved in American society as indicated by a recent Supreme Court ruling legalizing gay marriage throughout the country. Therefore, homosexuals now can insist that this practice is a part of their guaranteed freedom of choice as a sexual orientation. Moreover, this practice is openly condoned by some of the more liberal Christian churches and denominations in America, often leaving a strong impression among South Asian Muslims that all who consider themselves Christian hold these same views. Since South Asian Muslims typically reject homosexual practice as sinful and offensive, this creates a strong negative perception of Christianity in their minds.

The Bible and the Qur'an both denounce homosexual practice. Yet, South Asian Muslims have a negative perception of Christianity on this issue because some churches, liberal Christian denominations, and Christian organizations support and even advocate this practice. One example is from the American branch of World Vision, a Christian nonprofit organization, as reported by John Piper, on March 25, 2014:

> *Christianity Today* reports that "World Vision's American branch will no longer require its more than 1,100 employees to restrict their sexual activity to marriage between one man and one woman." World Vision president, Richard Sterns, clarified, "The new policy will not exclude someone from employment if they are in a legal same sex marriage." World Vision is in the top ten charities in America and took in over a billion dollars last year and serves over a 100 million people in 100 countries. (Piper 2014, 1)

A *Christianity Today* release on the following day stated:

> Only two days after announcing it would hire Christians in same-sex marriages, World Vision U.S. has reversed its ground-breaking decision after weathering intense criticism from Christian evangelical leaders. (Gracy and Weber 2014, 1)

World Vision quickly reversed its decision in response to outspoken criticism from many Christians in the United States, who strongly denounce this practice. This shows that when many Christians are united in speaking out against a decision, sometimes that decision can be changed. Yet, South Asian Muslims correctly perceive that Christians often fail to speak out against this practice, which reveals their perception of Christianity related to this ethical issue (cf. Chapters 4 and 5).

It is difficult for South Asian Muslims in America to distinguish between liberal and conservative Christians. Convictions related to controversial ethical issues can vary widely within the Christian community in America. The Muslim immigrant perception is that all Christians either support or tolerate these practices. Most of the participants in the interviews (cf. Chapters 4 and 5) have alluded to this perception.

Those in favor of same-sex marriage often argue that same-sex marriage is for simply enjoying the rights and personal sexual orientation protected by the law of the country. South Asian Muslims in America consider this argument a lame excuse for immoral behavior. They believe marriage must be a union between a man and a woman. Ibrahim B. Sayed stated:

> In the United States, proponents of equal marriage rights for same-sex couples point out that there are over 1,049 federal rights and benefits denied same-sex couples by excluding them from participating in marriage. A legal denial of rights or benefits afforded to others, they say, directly contradicts the 14th Amendment of the US Constitution which provides for equal protection and substantive due process under the law. (Sayed 2012, 3)

In postmodern American society, religious liberalism has much influence, and many churches in America are also influenced by these liberal ideas. Grant Wacker wrote an article, "Religious Liberalism and Modern Crisis of Faith," published by National Humanity Center, Duke University Divinity School. According to Wacker, religious liberalism:

> Served as an intellectual reaction against the evangelical Protestant heritage that pervaded most denominations. Evangelicalism stressed the supernatural character of Christianity, seeing the Bible as a transcription of God's will and human salvation solely through faith in Christ. (Wacker 2000 unpaginated)

Thus, religious liberalism is in opposition to many of the dominant emphases of conservative Christianity.

Since churches in America do not generally speak out and demonstrate against these emphases in the society, they appear to condone or tolerate them, and this contributes to the perception among South Asian Muslims in America that Christianity condones or tolerates same-sex marriage.

According to a 2015 Pew Research Center report by Carle Murphy, there is a notable trend among Christians toward favoring the acceptance of homosexuality by society. The Pew Research study included Catholics, mainline Protestants, Evangelical Protestants, Orthodox Protestants, and the black Protestant tradition, and covered a broad generational spectrum from the Silent Generation to the Millennial Generation. In every category, there was a consistent increase in Christians favoring the acceptance of homosexuality by society (Murphy 2015). In the interviews I conducted among a representative sampling of South Asian Muslims in the Boston area, there is no indication of a parallel trend among this group. This would suggest that, compared to Christians, Muslims are much less tolerant of homosexual activity and have much more severe punishment for this practice.

The teachings of the Bible and the Qur'an remain relatively static on this issue.

Unmarried Couples Living Together

Living together outside of marriage is a growing practice in American society. Many of these unmarried couples also have children and establish families. The ethical landscape of what is considered an acceptable family structure in American society is rapidly changing in the twenty-first century.

In this section, I describe the changing ethical attitudes toward this practice from Christian and Muslim perspectives, especially the religious ethical viewpoints. I especially examine the responses of South Asian Muslims in America to these practices and how their responses affect their perceptions of Christianity.

An unmarried couple (opposite sex) living in the same house and sexually active is generally referred to as "living together," or more specifically as "cohabitation." Cohabitation is defined by *The American Heritage Dictionary of the English Language* as "To live together in a sexual relationship when not legally married" (Morris 1978, 259). Cohabitation of unmarried, opposite sex couples is no longer a serious legal issue in the United States. However, it can be an issue in a conservatively religious society, especially in Muslim countries. In such a society, it is considered immoral when an unmarried male and female couple have a sexual relationship (fornication), and cohabitation is illegal and punishable by death in countries where shariah law is enforced.

Some couples in America who live together outside marriage choose not to marry in order to avoid legal commitments and obligations. Many unmarried couples in America remain unmarried even after becoming parents.

Cohabitation outside of marriage has become a prevalent practice in American society, and for South Asian Muslims this is uniformly denounced, because to them this is seen as immoral. From the Muslim religious perspective, this practice is strongly condemned.

For Muslims, premarital sex as well as sex outside marriage is fornication (*Zina*) and is denounced in the Qur'an. "And do not go near fornication, as it is immoral and an evil way" (Surah 17:32). Premarital sex is considered the same sin as adultery and the Qur'an is very clear about the serious punishment for an adulterer and adulteress. "The adulteress and adulterer should be flogged a hundred lashes each, and no pity for them" (Surah 24:2). Concerning this Qur'anic Surah, Raouf Ghattas and Carol B. Ghattas point out:

> The Qur'an orders punishment for those who commit adultery [male and female] by the application of a hundred lashes. We need to point out that this contradicts another verse in the Qur'an, which gives the punishment as death for the woman only. (Ghattas and Ghattas 2009, 195)

I agree with these writers that this Qur'anic Surah contradicts another Surah (Surah 4:15), where it calls for the death penalty for the woman only: "Retain them [the women] in the house until death overtakes them or Allah provides some other way for them." However, one thing is clear: outside of marriage, sexual relationship is not permitted in the Qur'an. The Qur'an says true believers will be successful and one of the marks (or evidences) of success is those "who guard their sex" (Surah 23:5).

The Qur'an strongly advocates marriage: "Marry off those who are single among you, and those of your male and female servants who are righteous" (Surah 24:32). "Those who cannot afford to marry should abstain from what is unlawful" (Surah 24:33).

So according to the teaching of the Qur'an, Islam denounces premarital sex and does not permit living together outside of marriage.

The Bible also undeniably condemns adultery and sexual immorality. Sexual immorality in the Bible includes fornication, premarital sex, and sex outside marriage, as well as any form of homosexual practice. But many people today argue that when a male and female agree to become married, living together before marriage and having premarital sex is not immoral. It has become common practice and tolerated in Western society. However, the Bible strongly denounces this: "But since there is so much immorality, each man should have his own wife and each woman her own husband. The husband should fulfill his marital duty to his wife, and likewise the wife to her husband" (1 Corinthians 7:2–3). The Bible is very clear that in order to control themselves from immoral sex outside of marriage, people should be married (1 Corinthians 7:9). Then they can fulfill their passion in a moral way.

Many other verses in the New Testament instruct abstinence from sexual immorality and about church disciplinary action for those who violate this instruction (1 Corinthians 5:1, 6:13–18; 2 Corinthians 12:21; Galatians 5:19; Ephesians 5:3; Colossians 3:5; 1 Thessalonians 4:3; Jude 7).

Jesus emphasized that lusting after a woman is committing adultery in a man's heart. He quoted from the Old Testament (Exodus 2:14) and the gospel writer Matthew recorded it: "You have heard that it was said, 'Do not commit adultery.' But I tell you that anyone who looks at a woman lustfully has already committed adultery with her in his heart" (Matthew 5:27). Living together or having a sexual relationship outside marriage is considered adultery or fornication according to the teaching of Jesus.

Jesus also emphasized the importance of marriage. Quoting from the Old Testament (Genesis 2:24), Jesus said, "'Haven't you read," he replied, "that at the beginning the Creator 'made them male and female', and said, 'For this reason a man will leave his father and mother and be united to his wife, and the two will become one flesh'" (Matthew 19:4–5). In this passage, scripture clearly indicates that sex is for marriage only. Sex is not just a pleasurable way of expressing mutual love. It's a question of two people becoming one flesh in the eyes of God. So the sanctity of marriage should be honored. Outside marriage, sex is not permitted in the Bible.

Sex between a husband and his wife is the only sexual relations approved by God. "Let marriage be held in honor by all, and let the marriage bed be kept undefiled; for God will judge fornicators and adulterers" (Hebrews 13:4).

Many passages in the Old Testament denounce sex outside of marriage. This is adultery, and any kind of sexual immorality is sin. God's warning against adultery was also incorporated into the Ten Commandments: "You shall not commit adultery" (Exodus 20:14).

Many passages in the Old Testament indicate the heavy punishment of sexual immorality: Deuteronomy 22:22 says, "If a man is found sleeping with another man's wife, both the man who slept with her and the woman must die."

"If a man commits adultery with another man's wife—with the wife of his neighbor—both the adulterer and the adulteress must be put to death" (Leviticus 20:10).

So the Bible and the Qur'an both denounce male and female living together and having sexual relationship outside marriage.

South Asian Muslims in America have a negative perception regarding unmarried couples living together, as well as those who become parents. This common practice in America affects their perception of Christianity, because they closely associate ethical norms with Christian influence in the society. The main reason for their negative perception about Christianity regarding this issue is that most of them are not aware that the Bible clearly denounces this practice. However, even if they are aware of the biblical teaching, they would probably still have a negative perception of Christianity because of some Christians who have sex outside marriage, and some homosexuals claim to be Christian, and some are even accepted into church membership.

Although the Old Testament passages shown above regarding the punishment of sexual immorality are parallel to the Qur'an, in modern-day America, its application (e.g., the death penalty) would be against the laws of the country. The Christian perspective looks also at the New Testament where Jesus articulated a different perspective regarding sexual immorality. In Matthew 5:27 (see above), Jesus stressed that to even look lustfully at a woman was tantamount to committing adultery with her "in your heart."

Jesus also gave a different way of looking at the punishment for sexual immorality. When confronted with a woman caught in adultery by a group of Jewish men intent on stoning her (John 8:1–11), instead of insisting on the death penalty called for by strict Jewish law, Jesus shifted the focus to the men eager to mete out the punishment, and said, "Let him who is without sin among you be the first to throw a stone at her." Since none were willing to claim sinlessness, they went away. Jesus said to the woman, "Neither do I condemn you; go and do not sin again." So Jesus did not say it was not sinful but enjoined the woman to not commit this sin again.

There is a growing perception among South Asian Muslims in America that Christian churches in this area either tolerate or accept unmarried couples living together, which is true of some churches and perhaps many churches but certainly not all. It would be a misperception to think all Christian churches tolerate or accept this practice. Many conservative Christians and many mainline evangelical Protestant churches and Catholic churches in America do not support this practice.

The South Asian Muslim perception is that churches should take a stronger public stand against it. Since they do not see many visible protests from churches against this practice (sex outside marriage), it affects their perception of Christianity in a negative way. In my interviews, all my participants shared this view (cf. Chapters 4 and 5); that is, the view that churches should publicly demonstrate against sex outside marriage.

ABORTION

In 1973 the United States Supreme Court handed down a decision legalizing abortion. After more than four decades, today opponents and supporters of this decision are still arguing over and demonstrating about this issue in the public arena, in the media, and in churches.

In this section, I discuss the moral aspects of abortion. I also examine this issue from Muslim and Christian perspectives, as well as responses of South Asian Muslims in America to this issue. I further discuss the effects of this moral issue on perceptions of Christianity among South Asian Muslims.

The American Heritage Dictionary of the English Language defines abortion as: "Any fatally premature expulsion of an embryo or fetus from the womb" (Morris 1978, 4).

In the United States abortion is legal because of the Supreme Court decision. Whether legal or illegal from the perspective of the courts, abortion is a serious moral issue from the religious (or ethical) perspective. My impression is that most discussions about abortion in the media and on social networks focus on politics and legal analysis, rather than on the ethical considerations.

In 2012, an article was published in the *European Journal of Social Science* entitled "Perspective on Abortion: Pro-Choice, Pro-Life, and What Lies in Between." written by Raquel Lopez. Lopez quoted directly from another scholar David Boonin:

> It is reasonable to agree that if an unborn is a human, the unborn is entitled to rights; and if a human is entitled to rights, it must have moral values. This statement appears to make abortion unethical from the standpoint that the unborn entity is being deprived from the right of choosing to live, considering someone else is making that choice; and, therefore, society should ban the practice of abortion. (Lopez 2012, 513)

Referring to this Raquel Lopez article, Sharah Breannes wrote in her blog in 2012 that abortion is murder and therefore is a serious moral issue. Breannes stated:

> In the article, *Perspectives on Abortion: Pro-Choice, Pro-Life, and What Lies in between,* Raquel Lopez states that 33.6% of women who get abortions are between the ages of 20 and 24 and 81.6% are not married to the father. Why should the helpless baby have to suffer because of a parent's inability to take care of it financially or mentally? Did your parents ever give up on you? The answer here is no. Everyone goes through rough times in their life, but that doesn't mean the baby has to suffer the consequences of the parental downfall

or instability. If a child is murdered, it goes against all moral values that we are taught. You can't walk down the street anywhere in the United States and find one person who thinks that murder is moral and that it is an okay way to deal with someone you don't want in your life. (Breannes 2012)

Most debates on the morality of abortion in which I have participated focus on the basic question of whether the fetus is a living person. I agree with the position of Aurora C. Griffin that human life begins with conception. Griffin points out:

> The premise based on natural science is that the life of each individual mammal begins at conception. Modern science has made it nearly impossible to defend the view that the fetus is not human, considering that from the moment of conception it has human DNA, so the issue centers on personhood. If the human is a person only when neurologically functioning as a human, then by that same argument it would be permissible to kill people while they are in deep sleep, in comas, or mentally handicapped. Similar arguments can be made for location and viability. The only time when we can consistently argue the human fetus becomes a person is when he or she becomes human: at conception. (Griffin 2011, 1)

This same view—that life begins at conception—is held by the Catholic Church and most conservative Protestant churches. Furthermore, pro-life advocates believe, and I am also convinced, that every fetus has a moral right to life. If the point is valid that life begins with conception, then religious and legal injunctions against murder would apply to the unborn fetus. It is a powerful argument that even though the fetus has no voice, neither do people in a coma or people who are mentally impaired.

There are two prominent opposing groups in the United States in an ongoing debate about abortion: pro-choice and pro-life. These debates are intense between these two groups even within some organized churches. Pro-choice people argue that women have the freedom of choice over their bodies to have an abortion. This argument often is presented as part of the rights of women. It is considered the discretion of the mother of the unborn fetus. Pro-choice advocates further argue that there may be a circumstance or situation that justifies an abortion, for example when the life of the mother is endangered; in such a case, it may be justified or sometimes even mandatory to save the life of the mother. Another circumstance often cited is when the pregnancy is the result of rape.

On the other hand, pro-life people believe abortion is the taking of a human life.

The question of morality of abortion is related to religion, because religion is generally the repository of morality. So in this work it is better to discuss abortion in terms of religious views and convictions when examining Christian and Muslim perspectives.

The Qur'an does not explicitly mention abortion, but the implication of the Qur'anic views on the sanctity of human life is not favorable for abortion. Ibrahim B. Syed states:

> In principle, the Qur'an condemns the killing of humans [except in the case of defense or as capital punishment], but it does not explicitly mention abortion. This leads Islamic theologians to take up different viewpoints: while the majority of early Islamic theologians permitted abortion up to day 40 of pregnancy or even up to day 120, many countries today interpret these precepts protecting unborn children more conservatively. Although there is no actual approval of abortion in the world of Islam, there is no strict, unanimous ban on it, either. Islam has not given any precise directions with regard to the issue of abortion. (Syed 1988–2012, 1)

Islamic theologians who oppose the idea of abortion defend their views based on a portion of the Qur'anic passage Surah 6:151: "Do not kill your children for fear of poverty for it is We [Allah] who shall provide sustenance for you as well as for them." They also find support from part of another passage, Surah 17:31: "killing them [children] is certainly a great wrong."

These two verses do not specifically clarify whether the word "children" refers only to children already born. Of course, anti-Muslim groups will argue that radical Islamic terrorist groups are killing living children and even unborn children when killing pregnant women.

In Muslim countries, the Islamic Council of Jurisprudence has the authority to issue a *Fatwah* (legal opinion) on matters related to abortion. They allow abortion only in certain circumstances, such as when pregnancy threatens the mother's life and when pregnancy results from rape. In some Muslim countries where *shariah* law is the law of the land, the Islamic Council of Jurisprudence in those countries has issued a *Fatwah,* stating that once a pregnancy reaches one hundred and twenty days, after that abortion is forbidden.

Although there are different views among Islamic jurists, the overall general rule is the right to life is God-given. No human should take away that right. Therefore, if life begins at conception, abortion is not permitted.

In numerous discussions and dialogues with South Asian Muslims, they believe there are a growing number of liberal Christians in America who believe that the Bible permits abortion. These liberal Christians argue that the Bible does not specifically say not to abort unborn babies. Even though there are no specific verses prohibiting abortion, if one believes that the unborn child is a human life, or that life begins at conception, then the Bible clearly teaches that abortion is wrong because of the sanctity of human life.

The Bible condemns the shedding of innocent blood. It follows that if the developing fetus is a member of the human race, all scriptures affirming the sanctity of life apply, including the following: "Whoever sheds the blood of man, by man shall his blood be shed; for in the image of God has God made man" (Genesis 9:6). "You shall not murder" (Exodus 20:13). "Cursed is the man who accepts a bribe to kill an innocent person" (Deuteronomy 27:25a). "There are six things which the LORD hates, seven that are detestable to Him: haughty eyes, a lying tongue, hands that shed innocent blood" (Proverbs 6:16–19).

Babies that are born and babies that are unborn are both innocent. The Bible verses above indicate that abortion is killing innocent human life. The position taken by the pro-choice people is that abortion is acceptable because life begins at birth. Some pro-choice people would say abortion is not acceptable when the fetus is viable if born at that stage of development. "Killing innocent human life" is a controversial choice of words, because many pro-life advocates believe life begins at conception.

The majority of South Asian Muslims in America consider abortion as a moral issue primarily because of the prevailing Islamic interpretation of the Qur'anic teaching. Their view is that abortion should be forbidden except in some special cases such as when the mother's life is in danger and when a pregnancy results from rape.

Since abortion is legal in America, South Asian Muslims have the opinion that if the rule of law allows abortion, and if this rule is against the convictions of Christians, then the churches should protest in public demonstrations. Their perception is that churches in America either tolerate or accept abortion because they do not see churches publicly demonstrating against this practice. In my interviews with South Asian Muslims (cf. Chapters 4 and 5) many participants shared this perception and seem to be unaware of numerous media reports of many public demonstrations of Christians against abortion as well as organized efforts by Christian groups to get Roe v. Wade overturned.

In January 2017, the Pew Research Center published an article, "Five Facts about Abortion," written by Michael Lipka and John Gramlich. This article reported the results of a Pew Research Center survey:

> About six-in-ten U.S. adults (59%) say abortion should be legal in all or most cases, compared with 37% who say it should be illegal all or most of the time. Public support for legal abortion is now as high as it's been in two decades of polling. More than four-in-ten Americans (44%) say having an abortion is morally wrong, while 19% think it is morally acceptable and 34% say it is not a moral issue. These views also differ by religious affiliation: About three-quarters of white evangelical Protestants (76%) say having an abortion is morally wrong, but 23% of religiously unaffiliated people agree. (Lipka and Gramlich 2017)

This Pew Research Center survey points out that 76 percent of "white evangelical Protestants" say that abortion is morally wrong. Almost all South Asian Muslims with whom I have discussed abortion are not aware that this significant proportion of Christians agrees with them in their view that abortion is immoral. They also are not aware that the Catholic Church is also in agreement with them. Concerning the Roman Catholic Church beliefs on abortion, David Granfield states:

> Throughout its history, the Catholic Church has resolutely opposed the practice of abortion. From the first recorded condemnation in ecclesiastical writings in the *Didache* [Teachings of the twelve apostles; First Century] ... to the most authoritative recent pronouncements ... we find no authoritative deviation from the doctrine that abortion, at any stage, is a serious sin against God, the Creator of human life. (Granfield 1969, 66)

Yet based on the interviews reported in this book, many South Asian Muslims have the perception that Christianity accepts or approves abortion (see Chapters 4 and 5). These interviews also indicated this perception is more prevalent among first-generation immigrants.

In numerous discussions with South Asian Muslim families in America, first-generation immigrants have expressed their concerns about what they consider immoral practices of their American-born teenage children and grandchildren. Some of these children are having premarital sex, which sometimes results in pregnancies, and, to the dismay of their parents, some of them hold the view that abortion is not a moral issue.

These Muslim parents believe their children are negatively influenced concerning the issue of abortion by their American friends, many of whom are from liberal Christian families. They usually fail to differentiate between conservative and liberal Christians. Consequently, many first-generation immigrants get the impression that immoral influences on their children and grandchildren are from Christian friends who accept the practice of abortion, and therefore they often develop the negative perception that Christianity allows or even accepts this practice.

When most South Asian Muslims immigrate to America, they come with the perception that America is a Christian nation and assume Christian influence in American society like the influence of Islam on the norms of morality in their homelands. They are astonished to soon learn of the legalization of abortion in America.

When they learn that over forty years ago, abortion was legalized by the Supreme Court, they assume this took place with the approval of Christianity or that Christianity could have prevented this legalization but failed to do so. So their perception is that Christian churches go along with these practices that are repulsive to them as Muslims. When they learn that many Christians agree with them about abortion, they wonder that churches do not publicly protest and demonstrate against these practices that to them are blatantly immoral.

They seem to be unaware that conservative Christians and the Catholic Church have had a strong public voice against this practice. Since the Supreme Court decision on abortion forty-four years ago, there have been many outspoken protests and demonstrations from the Christian community against this practice. In the democratic structures of the United States, especially considering the trends in America toward the secularization of society, Christianity can never have the kind of dominating influence that Islam has in the homelands of these Muslim immigrants.

Most conservative Christians agree with Muslims that abortion is a moral issue, and it is killing unborn children. In 2013, John Piper in his article "We Know They Are Killing Children—All of Us Know," points out: "When it comes to abortion, we know what we are doing—all America knows. We are killing children. Pro-choice and pro-life people both know this" (Piper 2013, 1).

In conclusion, the three major ethical issues (homosexuality and gay marriage, unmarried couples living together, and abortion) discussed in this chapter are not only controversial moral issues but are repugnant to South Asian Muslims, and also to many Christians as well. In this chapter, I discussed how these practices in American society are opposed by mainline conservative Protestant churches as well as by the Catholic Church.

Having grown up in a South Asian country, I realize that the way public demonstrations and protests are conducted in South Asia is very different from that in the United States. For one thing, violence is often a part of the protests in those countries, and this is not tolerated in the

United States. Christian churches cannot control the whole society to renounce these practices, but, of course, they can exert influence on society. South Asian Muslims in America have the perception that churches are not doing enough, and many Christians would agree with them.

These three controversial ethical practices, common in present-day American society, influence the perceptions of Christianity held by South Asian Muslims in America. These common practices affect their perception of Christianity even more when they see these practices are also found among Christians. As a consequence, the perception grows in the minds of South Asian Muslims that Christianity tolerates and often accepts these practices that are repugnant to them.

These are investigated through interviews with a representative sample of South Asian Muslims in America, and the resulting data are presented in the next chapter.

CHAPTER 4

PRESENTATION OF DATA

The literature available related to the focus of this book either did not specifically address South Asian Muslims in America or did not address the question of the perception of Christianity related to this focal group. Therefore, to acquire the data needed, interviews were conducted using a questionnaire related to perceptions of Christianity from a representative sample of South Asian Muslims and their family members.

The following guidelines were followed when conducting the interviews used for data gathering for this book.

1. Participants have their own thoughts and interpretations shaped by their life-experiences and convictions related to the questions.
2. Participants will answer all the interview questions openly and honestly, but may decline to answer some of the interview questions.
3. In cases where participants are uncomfortable with an audio recording of the interview, as the interviewer I need to take notes either during or immediately after the interview. Some of the participants will likely be uncomfortable with an audio recording of the interview, so as the interviewer I plan to take

notes either during or immediately after each interview rather than using an audio recorder.

4. Participants selected will be a representative sampling of South Asian Muslims in America.

5. In conducting interviews radical South Asian Muslims are not intentionally excluded, although the majority of South Asian Muslims in America are generally non-radical.

THE QUESTIONNAIRE DESCRIBED

The questionnaire included questions organized around three main areas of interest: theological, sociocultural, and ethical (moral). The questionnaire was prepared and interviews were conducted with fifty carefully chosen South Asian Muslims in America. The questionnaire used in the personal interviews is presented in Appendix B. Questions were designed to discern the perceptions of Christianity held by these South Asian Muslims as reflected in these three areas of interest. There were sixteen questions related to theological issues, nine questions related to sociocultural issues, and six related to ethical (moral) issues that affect perceptions of Christianity.

The questions were carefully crafted to assess the perceptions of Christianity from different perspectives held by the participants. The way participants respond to these questions provides helpful insights into their perceptions of Christians in each focal area of interest.

THE PARTICIPANTS DESCRIBED

Participants interviewed included a cross-section of the ethnic makeup of the larger population, and further included intellectuals and non-intellectuals, and a variety of professional backgrounds.

The chart below describes the general makeup of the participants interviewed:

Characteristics of Participants
(Number of persons interviewed)

Country of Origin

Pakistani .... Sixteen

Bangladeshi .... Twenty

Srilankan .... Three

Indian .... Nine

Maldivian .... Two

Gender

Women .... Five

Men .... Forty-five

Divisions of Islam

Sunni .... Forty

Shi'a .... Seven

Ahmadiyya .... Three

Sufi .... Thirty-eight

Deobandi .... Ten

Barelwi .... Twelve

Employment

Professional .... Forty

Non-professional .... Ten

Educational Background

College graduates .... Forty

Post Graduates .... Ten

Although this is a small sample of the total population of South Asian Muslims in Greater Boston, it is a fair representation of the South Asian Muslim population in America.

I included Muslims from all seven South Asian countries except Nepal and Bhutan, because I could find no Muslims from these countries in Greater Boston. Out of fifty participants, thirty-six are first generation immigrants, ten are second generation (who either immigrated with their parents or were born in the United States), and four are third generation, all of whom were born in the United States. This is a realistic representative sample of the larger population of Muslim families in America.

THE INTERVIEWING PROCESS

The interviewing process involved privately meeting one-on-one with each participant. Many participants would be uncomfortable with a tape recorder, so the participants wrote their responses to the questions on the form provided. For their comments related to each question, I would write on the form in front of them what they said as they looked on. Some of the participants were suspicious of my motives and fearful of some Muslim reprisals, so I constantly gave reassurances that their responses would be kept in strictest confidence and no one would know which responses and comments belong to which participants. I also told the participants that the information they provided was strictly for academic purposes.

The participants were free to skip a question if they were uncomfortable or unfamiliar with the subject of the question. I did not write the names of the participants on the forms during the interviews. Once an interview was finished, I made secret notes on the back of the form so I could associate the responses with a specific participant, but kept the forms strictly confidential, so only I would know which participant's responses were on which form.

Once the fifty interviews were completed, I randomly numbered the completed forms for easy reference. I was careful not to prompt or interject any influence or judgment, and the participants were encouraged to respond with their own opinions in an atmosphere of unbiased acceptance.

METHOD OF DATA PRESENTATION

The questionnaire form is included in Appendix B. The interview questions are also shown on the following pages in the text. Some of the questions were yes/no questions. Some of the questions were multiple-choice (e.g., A or B or C) and some were multiple-answer where a participant would check all that applied (e.g., A, B, C). Beside each question in the form are boxes with each possible answer, and the number of participants who answered with a particular response is recorded in the boxes. Every question allowed the participants to comment on that question. These comments were written on the questionnaire form.

From a study of the specific questions asked and the responses of the participants the reader can gain insights into the perceptions of Christianity held by those interviewed.

The data collected in the interviews are presented in two tables, one for the responses and one for the comments. The Responses Table is in Appendix C, and the Comments Table is presented in Appendix D. The Responses Table also has a comments column on the right side which simply shows the number of participants who made a comment on that particular question.

The Comments Table in Appendix D includes the actual written comments the various participants made for each question, with the reference number or the participant beside each comment. Each question is written at the top of a section, followed by the specific comments of participants who made comments related to that question.

There were only four participants who made no comments. There were a total of five-hundred eighty-six comments made, and these are all shown in the Comments Table in Appendix D. So on average each participant commented on more than one-third of the questions, which indicates a significant level of cooperation and interest in the interviewing process.

Data from the interviews are also presented on the following pages. The questions were organized around three areas of interest: theological, sociocultural, and ethical (moral).

THEOLOGICAL QUESTIONS

Question T1: Do you believe it is possible to be a good Muslim and also a Christian? Is it possible to be both a Muslim and embrace Christian ideology?

❑ Yes.

❑ No.   Explain.

Responses: All fifty participants checked the answer boxes; eleven checked yes, thirty-nine checked no, and fifteen made comments.

Question T2: What do you think are the major points of disagreement between Islam and Christianity? Check **all** that are points of disagreement:

☐ **A** Belief in Jesus Christ as the Son of God who came to earth from heaven.

☐ **B** Belief in resurrection of Jesus Christ from the dead.

☐ **C** Belief in Bible as Holy Scripture, inspired by God.

☐ **All of the above.** *(Distributed in Tally A + B + C)*
Any comment?

Responses: Forty-nine participants checked the answer boxes; forty-nine checked **A,** forty-nine also checked **B,** thirty-seven checked **C,** (those who checked **All of the above** were added to the count for A, B, and C), and thirteen made comments.

Question T3: Do you think that most doctrinal issues between Christians and Muslims are a result of simple misconceptions of Christianity?

☐ Yes.

☐ No.   Explain.

Responses: All fifty participants checked the answer boxes; fifteen checked yes, thirty-five checked no, and thirty-one made comments.

Question T4: Do you think that Christians and Muslims worship the same God? [Americans call Him God, Muslims call Him Allah, but only the name is different.] Or are there fundamental differences in how God and Allah are perceived. Different God or differently perceived?]

☐ **A** Different God.

☐ **B** Same God but differently perceived.
Explain.

Responses: Forty-nine participants checked the answer boxes; twenty-four checked **A**, twenty-five checked; **B**, and nineteen made comments.

Question T5: Do you think the Christian doctrine of the Trinity is polytheism (belief in multiple gods)? [The Christian doctrine of the Trinity believes that the one God includes God the Father, God the Son (Jesus Christ), and God the Holy Spirit]

- ❐ **A** Trinity doctrine is polytheism.
- ❐ **B** Trinity doctrine is not polytheism.
  Any comment?

Responses: Only twenty-seven participants checked the answer boxes; seventeen checked **A**, ten checked **B**, and thirty-four made comments.

Question T6: Do you believe that Jesus Christ is divine or merely a prophet?

- ❐ **A** Divine (Jesus was God).
- ❐ **B** Had divine power or wisdom.
- ❐ **C** Merely a prophet with no real divine power (godly power).
  Any comment?

Responses: Forty-nine participants checked the answer boxes; only two checked **A**, forty-three checked **B**, four checked **C**, and twenty made comments.

Question T7: Do you believe that Jesus Christ actually died on the cross? Or do you believe he did not actually die, but only swooned (fainted and appeared to be dead)? Or do you believe that it was not actually Christ who was killed on the cross, but some other person who appeared like him (cf. Surah 4:157)? Check **all** boxes you agree with below:

- ❐ **A** Yes, he died on the cross.
- ❐ **B** He did not die, but Allah lifted him up.
- ❐ **C** He only fainted, and appeared dead.
- ❐ **D** Someone else who appeared like him died on the cross.
- ❐ **E** Not sure what I believe about this.
  Any comment?

Responses: All fifty participants checked the answer boxes; no one checked **A**, forty-five checked **B**, only two checked **C**, six checked **D**, no one checked **E**, and eleven made comments. Some of the participants checked more than one box.

Question T8: Do you think that the Christian Bible (the Holy Book) has been corrupted?
- ☐ **A** Corrupted.
- ☐ **B** Not corrupted.   Any comment?

Responses: Forty-two participants checked the answer boxes; six checked **A**, thirty-six checked **B**, and twenty-nine made comments.

Question T9: Do you think that Sufi "veneration of Saints and Shrines and spiritual guides (pirs)" are the influence of Catholicism?
- ☐ Yes, they are the influence of Catholicism.
- ☐ No, they are not the influence of Catholicism.
  Any comment?

Responses: Forty-four participants checked the answer boxes; seventeen checked yes, twenty-seven checked no, and fourteen made comments.

Question T10: What is your opinion about the Sufi belief that humans can have a personal relationship with God?
- ☐ **A** I believe a person can have a personal relationship with God.
- ☐ **B** I do not believe a person can have a personal relationship with God.
  Any comment?

Responses: All fifty participants checked the answer boxes; seventeen checked **A**, thirty-three checked **B**, and fifteen made comments.

Question T11: From the Muslim perspective, is Christianity a religion of infidels?
- ☐ **A** Yes, all Christians are infidels.
- ☐ **B** Most Christians are infidels.
- ☐ **C** Some Christians are infidels.

❑ **D** No, Christianity is not a religion of infidels.
Any comment?

Responses: All fifty participants checked the answer boxes; two checked **A**, no one checked **B**, seventeen checked **C**, thirty-one checked **D**, and twelve made comments.

Question T12: Do you think the practices of Folk Islam are against the teachings of the Qur'an and Hadith?
❑ Yes.
❑ No.　　Please explain:

Responses: Thirty-four participants checked the answer boxes; twenty checked yes, fourteen checked no, and twenty made comments.

Question T13: Do you think Folk Islam is intermingled with Sufism in South Asia and was introduced by Sufi Missionaries?
❑ Yes.
❑ No.　　Any Comment?

Responses: Thirty-four participants checked the answer boxes; twenty-seven checked yes, seven checked no, and nine made comments.

Question T14: Do you think pirs are mediators between God and human beings?
❑ Yes.
❑ No.　　Any Comment?

Responses: Thirty-three participants checked the answer boxes; three checked yes, thirty checked no, and twenty made comments.

Question T15: Do you think South Asian Muslims are more open to Christianity because of the influence of syncretism practiced by Sufis?
❑ Yes.
❑ No.　　Please explain.

Responses: Thirty-four participants checked the answer boxes; thirty-one checked yes, only one checked no, and nine made comments.

Question T16: Do you agree with the view of Deobandi Sunni fundamentalists that Western culture is associated with Christianity?
- ☐ Yes.
- ☐ No.   Any Comment?

Responses: Fort-five participants checked the answer boxes; nineteen checked yes, twenty-six checked no, and fourteen made comments.

SOCIOCULTURAL QUESTIONS

The following questions related to sociocultural issues, were asked in the interviewing process. Participants checked the appropriate responses and proffered any comments they had to make. These questions are designated Question S1, Question S2, etc.

Question S1: Do you believe that American cultural practices are based on Christian values and teaching? (Such as living together outside of marriage, homosexuality, abortion, etc., legal in the United States)
- ☐ Yes.
- ☐ No.   Any comment?

Responses: All fifty participants checked the answer boxes; sixteen checked yes, thirty-four checked no, and nineteen made comments.

Question S2: Do you believe racial discrimination in the United States comes from the influence of Western Christianity (doctrine and teaching)?
- ☐ Yes.
- ☐ No.   Any comment?

Responses: Forty-eight participants checked the answer boxes; twenty-two checked yes, twenty-six checked no, and twenty-three made comments.

Question S3: Are individualistic emphases in American family and society a result of Christian influences?

☐ Yes.

☐ No.   Any comment?

Responses: Forty-nine participants checked the answer boxes; forty-two checked yes, seven checked no, and sixteen made comments.

Question S4: Is the free mixing of men and women, and gender equality in western society a Christian emphasis?

☐ Yes.

☐ No.   Any comment?

Responses: All fifty participants checked the answer boxes; forty-one checked yes, nine checked no, and sixteen made comments.

Question S5: Do you think the prevailing Christian attitude in American society is Anti-Muslim?

☐ Yes.

☐ No.   Any comment?

Responses: Forty-seven participants checked the answer boxes; forty-three checked yes, four checked no, and sixteen made comments.

Question S6: Do you think social integration into mainline American society compromises a Muslim's convictions and makes them appear to embrace Christian ideals?

☐ Yes.

☐ No.   Any comment?

Responses: All fifty participants checked the answer boxes; twenty-one checked yes, twenty-nine checked no, and eighteen made comments.

Question S7: Do you think Christianity believes in women's rights and does that compromise Muslim beliefs? (Women's rights are rights that promote a position of legal and social equality of women with men.)

☐ Yes.

☐ No.   Any comment?

Responses: All fifty participants checked the answer boxes; twenty-four checked yes, twenty-six checked no, and sixteen made comments.

Question S8: Do you believe Christianity supports women wearing dress that is sexually provocative?

☐ A Yes.

☐ B No.

☐ C Not sure.   Any comment?

Responses: All fifty participants checked the answer boxes; six checked A (yes), thirty-seven checked B (no), seven checked C (not sure), and twenty made comments.

Question S9: Do you believe body piercings and tattoos reflect Christian endorsement?

☐ A encourages them.

☐ B discourages them.

☐ C tolerates them.

☐ D I am not sure.   Any comment?

Responses: All fifty participants checked the answer boxes; three checked **A**, three checked **B**, thirty checked **C**, fourteen checked **D** (not sure), and fifteen made comments.

ETHICAL (MORAL) QUESTIONS

Question E1: Do you think the weak voice from some Christian churches in Greater Boston against homosexual practice and same-sex marriage implies silent support and sympathy towards these practices?

❏ Yes.
❏ No.   Explain.

Responses: All fifty participants checked the answer boxes; forty-six checked yes, four checked no, and eighteen made comments.

Question E2: Do you think that Christians teach that living together outside of marriage is OK?
❏ Yes.
❏ No.   Any comment?

Responses: Forty-one participants checked the answer boxes; seven checked yes, thirty-four checked no, and thirty made comments.

Question E3: Do you think that Christians teach that legalized abortion is OK?
❏ Yes.
❏ No.   Any comment?

Responses: Forty-one participants checked the answer boxes; eight checked yes, thirty-three checked no, and twenty-five made comments.

Question E4: Do you believe it is a Christian practice to approve an unmarried couple becoming parents?
❏ Yes.
❏ No.   Any comment?

Responses: Thirty-nine participants checked the answer boxes; three checked yes, thirty-six checked no, and thirty made comments.

Question E5: Do you believe that Christianity approves the common American practice of drinking alcohol and wine at social gatherings?
❏ Yes.
❏ No.   Any comment?

Responses: All fifty participants checked the answer boxes; thirty-two checked yes, eighteen checked no, and twelve made comments.

Question E6: Do you think the recent ruling of the Supreme Court, legalizing homosexual marriage throughout the United States was a result of Christian (Church) influence?

☐ Yes, strongly influenced by Christian church.

☐ No, it is a secular Court.

Any comment?

Responses: Forty-six participants checked the answer boxes; one only checked yes, forty-five checked no, and fourteen made comments.

In conclusion, the participants comprise a representative sample of the larger population of South Asian Muslims in America. The participants responded well and almost all of them commented on the various questions.

The responses were generally as I had expected them to answer, based on many years of interacting with South Asian Muslims in America. However, I was surprised at the number (ninety-three percent) who said the Bible is not corrupted, although seventy-six percent also recognize that "Belief in Bible as Holy Scripture, inspired by God" is a major point of disagreement between Islam and Christianity.

Those participants who were well educated occasionally responded somewhat differently from the other participants. To some extent, because I am recognized by the participants as a Christian practitioner, they may have been inclined to respond less critically of Christianity that they might otherwise have done. Conducting these interviews was a very rewarding experience for me because of the cooperative attitude and interest of the participants.

The data and comments presented in this chapter form the basis for the analysis in the following chapter.

CHAPTER 5

ANALYSIS OF DATA

In this chapter I analyze the data presented in Chapter 4. As I mentioned in Chapter 1, I chose the thematic approach as the methodology employed for data analysis, because these data best lend themselves to being presented around the chosen theme: South Asian Muslims perceptions of Christianity.

Every question is designed to elicit from the participants responses and comments that inform some aspect of the participant's perception of Christianity. I examine every question and the responses as well as the comments of the participants in the light of the fundamental goal of discovering perceptions of Christianity held by the participants.

The reader may refer to the data presentation tables in Appendix C and Appendix D to better understand the analysis of the responses and the comments.

In this chapter, I examine every question and the responses of the participants as shown in the Responses Table in Appendix C and the Comments Table in Appendix D, and analyze these in terms of what this reveals about their perceptions of Christianity.

Beginning with the sociocultural questions (Question S1, Question S2, etc.), and continuing with the ethical and theological questions, I examine each question one-by-one, calculate the percentages of the various responses, analyze the responses and the comments, then discuss the insights these responses reveal about the participants' perceptions of Christianity.

198

THEOLOGICAL QUESTIONS ANALYZED

Question T1: Do you believe it is possible to be a good Muslim and also a Christian? Is it possible to be both a Muslim and embrace Christian ideology?

☐ Yes.

☐ No.   Explain.

Responses: Out of fifty participants who answered this question, twenty-two percent said yes, seventy-eight percent said no, and there were fifteen who made comments.

Analysis of Responses Question T1: The purpose of this question is to investigate whether South Asian Muslims believe they can embrace Christian ideology while remaining a good Muslim. The percentages indicate that a strong majority of the participants believe it is **not** possible to be a good Muslim and also be a Christian or embrace Christian ideology.

Those who answered no, seventy-eight percent, clearly have the perception that Christian ideology is incompatible with Muslim convictions. The other twenty-two percent believe it is somehow possible to remain a good Muslim while being a Christian and embracing Christian ideology.

Analysis of Comments Question T1: It should be noted that of the fifteen who made comments only one had checked yes to the question, and this comment was that some Christian ideologies are similar to Islam. The others explained why it is impossible to be a good Muslim and a Christian or to embrace Christian ideals. These commented that it is not possible or that it will compromise Muslim conviction and beliefs.

Based on these comments, the perception of the majority of South Asian Muslims in America is that Christian religion is so different from Islam that a person cannot be both.

Question T2: What do you think are the major points of disagreement between Islam and Christianity? Check **all** that are points of disagreement:

- ☐ **A** Belief in Jesus Christ as the Son of God who came to earth from heaven.
- ☐ **B** Belief in resurrection of Jesus Christ from the dead.
- ☐ **C** Belief in Bible as Holy Scripture, inspired by God.
- ☐ **All of the above**.
  Any comment?

Note: Here the participants can check multiple boxes indicating **all** points of disagreement between Christians and Muslims. For those who checked "all of the above" this was added to the tally count for **A** and **B** and **C**.

Responses: Out of forty-nine participants who answered this question, one-hundred percent checked **A**, also one-hundred percent checked **B**, and seventy-six percent checked **C**. There were thirteen who made comments.

Analysis of Responses Question T2: This question is intended to discover the major points of disagreement between Islam and Christianity in the minds of the participants. All the participants say: belief in Jesus as the Son of God and belief that Jesus was resurrected, are major disagreements between Christianity and Islam. Seventy-six percent say that belief in the Bible as Holy Scripture inspired by God is a major point of disagreement.

This indicates that certain major Christian doctrines cannot be accepted by a very large percentage of South Asian Muslims, hence the perception of Christianity that it is doctrinally at variance with Islam.

Analysis of Comments Question T2: All who made comments reinforced their rejection of the doctrines of Jesus as Son of God and His resurrection from the dead, and more than thirty-eight percent of the comments referred to belief in the Bible.

This suggests their perception of Christianity is negatively affected by the Christian doctrine of Jesus as the Son of God, and the doctrine of His resurrection from the dead, both of which they all reject.

In contrast, the Christian doctrine of the Bible as Holy Scripture inspired by God is not rejected by all these participants, as only seventy-six percent checked C.

Of those who made comments, eight (sixty-two percent) did **not** check C, indicating they did not think belief in the Bible as Holy Scripture inspired by God, is a major point of disagreement. However of the five who did check C, four wrote qualifying comments which I think were saying:

1. This is a major point of disagreement between Islam and Christianity, but I believe in the Bible as Holy Scripture inspired by Allah, because the Quran affirms the Bible.
2. While this is a major point of disagreement, it is not for me because I accept the Bible.
3. This is a major point of disagreement between Islam and Christianity, but I have high regard for the Bible, it is revelation from God.
4. I believe the Bible is Holy Scripture, but is corrupted by translation. Hebrew and Greek Bible are OK.

What this says about their perception of Christianity is that for the twenty-four percent who did not check C, they can easily accept the Christian Bible as Holy Scripture inspired by God. And for those who did check C, but added qualifying comments, these also tend to affirm the Bible as Holy Scripture. Those who affirm the Bible as Holy Scripture inspired by God indicates that on this point there is a positive perception of Christianity, because this perception implies common ground between Christianity and Islam.

Question T3: Do you think that most doctrinal issues between Christians and Muslims are a result of simple misconceptions of Christianity?

◻ Yes.

◻ No.   Explain.

Responses: Out of fifty participants who answered this question, thirty percent said yes, seventy percent said no, and there were thirty-one who made comments.

Analysis of Responses Question T3: The purpose of this question is to determine whether the participants think doctrinal differences between Christian and Muslim are because of misconceptions of Christianity. These percentages indicate that a large majority of the participants said that doctrinal differences are not because of misconceptions of Christianity. However, it is significant that thirty percent admitted that many doctrinal differences are because they do not fully understand Christian teaching.

This indicates a perception of Christianity among these South Asian Muslims that serious doctrinal differences do exist between Christianity and Islam. However, thirty percent of the participants seemed unsure whether these differences are inherent or because of misconceptions of Christianity.

Analysis of Comments Question T3: To summarize these comments, almost all are saying there are real doctrinal differences, not just misconceptions. About eighty-four percent of the comments state this.

These comments indicate there are real, serious doctrinal differences, which clearly reveal a perception of incompatibility between Christianity and Islam.

Question T4: Do you think that Christians and Muslims worship the same God? [Americans call Him God, Muslims call Him Allah, but only the name is different. Or are there fundamental differences in how God and Allah are perceived. Different God or differently perceived?]

- ☐ A Different God.
- ☐ B Same God but differently perceived.   Explain.

Responses: Out of forty-nine participants who answered this question, forty-nine percent said yes, fifty-one percent said no, and there were thirteen who made comments.

Analysis of Responses Question T4: The purpose of this question is to investigate whether these participants believe Allah and God are the same. About half said yes and half said no, indicating that generally South Asian Muslims are equally divided on this question.

The perception of Christianity implied by this is inconclusive, because the concept held by South Asian Muslims of whether the Christian God is the same as the Muslim Allah is evenly divided. It is possible to conclude that about half of South Asian Muslims believe that Allah and God are the same.

Analysis of Comments Question T4: A strong majority of the comments emphasized the difference between Allah and God.

While the responses indicated a fifty-fifty split in the opinion of the participants, the comments strongly emphasized the differences in opinion. Because of the divergence of opinions, with the responses indicating one thing and the comments indicating another, we can only note an inconsistency in the Muslim perception on this issue.

Question T5: Do you think the Christian doctrine of the Trinity is polytheism (belief in multiple gods)? [The Christian doctrine of the Trinity believes that the one God includes God the Father, God the Son (Jesus Christ), and God the Holy Spirit]

- ☐ **A** Trinity doctrine is polytheism.
- ☐ **B** Trinity doctrine is not polytheism.
  Any comment?

Responses: Out of only twenty-seven participants who answered this question, seventy-four percent say the Trinity is polytheism, twenty-six percent say it is not, and there were thirty-four who made comments.

Analysis of Responses Question T5: The purpose of this question is to find out whether South Asian Muslims believe the Christian doctrine of the Trinity is polytheism or not. All fifty participants responded, but twenty-three did not check an answer box, yet commented on the question. Of those who did check an answer box, about three-fourths believe this doctrine is polytheism, which they strongly reject as sinful.

This reveals that a strong majority of the participants believe this doctrine is polytheism, which indicates a negative perception of Christianity on this point.

Analysis of Comments Question T5: Of those who made comments, twenty-three (sixty-eight percent) did not check an answer box. Twenty-two of the thirty-four who made comments said they were unsure or confused about this doctrine. This suggests there is quite a bit of confusion and uncertainty about this particular Christian doctrine. The other comments were supporting the belief that this doctrine is polytheism.

The perception of Christianity held by the participants is divided on this issue; however, it can be said that a strong majority of these Muslims say this is polytheism, which is an unpardonable sin.

Question T6: Do you believe that Jesus Christ is divine or merely a prophet?
- ☐ **A** Divine (Jesus was God).
- ☐ **B** Had divine power or wisdom.
- ☐ **C** Merely a prophet with no real divine power (godly power).
  Any comment?

Responses: Out of forty-nine participants who answered this question, only four percent said **A**, eighty-eight percent said **B**, eight percent said **C**, and there were twenty who made comments.

Analysis of Responses Question T6: This question is intended to reveal what South Asian Muslims believe about Jesus Christ, especially about His divinity. A very high percentage believes Jesus Christ had divine power or wisdom, but was not himself divine.

This suggests that most of these participants have a negative perception about the divinity of Jesus Christ (a major Christian doctrine), although they agree He did have divine power or wisdom.

Analysis of Comments Question T6: Most comments suggest a belief in Jesus Christ as only a prophet, but like other prophets He was given power from God. To most who made comments Jesus Christ was not divine.

Although fewer than half of the participants made comments, for those who did comment, their perception of Christianity is that Jesus Christ was only a prophet and not divine.

Question T7: Do you believe that Jesus Christ actually died on the cross? Or do you believe he did not actually die, but only swooned (fainted and appeared to be dead)? Or do you believe that it was not actually Christ who was killed on the cross, but some other person who appeared like him (cf. Surah 4:157)? Check **all** boxes you agree with below:

- ❏ **A** Yes, he died on the cross.
- ❏ **B** He did not die, but Allah lifted him up.
- ❏ **C** He only fainted, and appeared dead.
- ❏ **D** Someone else who appeared like him died on the cross.
- ❏ **E** Not sure what I believe about this.
  Any comment?

Responses: For this question the participants could check **all boxes** that they agreed with. Out of fifty participants who answered this question, no one checked **A**, ninety percent checked **B**, four percent checked **C**, and twelve percent checked **D**. No one checked **E**. There were eleven who made comments.

Analysis of Responses Question T7: This question is intended to uncover what the participants believe about the crucifixion of Jesus Christ. The vast majority of the participants believe that Allah lifted Jesus up so He would not die on the cross. Some believe that someone took his place on the cross; who appeared to the crowd to be like Jesus. Three checked both **B** and **D**. Only two of the participants checked **C**, that Jesus fainted and appeared dead.

In reference to the Christian doctrine of Crucifixion, the vast majority hold the perception that Jesus was not crucified but rather was lifted up into heaven by God.

Analysis of Comments Question T7: Because the dominant belief (**B** box) is that Allah lifted Jesus up so he would not die on the cross, only four of those who checked the **B** box commented in support of this conviction. Five of the six who checked the **D** box (belief that someone else was crucified in place of Jesus) also commented in support of their conviction. The two who checked the **C** box, also commented in support of their belief that Jesus did not die but only fainted.

This reveals that the vast majority of the participants hold the strong perception that Jesus did not die on the cross. This includes all three groups: those who believe Allah lifted Him up, those who believe he fainted, and those who believe someone else died in place of Jesus. Hence there is the consistent perception that the Christian doctrine of the Crucifixion of Jesus is a false doctrine.

Question T8: Do you think that the Christian Bible (the Holy Book) has been corrupted?

☐ A Corrupted.

☐ B Not corrupted.   Any comment?

Responses: Out of forty-two participants who answered this question fourteen percent said the Bible has been corrupted; eighty-six percent said it has not been corrupted, and there were twenty-nine who made comments.

Analysis of Responses Question T8: The purpose of this question is to discover whether or not the participants believe the Bible is corrupted. The very strong majority of the participants believe the Bible has not been corrupted.

The perception of Christianity this reveals is that most participants accept the authenticity of the Bible as the holy book of Christians. The perception held by the minority of participants is that the Bible has been corrupted.

Analysis of Comments Question T8: A very strong majority of those who made comments think that the translation of the Bible corrupts or distorts the meaning of the original text, and yet most of these believe the original text is correct.

This suggests that the perception of Christianity as related to the authenticity of the Bible is that the original text is reliable, but many think the translations are corrupted.

Question T9: Do you think that Sufi "veneration of saints and shrines and spiritual guides (pirs)" are the influence of Catholicism?

☐ Yes, they are the influence of Catholicism.

☐ No, they are not the influence of Catholicism.

Any comment?

Responses: Out of forty-four participants who answered this question, thirty-nine percent said yes, sixty-one percent said no, and there were fourteen who made comments.

Analysis of Responses Question T9: This question is intended to discern whether Catholicism influenced certain practices and emphases of Sufis, such as veneration of saints and shrines, and pirs (spiritual guides and intermediaries). About two out of every three who commented, believe these practices and emphases were not influenced by Catholicism. One-third do believe there is Catholic influence.

This indicates a perception among one-third of the participants that there is a Christian influence of Catholicism on some of the practices of the Sufis. The other two-thirds of the participants say there is no Catholic influence on these practices and emphases.

Analysis of Comments Question T9: All who answered yes (five comments) and made comments said there are similarities between Sufi and Catholic practice and emphasis. The others were not sure (five comments) or thought there was some other influence such as paganism or animism.

The perception of Christianity is only as relates to Catholic influence, and the strong majority of participants hold the perception that there is no Catholic influence at least as relates to Sufism.

Question T10: What is your opinion about the Sufi belief that humans can have a personal relationship with God?

☐ A I believe a person can have a personal relationship with God.

❒ **B** I do not believe a person can have a personal relationship with God.   Any comment?

Responses: Out of fifty participants who answered this question, thirty-four percent said yes, sixty-six percent said no, and there were fifteen who made comments.

Analysis of Responses Question T10: The purpose of this question is to discover whether the participants agree with the Sufi belief that humans can have a personal relationship with God. A strong majority of the participants (two-thirds) believe it is not possible for a human to have a personal relationship with God. If the participants are a true representative sample of the South Asian Muslim population, this means that two out of every three of these immigrants reject the possibility of a personal relationship with God, and thus remove themselves from the consideration of entering into such a relationship.

This is at the very heart and core of the Christian concept of a loving, personal, God, and only highlights the radical difference in how God is described by the Christian and Allah is described by the Muslim. Allah becomes a remote, aloof, divine judge, so very different from a "Father God" as emphasized in the teaching of Jesus, a heavenly Father with whom we walk in life.

Analysis of Comments Question T10: Out of the nine who checked the No box and made comments, they explained why they believe it is not possible to have a personal relationship with Allah, emphasizing that he is not human. Of the six who checked the Yes box and made comments, they explained why they believe this is possible emphasizing that it is only a spiritual relationship.

The dominant perception (sixty-six percent) among these participants is that the concept of a personal relationship with God is a Christian emphasis, not Muslim; however, it is significant that thirty-four percent of the participants believe a personal spiritual relationship with God is possible.

Question T11: From the Muslim perspective, is Christianity a religion of infidels?

☐ **A** Yes, all Christians are infidels.
☐ **B** Most Christians are infidels.
☐ **C** Some Christians are infidels.
☐ **D** No, Christianity is not a religion of infidels.
  Any comment?

Responses: Out of fifty participants who answered this question, four percent said **A**, no one checked **B**, thirty-four percent said **C**, sixty-two percent said **D**, and there were twelve who made comments.

Analysis of Responses Question T11: This question intended to investigate whether South Asian Muslims perceive Christianity as a religion of infidels. The majority of the participants said Christianity is **not** a religion of infidels. However, about one-third of the participants believe some Christians are infidels.

This indicates the perception of the majority of the participants that Christianity is not a religion of infidels who hold false doctrinal beliefs. The perception of a significant minority of participants is that **some** Christians are infidels.

Analysis of Comments Question T11: There are two themes in the comments, one that false belief makes a person an infidel; the other is that immoral behavior makes a person an infidel. The implied definition of infidel varies from participant to participant. The majority of the participants say that not all Christians are infidels, although some **believe** like infidels and some **act** like infidels.

Half of the comments say some Christians are infidels based on what they believe or how they act. Two of the twelve comments said all Christians are infidels because they believe that Jesus Christ is God or the Son of God. One-third of the comments say Christianity is not a religion of infidels. Their perception of Christianity follows their comments.

Question T12: Do you think the practices of Folk Islam are against the teachings of the Qur'an and Hadith?
☐ Yes.
☐ No.   Please explain.

Responses: Out of thirty-four participants who answered this question, fifty-nine percent said yes, forty-one percent said no, and there were twenty who made comments.

Analysis of Responses Question T12: The purpose of this question is to examine what the participants believe about folk Islamic beliefs and practices. The reason for this examination is based on the fact that folk Islam has some beliefs and practices that are similar to those in traditional Christianity, which may incline some to more openness to Christianity. If the typical Muslim believes the practices of folk Islam are against the Qur'an and Hadith, then this individual will tend to reject folk Islam and move farther away from those practices that are similar to those found in Christianity. The percentages indicate that the majority of the participants believe the practices of folk Islam are not supported by the Qur'an and Hadith. The forty-one percent who believe folk Islam is supported by the Qur'an and Hadith would look more favorably on these practices.

For those who believe folk Islam is supported by the Qur'an and Hadith, they would be more accepting of those practices in Christianity that are similar to those in folk Islam, and this would likely be reflected in a more positive perception of Christianity.

Analysis of Comments Question T12: The participants who made comments reflect a division that follows their responses to the questions above. Of those who made comments sixty-two percent made negative comments about folk Islam, which corresponds to the answers given above. On the other hand, thirty-eight percent of the comments were favorable to folk Islamic practices. This indicates a significant number of the participants look with favor on some of these practices which may make them more open to Christianity.

It is reasonable to assume that those who favor folk Islamic practices are more likely to have a more positive perception of Christianity.

Question T13: Do you think Folk Islam is intermingled with Sufism in South Asia and was introduced by Sufi Missionaries?

□ Yes.

□ No.   Any comment?

Responses: Out of thirty-four participants who answered this question, seventy-nine percent said yes, twenty-one percent said no, and there were nine who made comments.

Analysis of Responses Question T13: This question has the objective to reveal the extent of the awareness of the connectivity between Sufism and folk Islam in the minds of the South Asian Muslims. The rationale behind this question relates to the fact that there are similarities between some of the practices of Sufism and those of Christianity, which cause Sufis to be more open and responsive to Christianity. If South Asian Muslims look with favor on Sufism, which is quite popular in South Asia, they may have a more favorable perception of Christianity. A strong majority of the participants said there is a close relationship between folk Islam and Sufism. Those who disagree were a small minority.

This would indicate that the majority of the participants might have a more positive perception of and openness to Christianity which is true of Sufi Muslims.

Analysis of Comments Question T13: The very small number of comments and the small majority who commented positively about the connection of folk Islam and Sufism, the result of this investigation is inconclusive.

Even though the comments were inconclusive about a more positive perception of Christianity, the analysis of the responses might suggest a more positive perception of Christianity among the seventy-nine percent who checked yes.

Question T14: Do you think pirs are mediators between God and human beings?
- ☐ Yes.
- ☐ No.   Any Comment?

Responses: Out of thirty-three participants who answered this question, nine percent said yes, ninety-one percent said no, and there were twenty who made comments.

Analysis of Responses Question T14: The purpose of this question is to determine if the participants believe in the concept of a mediator between God and humans. A very strong majority (ninety-one percent) reject the idea of mediators between humans and God.

The question was formulated to see if South Asian Muslims accept the Muslim concept of *pirs* (mediators between humans and God), which is a parallel to the Catholic priests in Christianity.

Because there is a strong rejection of the concept of *pirs* this would suggest these Muslims do not like the Catholic concept of priests who mediate between God and humans.

Analysis of Comments Question T14: About ninety percent of the comments were negative, which correlates with the answers checked, and reject the idea of mediators between humans and God.

The strong negative comments indicate that a very strong majority of the participants do not accept the idea of mediators. This would indicate that the majority of South Asian Muslims in America hold the perception that Christianity as practiced by Catholicism is negative and is therefore not likely to appeal to them.

Question T15: Do you think South Asian Muslims are more open to Christianity because of the influence of syncretism practiced by Sufis?

☐　Yes.

☐　No.　　　Please explain.

Responses: Out of thirty-four participants who answered this question, ninety-seven percent said yes, only three percent said no, and there were nine who made comments.

Analysis of Responses Question T15: The purpose of this question is to investigate whether the participants believe the influence of syncretism as practiced by Sufis causes South Asian Muslims to be more open to Christianity. Only one participant checked no to the question, so a very strong majority of the participants think this influence does create more openness to Christianity.

The idea of syncretism suggests that the two religions under discussion, Islam and Christianity, could both be put together into the life of an adherent. Typically syncretism implies compromise on the part of the two religions, so at least some of the beliefs and practices of both can be embraced simultaneously. Applying this idea to Muslims and Christians in America would mean that at least some Christian ideology could be embraced by these immigrants, and they would have a more positive perception of Christianity.

Analysis of Comments Question T15: These comments support the concept of more openness or tolerance toward other religions. The impression given by these comments is generally positive.

The implication of this response regarding the perception of Christianity is that those who responded to this question are willing to see Christianity in a positive light.

Question T16: Do you agree with the view of Deobandi Sunni fundamentalists that Western culture is associated with Christianity?

❑ Yes.

❑ No.   Any Comment?

Responses: Out of forty-five participants who answered this question, forty-two percent said yes, fifty-eight percent said no, and there were fourteen who made comments.

Analysis of Responses Question T16: This question intends to discover whether the participants agree with the perception that Christianity is associated with Western culture. The percentages indicate that the majority of the responses do not see an association of Western culture with Christianity. A significant minority believe there is an association between Western culture and Christianity.

There is a divided view about whether or not an association exists between Western culture and Christianity, which reveals differences in the participants' perception of Christianity. To the minority of participants this reflects a more negative perception of Christianity; whereas to the majority of participants this reflects a more positive perception.

Analysis of Comments Question T16: Generally when these participants associate Christianity and Western culture, this is not a positive perception. The comments are about evenly divided between those who associate Western culture and Christianity and those who do not.

Among the participants a small majority said Christianity is not associated with Western culture and this suggests these participants have a more positive and favorable perception of Christianity.

SOCIOCULTURAL QUESTIONS ANALYZED

Question S1: Do you believe that American cultural practices are based on Christian values and teaching? (Such as living together outside of marriage, homosexuality, abortion, etc., legal in the United States)

☐ Yes.

☐ No.

Any comment?

Responses: Out of fifty participants who answered this question, thirty-two percent said yes, sixty-eight percent said no, and there were nineteen who made comments.

Analysis of Responses Question S1: This question specifically mentions unmarrieds living together, homosexuality, and abortion, three practices considered immoral by South Asian Muslims. The question seeks to discover how closely the participants associate practices like these in the American sociocultural milieu with the influence of Christianity. The percentages indicate that most participants think these practices **are not** based on Christian values and teaching.

This means that almost two out of every three of the participants **do not** associate these practices observed in American culture as related to Christian values and teaching. This does not imply a close association of these practices with Christian values and teaching, which naturally influences their perception of Christianity in a positive way.

A further detailed study of the individual responses on the

questionnaire form showed that thirty-six of the participants were first generation immigrants, ten were second generation, and four were third generation. Below is a chart showing how they responded to question S1:

Participants	Total	Said yes	Said No
First Generation	36	14	22
Second Generation	10	1	9
Third Generation	4	1	3
Totals	50	16	34

This clearly shows that the second and third generation participants did not mentally connect Christian values and teaching with these practices in American society, while about thirty-nine percent of the first generation said yes, a much higher percentage than the second and third generation.

In this book I have repeatedly shown how the vast majority of Muslim immigrants from South Asia come with the predetermined idea that American society reflects Christian endorsement. So when they first arrive in America, they tend to believe the social practices of unmarried couples living together, homosexuality, and abortion reflect Christian values and teaching.

These data indicate that over time, as Muslim immigrants become better informed about Christianity, there is a shift away from thinking that **all** practices in American society reflect Christian values.

Also, the fact that only two of the second and third generation said these practices were based on Christian values and teaching clearly shows that subsequent generations have a much more positive perception of Christianity as regards these practices in American society.

Analysis of Comments Question S1: See Appendix D for the actual verbatim comments made by the participants.

The participants' comments consistently include three criticisms. One is that Christian churches in the America area tolerate these practices. Another is that they have a weak voice in society (do not publicly speak out) against these practices. And a third is that many Christians have been seen practicing these behaviors.

This reflects a perception of Christianity held by South Asian Muslims that views the Christian church as tolerating and even practicing behaviors Muslims consider sinful.

Question S2: Do you believe racial discrimination in the United States comes from the influence of Western Christianity (doctrine and teaching)?

❏ Yes.

❏ No.   Any comment?

Responses: Out of forty-eight participants who answered this question, forty-six percent said yes, fifty-four percent said no, and there were twenty-three who made comments.

Analysis of Responses Question S2: This question seeks to discover the responses about connection between Christian teaching and racial discrimination in American society. Only slightly less than half and those saying no and only slightly more than half agree. This is not a definitive difference, so all that can be concluded is that the South Asian Muslim population is about evenly divided on this issue.

Of the total who said yes, seventy percent were first generation immigrants. About half of the second and third generation also said yes. A yes answer suggests a negative perception of Christianity because of the negative connotation of racial discrimination among Muslims. The total responses suggest the Muslim population is divided on the question of racial discrimination being the influence of Christianity.

Analysis of Comments Question S2: The comments of the participants indicate they do not generally think this is a Christian teaching; however many of them said it is practiced by Christians and by the churches. Some say this practice has been among Christians historically.

Question S3: Are individualistic emphases in American family and society a result of Christian influences?

❏ Yes.

❏ No.   Any comment?

Responses: Out of forty-nine participants who answered this question, eighty-six percent said yes, fourteen percent said no, and there were thirteen who made comments.

Analysis of Responses Question S3: This question seeks to determine the percentage of South Asian Muslims who believe that individualism in American society is a result of Christian influence.

This suggests that a very large part of the larger population of South Asian Muslims in America have the perception that Christianity has caused this emphasis on individualism in American society.

Analysis of Comments Question S3: Many of the participants commented that American Christians put too much emphasis on privacy. This suggests that they associate privacy with individualistic emphases. Their comments indicate that a significant number of them hold the perception that Christianity emphasizes individualism.

Question S4: Is the free mixing of men and women, and gender equality in western society a Christian emphasis?
- ☐ Yes.
- ☐ No.   Any comment?

Responses: Out of forty-eight participants who answered this question, eighty-two percent said yes, eighteen percent said no, and there were sixteen who made comments.

Analysis of Responses Question S4: This question undertakes to discover if South Asian Muslims believe Christianity emphasizes the free mixing of men and women, and gender equality. Eighty-two percent is a large percentage of the participants who hold this belief.

This indicates that a prevalent perception of Christianity among South Asian Muslims is that this is a Christian emphasis.

Analysis of Comments Question S4: The majority of the comments focused on Christians practicing the free mixing of men and women. Some mentioned that Christian churches tolerate this practice. This indicates the perception that Christianity allows this free gender mixing.

Question S5: Do you think the prevailing Christian attitude in American society is Anti-Muslim?

☐ Yes.

☐ No.   Any comment?

Responses: Out of forty-seven participants who answered this question, ninety-one percent said yes, nine percent said no, and there were sixteen who made comments.

Analysis of Responses Question S5: This question attempts to discover if there is a perception that Christians in America have an anti-Muslim bias. Ninety-one percent is a very large percentage of the participants who hold this view.

This gives a very strong indication that South Asian Muslims in America hold the perception that Christians in American are anti-Muslim.

Analysis of Comments Question S5: Almost all who made comments had said that the prevailing Christian attitude in America is anti-Muslim. The comments of the participants indicate that they think most Americans are Christians, so when many of the participants commented that most Americans are prejudiced against Muslims, this indicates that they also believe most Christians are anti-Muslim. There were a number of comments that terrorist activity has increased the anti-Muslim sentiment.

The comments reflect a perception that Christianity in America has an anti-Muslim attitude.

Question S6: Do you think social integration into mainline American society compromises a Muslim's convictions and makes them appear to embrace Christian ideals?

☐ Yes.

☐ No.   Any comment?

Responses: Out of fifty participants who answered this question, forty-four percent said yes, fifty-six percent said no, and there were eighteen who made comments.

Analysis of Responses Question S6: This question seeks to discern if immigrants think their Muslim convictions are compromised if they integrate into American society. The data indicate that slightly less than half think integration into American society would compromise their religious beliefs, while about the same percentage believe it is possible to integrate without compromising their convictions. So the data are not determinative, since about the same percentage are on both sides of this issue.

We can conclude, South Asian Muslims are about evenly divided on the question of integrating into American society. If Muslim convictions are not compromised by integration into American society, then these Muslims who say it is possible, are saying integration can be done without embracing Christian ideology. If they were to embrace Christianity, that would mean compromising their convictions.

Analysis of Comments Question S6: In their comments, about half of the participants explained why they believe integration into American society would compromise their Muslim faith. The other half explained why they believe integration is important, while finding ways not to compromise their faith.

This indicates that about half of the participants have the perception that Christian influence in American society is so pervasive that to integrate would mean compromising their Muslim convictions. The other half evidently hold the perception that the influence of Christianity is not so dominant in American society as to prevent Muslims integrating without compromising their convictions.

Question S7: Do you think Christianity believes in women's rights and does that compromise Muslim beliefs? (Women's rights are rights that promote a position of legal and social equality of women with men.)

☐ Yes.

☐ No.   Any comment?

Responses: Out of fifty participants who answered this question, forty-eight percent said yes, forty-two percent said no, and there were sixteen who made comments.

Analysis of Responses Question S7: If we focus on the primary question here, it undertakes to determine if the participants believe Christianity supports women's rights. About half of the participants believe that Christianity does support women's rights; however about half also disagree. Because the percentages are very close we can only conclude that the South Asian Muslim population is about evenly divided on this question.

This indicates that there is no clear leaning one way or the other; however the fact that about half of the participants do believe that Christianity supports women's rights would suggest that this proportion of Muslims hold the perception that Christians believe that women should definitely have equal rights with men in the society.

Analysis of Comments Question S7: Of the participants who made comments, about half insist that Islam also grants rights to women. A few more than half say that in America it goes too far, allowing women to dominate.

Because of the preset idea that Christianity is closely associated with American society, this suggests that the general perception is that Christianity supports women's rights in America, while many of the participants believe it goes too far.

Question S8: Do you believe Christianity supports women wearing dress that is sexually provocative?
- ❏ A Yes.
- ❏ B No.
- ❏ C Not sure.　　Any comment?

Responses: Out of fifty participants who answered this question, seven said they were not sure, so these will be discounted. Of the remaining forty-three participants, fourteen percent said yes, eighty-six percent said no, and there were twenty who made comments.

Analysis of Responses Question S8: This question attempts to find if the participants believe that Christianity approves of women wearing sexually provocative attire. This question included a response: "not sure" and six individuals said they were not sure, so in the calculation they were discounted. The percentages suggest that if you asked this question to five random South Asian Muslims in America, more than four of them would say no.

So we could conclude that while most South Asian Muslims do not approve of sexually provocative dress, they nevertheless do not blame Christianity as supporting this practice. This would indicate that their perception of Christianity is that most Christians would agree with them in disapproving this practice.

Analysis of Comments Question S8: Fourteen out of twenty (seventy percent) of the comments mentioned either that Christianity tolerates sexually provocative dress or Christian women practice it or the Church allows it.

This indicates a perception that Christianity tolerates sexually provocative dress for women.

Question S9: Do you believe body piercings and tattoos reflect Christian endorsement?

- ☐ A encourages them.
- ☐ B discourages them.
- ☐ C tolerates them.
- ☐ D I am not sure.   Any comment?

Responses: Out of fifty participants who answered this question, fourteen said they were not sure, and so will be discounted. Of the remaining thirty-six, eight percent said "encourages them," another eight percent said, "discourages them," and eighty three percent said "tolerates them." There were fifteen who made comments.

Analysis of Responses Question S9: This question is designed to reveal what these Muslims believe about Christian endorsement of body piercings and tattoos, a practice that is particularly repugnant to most Muslims in America. Only eight percent of those who answered the question believe that Christians encourage these practices. Another eight percent believe Christians disapprove or discourage them. Yet, about eighty-three percent believe Christianity tolerates these practices.

So their perception is that a strong majority of Christians tolerate these practices, whereas most Muslims would strongly disapprove.

Analysis of Comments Question S9: Examining these comments, it is observed that the words pagan, animistic, and evil are associated with these practices. It is also observed that six of the fifteen comments state that it is tolerated and/or practiced by Christians.

It can be concluded from these responses that most of these participants have the perception that Christianity either tolerates or allows these practices.

ETHICAL (MORAL) QUESTIONS ANALYZED

Question E1: Do you think the weak voice from some Christian churches in America against homosexual practice and same-sex marriage implies silent support and sympathy towards these practices?

❐ Yes.

❐ No.   Explain.

Responses: Out of fifty participants who answered this question, ninety-two percent said yes, eight percent said no, and there were eighteen who made comments.

Analysis of Responses Question E1: The purpose of this question is to find if these participants think that Christian churches, by not speaking out publicly against homosexuality and gay marriage, are giving silent support for and sympathizing with these practices. The fact that ninety-two percent say yes, indicates a very strong opinion that they believe Christian churches are supporting and sympathizing with these practices.

This clearly reveals that nine out of ten of these participants have the perception that Christianity is in favor of homosexual practice and gay marriage.

Analysis of Comments Question E1: Out of eighteen comments, sixteen included a complaint that churches should publicly protest against these practices, but do not do so.

This implies a perception that within Christianity there is no united Christian voice speaking out against these practices.

Question E2: Do you think that Christians teach that living together outside of marriage is OK?

- ☐ Yes.
- ☐ No.   Any comment?

Responses: Out of forty-one participants who answered this question, seventeen percent said yes, eighty-three percent said no, and there were thirty who made comments.

Analysis of Responses Question E2: This question seeks to discern if South Asian Muslims in America believe Christians approve unmarried couples living together. The percentages suggest that four out of every five do not blame Christianity for the prevalence of this practice today in America.

This suggests that on this topic, there is a strong positive perception of Christianity, since they believe Christians agree with the Muslim position regarding this practice.

Analysis of Comments Question E2: There were thirty comments, which is significant out of fifty participants. Eighty-three percent of the comments indicate an awareness that some Christians are living together outside marriage. Twenty-three percent of the comments said that churches or Christians tolerate this practice.

This implies a perception that Christianity allows the practice of living together outside marriage.

Question E3: Do you think that Christians teach that legalized abortion is OK?

- ☐ Yes.
- ☐ No.   Any comment?

Responses: Out of forty-one participants who answered this question, twenty percent said yes, eighty percent said no, and there were twenty-five who made comments.

Analysis of Responses Question E3: This question is meant to discover if South Asian Muslims believe that Christians approve of legalized abortion. The percentages indicate that four out of every five South Asian Muslims in America do not have the perception that Christianity condones legalized abortion.

Analysis of Comments Question E3: Twenty-five of the fifty participants made comments about this issue. About half of the comments said that it is tolerated by Christians and churches. Some said that Christians practice abortion. About half also accuse the Christians of not speaking out publicly against this practice, and some say Christians are hypocritical and compromise the Christian faith.

This suggests a generally negative perception of Christianity.

Question E4: Do you believe it is a Christian practice to approve an unmarried couple becoming parents?

❒ Yes.
❒ No.   Any comment?

Responses: Out of thirty-nine participants who answered this question, eight percent said yes, ninety-two percent said no, and there were thirty who made comments.

Analysis of Responses Question E4: The purpose of this question is to discover whether the participants think Christians approve of unmarrieds becoming parents. The percentages indicate a strong interest in this topic and a strong perception that Christianity does not approve this practice.

Analysis of Comments Question E4: Twenty-three (seventy-seven percent) of the comments said that Christians practice having children outside marriage. A few accused the church of tolerating this practice.

This high percentage of participants (ninety-two percent) indicate that their perception is that it is a not a Christian practice to approve unmarrieds becoming parents; however the comments strongly indicate the perception that many Christians are practicing this behavior. Although the church does not openly approve unmarrieds having children out of wedlock, the fact that it is commonly tolerated, creates a negative perception of Christianity among the South Asian Muslims in America.

Question E5: Do you believe that Christianity approves the common American practice of drinking alcohol and wine at social gatherings?

☐ Yes.

☐ No.   Any comment?

Responses: Out of fifty participants who answered this question, sixty-four percent said yes, thirty-six percent said no, and there were twelve who made comments.

Analysis of Responses Question E5: This question is intended to discover if the participants believe Christians approve of drinking alcohol in social gatherings. The percentages tell us that the majority participants think that Christianity approves the practice of drinking alcohol in social settings.

The perception of South Asian Muslims is that Christianity approves the drinking of alcohol in social gatherings, which is a correct perception because the Bible allows drinking of alcohol, but condemns drunkenness. (Ephesians 5:18)

Analysis of Comments Question E5: Examining the comments reveals that about seventy-five percent said that this is a common practice in America, even in churches and among Christians. This indicates that a large percentage of South Asian Muslims have this impression.

For Muslims this creates a negative perception of Christianity.

Question E6: Do you think the recent ruling of the Supreme Court, legalizing homosexual marriage throughout the United States was a result of Christian (Church) influence?

- ❏ Yes, strongly influenced by Christian church.
- ❏ No, it is a secular court.
  Any comment?

Responses: Out of forty-six participants who answered this question, only two percent said yes, ninety-eight percent said no, and there were fourteen who made comments.

Analysis of Responses Question E6: This question is meant to discover whether the Supreme Court action legalizing gay marriage resulted from Christian influence. This huge percentage said this action of the Supreme Court is not caused by Christian influence.

This indicates that South Asian Muslims have the positive perception that Christianity is not responsible for this Supreme Court ruling.

Analysis of Comments Question E6: Twelve out of fourteen of the participants who made comments said that Christians or churches should publicly protest this ruling. This is a very strong opinion that criticizes the church and Christians for not speaking out against this Supreme Court ruling.

This implied criticism against Christian churches reflects the perception of Christianity among South Asian Muslims.

In conclusion, In this chapter I presented an analysis of responses and comments of participants about some of the major sociocultural and ethical emphases and practices in American society such as homosexuality, same sex marriage, living together outside of marriage, abortion, prejudices against Muslims, gender equality, liberal feminism, and immodest dress of women. The analysis of the data and comments indicate that many of the South Asian Muslims in America have strong feelings about these practices, some of which they consider to be immoral.

Most participants do not blame Christianity or Christian teaching for these practices in America society, yet they have a negative perception of Christians and Christian churches because they tolerate these practices and, from the Muslim perspective, fail to speak out strongly in protest and exert influence in society against them.

Similarly, I analyzed the responses and comments of participants about theological questions. Many of these questions are related to doctrinal issues such as the Trinity, Jesus as the Son of God, the death and Resurrection of Jesus, and the authenticity of the Bible. I observed that generally South Asian Muslims strongly oppose these Christian doctrines, with the exception of the authenticity of the Bible, which most accept, but not the translations. This was further corroborated by the comments of the participants.

There were some significant insights gained from a careful study of the responses and analysis of the data as presented below:

➤ During the interviewing process, I observed that first generation immigrants tended to hold onto perceptions of Christianity that were established before they left their South Asian homelands.

➤ I noticed perceptions of Christianity are often very different when comparing the responses of first generation Muslim immigrants to the responses of second and third generation participants.

➤ A careful analysis of the responses confirms the conviction that many of the perceptions of Christianity generally held by Muslims everywhere are also applicable to South Asian Muslims in America. This is especially true about Christological issues. On the other hand, there are some uniquenesses among South Asian Muslims, for example the popularity of folk Islam and Sufism are much more prevalent among South Asian Muslims.

➤ A very strong majority of the responses indicated the predominant perception that American Christians have a strong anti-Muslim bias and hold prejudices against Islam and Muslims.

➤ The majority believe it is possible to integrate into mainline American society without compromising one's Muslim convictions, which was an unexpected response.

➤ Generalization from the data analysis would indicate that about half of South Asian Muslims in America believe that the issue of women's rights is overemphasized in American society.

➤ One significant observation is that Sufism has considerable popularity among South Asian Muslims and the influence of

Sufism, especially the Sufi emphasis on the belief that a personal relationship with God is possible. This emphasis fits with the major Christian emphasis on the attribute of God as a loving, caring, intimate, personal God who is known in relationship, and is distinct from the usual Muslim teaching that rejects the idea of humans having any personal relationship with Allah. This Sufi influence may cause South Asian Muslims to be more open to Christianity, when compared to Muslims in general. As a result they would more likely have a more positive perception of Christianity due to this similarity of emphasis.

➤ I gained a new insight related to the perception of the Christian Bible held by South Asian Muslims. The majority of participants, both intellectuals and non-intellectuals, hold the positive view that the original text of the Bible is not corrupted. This was different from the Muslim perception in general that the Bible is corrupted. However, a strong perception remains that translations of the Bible corrupt its true meaning.

CONCLUSION

The research for this book was undertaken focusing on a specific group—the South Asian Muslims. The interviews were conducted in Greater Boston; however, the responses of the participants are typical of South Asian Muslims throughout America. These interviews focused on perceptions of Christianity held by this group from three distinct perspectives: theological, sociocultural, and ethical (moral).

Throughout this book, I mentioned the predetermined ideas related to perceptions of Christianity that South Asian Muslims bring with them to the United States when they immigrate.

Two basic sources of reference material were used that inform the research for this book: (1) I examined numerous scholarly writings related to the focal area: perceptions of Christianity among Muslims in general, and (2) I conducted personal interviews with South Asian Muslims, guided by a topical questionnaire, with a representative cross-section of South Asian Muslims in the Greater Boston area. Responses to the questionnaire comprise the data presented and analyzed in Chapters 4 and 5 of this book.

The literature I reviewed contributed many relevant insights included in this book. Many of these insights will prove useful to those involved in ministry among South Asian Muslims in America.

The literature provided insights into the background of historical influences that imparted many misperceptions of theological issues to South Asian Muslims.

I concentrated some research on Islamic revivalist movements, as well as on radical Islamic movements in South Asia, to investigate the influence of these movements on perceptions of Christianity held by South Asian Muslims. I found that these movements contributed many negative perceptions of Christianity.

The three main perspectives explored in this book (theological, sociocultural, and ethical) provided helpful insights on perceptions of Christianity held by the focal group. I found how some sociocultural emphases and practices in American society helped to shape perceptions of Christianity among South Asian Muslims. Because of many previously imparted ideas brought with them when they immigrate, they naturally associate Christianity with these emphases and practices found in their new homeland.

My research also revealed that some South Asian first-generation Muslim immigrants integrate into American culture to some extent, but they do not successfully acculturate to the same extent as their children. More complete acculturation or adaptation is usually accomplished by children of immigrants, especially those born in America.

My research further revealed that the vast majority of South Asian Muslims in America have strong ethical and moral convictions about certain practices and customs they observe in American society. Some of these addressed in this book include: homosexuality, same-sex marriage, unmarried couples living together, and abortion.

There are also some serious ethical and moral issues related to common practices in American society that most South Asian Muslims believe are incompatible with Islam.

Most of these immigrants do not have the perception that Christianity is directly responsible for or condones the behaviors associated with these practices, although they do believe Christians and Christian churches could be and should be a much stronger influence in American society opposing such behaviors. This belief has a bearing on their overall perception of Christianity.

Many from the South Asian Muslim community stated in the interviews that they would stand together with Christians in demonstrations against these practices. Although they do not believe Christianity supports these practices, they criticize Christianity for tolerating them.

In my preparatory literary research and in the interviews I conducted for this book, I realized that Christian practitioners will be more effective in their ministry if they understand the worldview and religious convictions of their target group.

My analysis of the data gathered from the personal interviews research, both from the literature reviewed and from the interviews and analysis, indicated that, compared to first-generation South Asian Muslim immigrants, the children and grandchildren of these immigrants, especially those born in the United States, have somewhat different perceptions related to sociocultural emphases in American society.

Full integration into American culture is evidently very difficult for first-generation South Asian Muslim immigrants. This observation was reinforced in the personal interviews with these immigrants and their families. I believe this is at least partly because predetermined ideas related to American culture and customs are still retained many years after immigration to America.

I further observed that perceptions of Christological issues held by South Asian Muslims tend to remain essentially like other Muslims ethnic groups; however, I am convinced that the influence of Sufism and folk Islam makes South Asian Muslims more open to Christianity. This opinion was reinforced by a majority of the interviewees who hold the same view. In my opinion, this is true because of the similarity between some Sufi practices and those of Christians, such as worship styles and similar emphases such as a personal relationship with God (Allah).

The interviews revealed that the majority of South Asian Muslims believe that anti-Muslim bias is prevalent among Christians in America.

In the interviews, many South Asian Muslims expressed their opinion that liberal feminism and women's rights are overemphasized in American society.

Careful study of the data from interviews further indicated that most South Asian Muslims have a positive view related to the authenticity of the Bible, but they also believe that translations corrupt the meaning and message of the Bible.

During the interviewing process, I observed an unexpected shift in perceptions of Christianity among first-generation immigrants. The responses did not fit with what I had come to expect that recently arrived immigrants would probably think. So this indicated that over time there had been some change in perception, just from the natural interactions that occur here in America. Something caused a modification of perceptions that the immigrants brought with them from South Asia.

Also, in the process of conducting the interviews, I observed that the second and third generation of South Asian Muslim immigrants had perceptions of Christianity noticeably different from their parents, which is to be expected because of growing up in a different culture.

After many years in ministry among Muslims in South Asia and South Asian Muslims in America, the research I conducted for this book provided many insights helpful in my ongoing ministry.

For Christian practitioners this book can serve as a foundation for developing ministry tools to achieve more effective communication of the gospel of Jesus Christ to South Asian Muslims.

It is my sincere hope this book will also provide useful resource material for academicians who continue research on this specific area of concern.

APPENDICES

APPENDIX A
Summary Table: Part of Chapter 1

Theological Influences that Historically Have Shaped Perceptions of Christianity among South Asian Muslims in America

Reform Movement	What South Asian Muslims think Christians believe (perceptions)
Deobandi	What the Qur'an says about Christianity and the Bible is what we believe.
	Christianity is associated with western secular education and to be avoided.
	Extreme Deobandi today (few in America \) are associated with militant Taliban with perception of Christianity as the enemy of Islam.
Barelwi	Elevated Muhammad to divine status equal to Jesus. (Some found among South Asian Muslims in the Boston area.)
	Extreme Barelwi support Jihadi movement against Christianity. Charges of blasphemy used to persecute Christians. Rarely found in Boston.
Tablighi Jama'at	Strong advocate of proselytizing of non-Muslims—Christianity is not a true religion like Islam. (They are very strong and active among South Asian Muslims in Greater Boston and becoming more popular.)
Ahmadiyya	Unlike other Muslims they believe in "Swoon Theory" that Jesus was crucified but did not die on the cross, and later died a natural death. (In the Boston area there are many South Asian adherents of Ahmadiyya, with perceptions that cause them to reject Christianity.)

Popular Movement	What South Asian Muslims think Christians believe (perceptions)
Syncretism	Emphasize personal relationship with Creator (Allah). Positive perception of Christianity in emphasis on personal relationship with God. Also emphasize devotion and meditation, similar to emphasis in Christianity. (Much influence of Sufism among Muslims in Boston.)
Sufism	Syncretism only found in Sufism and folk Islam. Adopt indigenous cultural practices of non-Muslims. Open to merging with Christianity. Perception of Christianity and Islam compatible. Embraces universalism. (in Greater Boston only found among moderate Muslims)
Folk Islam	Perception of Christianity in agreement with their emphases and practices. Perception of Christianity as compatible with Folk Islam because of Folk Islam's emphasis on universalism. (Seldom found among South Asian Muslims in Greater Boston).

Radical Movement	What South Asian Muslims think Christians believe (perceptions)
Islamism	Christianity does not include all spheres of life, whereas Islam does. Perception of Christianity as false religion, an enemy of Islam. (Although small in number, increasing influence among South Asians in Greater Boston.)

Questionnaire for Interviewing
South Asian Muslims

Theological (Doctrinal) Questions:

1. Do you believe it is possible to be a good Muslim and also a Christian? Is it possible to be both a Muslim and embrace Christian ideology?
   - ☐ Yes.
   - ☐ No.   Explain.

2. What do you think are the major points of disagreement between Islam and Christianity?
   Check all that are points of disagreement:
   - ☐ Belief in Jesus Christ as the Son of God who came to earth from heaven.
   - ☐ Belief in resurrection of Jesus Christ from the dead.
   - ☐ Belief in Bible as Holy Scripture, inspired by God.
   - ☐ All of the above.
     Any comment?

3. Do you think that most doctrinal issues between Christians and Muslims are a result of simple misconceptions of Christianity?
   - ☐ Yes.
   - ☐ No.   Explain.

4. Do you think that Christians and Muslims worship the same God? [Americans call Him God, Muslims call Him Allah, but only the name is different. Or are there fundamental differences in how God and Allah are perceived. Different God or differently perceived?]
   - ☐ Different God.
   - ☐ Same God but differently perceived.   Explain.

5. Do you think the Christian doctrine of the Trinity is polytheism (belief in multiple gods)? [The Christian doctrine of the Trinity

believes that the one God includes God the Father, God the Son (Jesus Christ), and God the Holy Spirit]

- ☐ Trinity doctrine is polytheism.
- ☐ Trinity doctrine is not polytheism.
  Any comment?

6. Do you believe that Jesus Christ is divine or merely a prophet?
   - ☐ Divine (Jesus was God).
   - ☐ Had divine power or wisdom.
   - ☐ Merely a prophet with no real divine power (godly power).
     Any comment?

7. Do you believe that Jesus Christ actually died on the cross? Or do you believe he did not actually die, but only swooned (fainted and appeared to be dead)? Or do you believe that it was not actually Christ who was killed on the cross, but some other person who appeared like him (cf. Surah 4:157)? Check all boxes you agree with below:
   - ☐ Yes, he died on the cross.
   - ☐ He did not die, but Allah lifted him up.
   - ☐ He only fainted, and appeared dead.
   - ☐ Someone else who appeared like him died on the cross.
   - ☐ Not sure what I believe about this.
     Any comment?

8. Do you think that the Christian Bible (the Holy Book) has been corrupted?
   - ☐ Corrupted.
   - ☐ Not corrupted.   Any comment?

9. Do you think that Sufi "veneration of Saints and Shrines and spiritual guides (pirs)" are the influence of Catholicism?
   - ☐ Yes, they are the influence of Catholicism.
   - ☐ No, they are not the influence of Catholicism.
     Any comment?

10. What is your opinion about the Sufi belief that humans can have a personal relationship with God?
    - ❏ I believe a person can have a personal relationship with God.
    - ❏ I do not believe a person can have a personal relationship with God. Any comment?

11. From the Muslim perspective, is Christianity a religion of infidels?
    - ❏ Yes, all Christians are infidels.
    - ❏ Most Christians are infidels.
    - ❏ Some Christians are infidels.
    - ❏ Christianity is not a religion of infidels. Any comment?

12. Do you think the practices of Folk Islam are against the teachings of the Qur'an and Hadith?
    - ❏ Yes.
    - ❏ No.   Please explain.

13. Do you think Folk Islam is intermingled with Sufism in South Asia and was introduced by Sufi Missionaries?
    - ❏ Yes.
    - ❏ No.   Any Comment?

14. Do you think pirs are mediators between God and human beings?
    - ❏ Yes.
    - ❏ No.   Any Comment?

15. Do you think South Asian Muslims are more open to Christianity because of the influence of syncretism practiced by Sufis?
    - ❏ Yes.
    - ❏ No.   Please explain.

16. Do you agree with the view of Deobandi Sunni fundamentalists that Western culture is associated with Christianity?
    - ❏ Yes.
    - ❏ No.   Any Comment?

Sociocultural Questions:

1. Do you believe that American cultural practices are based on Christian values and teaching? (Such as living together outside of marriage, homosexuality, abortion, etc., legal in the United States)
   ☐ Yes.
   ☐ No.   Any comment?

2. Do you believe racial discrimination in the United States comes from the influence of Western Christianity (doctrine and teaching)?
   ☐ Yes.
   ☐ No.   Any comment?

3. Are individualistic emphases in American family and society a result of Christian influences?
   ☐ Yes.
   ☐ No.   Any comment?

4. Is the free mixing of men and women, and gender equality in western society a Christian emphasis?
   ☐ Yes.
   ☐ No.   Any comment?

5. Do you think the prevailing Christian attitude in American society is Anti-Muslim?
   ☐ Yes.
   ☐ No.   Any comment?

6. Do you think social integration into mainline American society compromises a Muslim's convictions and makes them appear to embrace Christian ideals?
   ☐ Yes.
   ☐ No.   Any comment?

7. Do you think Christianity believes in women's rights and does that compromise Muslim beliefs? (Women's rights are rights

that promote a position of legal and social equality of women with men.)

☐ Yes.

☐ No. Any comment?

8. Do you believe Christianity supports women wearing dress that is sexually provocative?

☐ Yes.

☐ No.

☐ Not sure. Any comment?

9. Do you believe body piercings and tattoos reflect Christian endorsement?

☐ encourages them.

☐ discourages them.

☐ tolerates them.

☐ I am not sure.
Any comment?

Ethical (moral) Questions:

1. Do you think the weak voice from some Christian churches in America against homosexual practice and same-sex marriage implies silent support and sympathy towards these practices?

☐ Yes.

☐ No. Explain.

2. Do you think that Christians teach that living together outside of marriage is OK?

☐ Yes.

☐ No. Any comment?

3. Do you think that Christians teach that legalized abortion is OK?

☐ Yes.

☐ No. Any comment?

4. Do you believe it is a Christian practice to approve an unmarried couple becoming parents?

☐ Yes.

☐ No.   Any comment?

5. Do you believe that Christianity approves the common American practice of drinking alcohol and wine at social gatherings?

☐ Yes.

☐ No.   Any comment?

6. Do you think the recent ruling of the Supreme Court, legalizing homosexual marriage throughout the United States was a result of Christian (Church) influence?

☐ Yes, strongly influenced by Christian church.

☐ No, it is a secular court.

Any comment?

APPENDIX C
Responses to Questionnaire

Theological (Doctrinal): Questions | Responses

	Yes	No		Comments
T1 Do you believe it is possible to be a good Muslim and also a Christian? Is it possible to be both a Muslim and embrace Christian ideology? ☐ Yes. ☐ No. Explain.	11	39		15

	A	B	C	Comments
T2 What do you think are the major points of disagreement between Islam and Christianity? Check **all** that are points of disagreement: ☐ **A** Belief in Jesus Christ as the Son of God who came to earth from heaven. ☐ **B** Belief in resurrection of Jesus Christ from the dead. ☐ **C** Belief in Bible as Holy Scripture, inspired by God. ☐ **All of the above.** *(Distributed in Tally A + B + C)* Any comment?	49	49	37	13

	Yes	No		Comments
T3 Do you think that most doctrinal issues between Christians and Muslims are a result of simple misconceptions of Christianity? ☐ Yes. ☐ No. Explain.	15	35		31

	A	B		Comments
T4 Do you think that Christians and Muslims worship the same God? [Americans call Him God, Muslims call Him Allah, but only the name is different. Or are there fundamental differences in how God and Allah are perceived. Different God or differently perceived?] ☐ **A** Different God. ☐ **B** Same God but differently perceived. Explain.	24	25		13

	A	B		Comments
T5 Do you think the Christian doctrine of the Trinity is polytheism (belief in multiple gods)? [The Christian doctrine of the Trinity believes that the one God includes God the Father, God the Son (Jesus Christ), and God the Holy Spirit] 　❑　**A** Trinity doctrine is polytheism. 　❑　**B** Trinity doctrine is not polytheism. Any comment?	20	7		34

	A	B	C	Comments
T6 Do you believe that Jesus Christ is divine or merely a prophet? 　❑　**A** Divine (Jesus was God). 　❑　**B** Had divine power or wisdom. 　❑　**C** Merely a prophet with no real divine power (godly power). Any comment?	2	43	4	20

	B	C	D	Comments
T7 Do you believe that Jesus Christ actually died on the cross? Or do you believe he did not actually die, but only swooned (fainted and appeared to be dead)? Or do you believe that it was not actually Christ who was killed on the cross, but some other person who appeared like him (cf. Surah 4:157)? Check **all** boxes you agree with below: 　❑　**A** Yes, he died on the cross (*No A or E in Responses*). 　❑　**B** He did not die, but Allah lifted him up. 　❑　**C** He only fainted, and appeared dead. 　❑　**D** Someone else who appeared like him died on the cross. 　❑　**E** Not sure what I believe about this. Any comment?	45	2	6	11

	A	B		Comments
T8 Do you think that the Christian Bible (the Holy Book) has been corrupted? 　❑　**A** Corrupted. 　❑　**B** Not corrupted.　Any comment?	6	36		29

	Yes	No		Comments
T9 Do you think that Sufi "veneration of saints and shrines, and spiritual guides (pirs)" are the influence of Catholicism? 　❑　Yes, they are the influence of Catholicism. 　❑　No, they are not the influence of Catholicism.　Any comment?	17	27		14

	A	B		Comments

T10 What is your opinion about the Sufi belief that humans can have a personal relationship with God.
    ☐ **A** I believe a person can have a personal relationship with God.
    ☐ **B** I do not believe a person can have a personal relationship with God.
    Any comment?
	17	33		15

	A	C	D	Comments

T11 From the Muslim perspective, is Christianity a religion of infidels?
    ☐ **A** Yes, all Christians are infidels.
    ☐ **B** Most Christians are infidels.
    ☐ **C** Some Christians are infidels.
    ☐ **D** No, Christianity is not a religion of infidels.
    Any comment? (*No B in responses*)
	2	17	31	12

	Yes	No		Comments

T12 Do you think the practices of Folk Islam are against the teachings of the Qur'an and Hadith?
    ☐ Yes.
    ☐ No.   Please explain.
	20	14		20

T13 Do you think Folk Islam is intermingled with Sufism in South Asia and was introduced by Sufi Missionaries?
    ☐ Yes.
    ☐ No.   Any Comment?
	27	7		9

T14 Do you think pirs are mediators between God and human beings?
    ☐ Yes.
    ☐ No.   Any Comment?
	3	30		20

T15 Do you think South Asian Muslims are more open to Christianity because of the influence of syncretism practiced by Sufis?
    ☐ Yes.
    ☐ No.
    Please explain.
	33	1		9

T16 Do you agree with the view of Deobandi Sunni fundamentalists that Western culture is associated with Christianity?
    ☐ Yes.
    ☐ No.   Any Comment?
	19	26		14

Sociocultural Questions | Responses

	Yes	No		Comments
S1 Do you believe that American cultural practices are based on Christian values and teaching? (Such as living together outside of marriage, homosexuality, abortion, etc., legal in the United States) ❑　Yes. ❑　No.　Any comment?	16	34		19
S2 Do you believe racial discrimination in the United States comes from the influence of Western Christianity (doctrine and teaching)? ❑　Yes. ❑　No.　Any comment?	22	26		23
S3 Are individualistic emphases in American family and society a result of Christian influences? ❑　Yes. ❑　No.　Any comment?	42	7		13
S4 Is the free mixing of men and women, and gender equality in western society a Christian emphasis? ❑　Yes. ❑　No.　Any comment?	41	9		16
S5 Do you think the prevailing Christian attitude in American society is Anti-Muslim? ❑　Yes. ❑　No.　Any comment?	43	4		16
S6 Do you think social integration into mainline American society compromises a Muslim's convictions and makes them appear to embrace Christian ideals? ❑　Yes. ❑　No.　Any comment?	21	29		18
S7 Do you think Christianity believes in women's rights and does that compromise Muslim beliefs? (Women's rights are rights that promote a position of legal and social equality of women with men.) ❑　Yes. ❑　No.　Any comment?	24	26		16

	A	B	C	
S8 Do you believe Christianity supports women wearing dress that is sexually provocative? ☐ A Yes. ☐ B No. ☐ C Not sure. Any comment?	6	37	7	20

	A	B	C	D	
S9 Do you believe body piercings and tattoos reflect Christian endorsement? ☐ A encourages them. ☐ B discourages them. ☐ C tolerates them. ☐ D I am not sure. Any comment?	3	3	30	14	15

Ethical (moral): Questions | Responses

	Yes	No		Comments
E1 Do you think the weak voice from some Christian churches in Greater Boston against homosexual practice and same-sex marriage implies silent support and sympathy towards these practices? ☐ Yes. ☐ No. Explain.	46	4		18
E2 Do you think that Christians teach that living together outside of marriage is OK? ☐ Yes. ☐ No. Any comment?	7	34		30
E3 Do you think that Christians teach that legalized abortion is OK? ☐ Yes. ☐ No. Any comment?	8	33		25
E4 Do you believe it is a Christian practice to approve an unmarried couple becoming parents? ☐ Yes. ☐ No. Any comment?	3	36		30
E5 Do you believe that Christianity approves the common American practice of drinking alcohol and wine at social gatherings? ☐ Yes. ☐ No. Any comment?	32	18		12

	Yes	No		Comments
E6 Do you think the recent ruling of the Supreme Court, legalizing homosexual marriage throughout the United States was a result of Christian (Church) influence? ☐ Yes, strongly influenced by Christian church. ☐ No, it is a secular court. Any comment?	1	45		14

APPENDIX D
Questionnaire Comments

<u>T = Theological Questions S = Sociocultural Questions; E = Ethical (moral) Questions;</u>

T1	Q: Do you believe it is possible to be a good Muslim and also a Christian? Is it possible to be both a Muslim and embrace Christian ideology? ❏ Yes. ❏ No. Explain.	
Q	Comments Participant Reference Numbers↓	
T1	Fundamental beliefs and practices are different between Islam & Christianity	1,2
	No one can do both.	3,15
	To a Muslim it is compromise	4,5,6
	No one can practice both, but we may agree on some points	7
	For Muslims it will be a compromise	8
	Islam and Christianity are entirely different faiths. There are many doctrinal differences.	9
	Anybody at a time cannot practice both.	11
	The two are totally different religions. We cannot maintain a double standard.	12
	Some Christian ideologies are similar to Islam	41
	It will be a compromising of Muslim faith	45
	To embrace Christian ideology means to embrace Christianity	49

T2	Q: What do you think are the major points of disagreement between Islam and Christianity? Check **all** that are points of disagreement: ❏ A Belief in Jesus Christ as the Son of God who came to earth from heaven. ❏ B Belief in resurrection of Jesus Christ from the dead. ❏ C Belief in Bible as Holy Scripture, inspired by God. ❏ **All of the above.** Any comment?	
Q	Comments Participant Reference Numbers↓	
T2	Jesus' crucifixion and resurrection and he is called Son of God. How can God have a son – unpardonable sin.	1
	No Muslim can accept it.	2
	I strong disbelieve, but I believe in the Bible as Holy Scripture inspired by God.	3,4
	Muslims cannot accept that Jesus was Son of God. If he was the son of God, then how could he die.	5

Q	Comments	Participant Reference Numbers↓
T2	I believe the Bible is Holy Scripture, but is corrupted by translation; Hebrew and Greek Bible are OK.	6
	I disagree with all of this.	7
	I believe the Bible is the Holy Scriptures inspired by Allah because the Qur'an affirms the Bible	8
	Especially son of God and Crucifixion (does not accept)	30
	I have high regard for the Bible. It is revelation from God.	36
	Crucifixion and resurrection and divinity of Jesus are main points of disagreement	39
	I accept the Bible	41
	I don't have any problem to accept the Bible as holy Scripture, but I have problem to accept Jesus as the son of Allah, his crucifixion and resurrection	49

T3	**Q:** Do you think that most doctrinal issues between Christians and Muslims are a result of simple misconceptions of Christianity? ❐ Yes. ❐ No. Explain.	

Q	Comments	Participant Reference Numbers↓
T3	There are many doctrinal differences	1
	It is more than misconception.	2
	Doctrines are totally different.	3,4
	There are some misconceptions, but many doctrinal differences.	5
	Christians do not accept Muhammad as a prophet.	6
	It is not simply misunderstand, but there are some fundamental beliefs that separate each other. We do not believe that Jesus Christ is son of God and was crucified.	7
	Totally doctrinal issues.	8
	Christians do not recognize Muhammad as a prophet	9
	It is not simply misconception, it is doctrinal clash with Islam	10
	Islam and Christianity are entirely different faiths. There are major differences in doctrine.	11
	Both (Islam and Christianity) are not exposed enough to each other about their respective doctrines.	12
	Islamic confession* is the fundamental different between Islam and Christianity. (Islamic confession states: "There is no God but Allah, and Muhammad is His messenger.")	13
	Christians worship Jesus as God	14
	Christian doctrines and Islamic doctrines are entirely different. It is not simply a misconception.	20

Q	Comments	Participant Reference Numbers↓
T3	Christianity and Islam are totally different from each other.	22
	Contradictory teaching (Christian and Muslim)	23
	The Qur'anic teachings and Biblical teaching are different	24
	It is not simply misconception, but there are much differences between the Qur'an and the Bible	28
	There are much differences between the Qur'anic teaching and the biblical teaching.	29
	It is not simply a misconception. There is a great contradiction between Qur'anic teaching and biblical teaching	31
	No, it is not simply misunderstanding, because the Qur'anic teaching *Shahadah* (Islamic confession) is total different than Christian confession (of sin).	36
	Because Muslims do not like to read the Bible	41
	The Qur'anic teaching is entirely different than the teaching of the Bible	43
	Christian doctrines are against the Qur'anic teaching	44
	This is against the Qur'anic teaching.	45
	Muslims attitude is not to agree which are not found in the Qur'an	46
	Because it is against Islamic doctrine and Qur'anic teaching	47
	It is not simply misperception, but the Qur'anic teachings are entirely different	48
	There are many doctrinal issues	49
	The Qur'anic teaching and the Bible teaching is contradictory	50

Q		
T4	**Q:** Do you think that Christians and Muslims worship the same God? [Americans call Him God, Muslims call Him Allah, but only the name is different. Or are there fundamental differences in how God and Allah are perceived. Different God or differently perceived?] ❏ **A** Different God. ❏ **B** Same God but differently perceived. Explain.	

Q	Comments	Participant Reference Numbers↓
T4	At least Christians worship one God.	1
	We worship one God; Christians worship different God	2
	Christians believe that God came down to us.(God cannot do that)	3
	We Muslims worship Allah; Christians worship God.	4,5
	Allah is equal to the Jewish God. The Christian god is like pagan god; Allah is the supreme being.	6
	He is not close to us.	7
	We worship Allah only. Christians worship Jesus who is simply a prophet.	8

Q	Comments	Participant Reference Numbers↓
T4	Because Islam is absolute monotheism. We worship different gods.	12
	I am not sure	16
	The nature of Allah is different.	41
	God is love – Christians believe that, as Muslims we cannot have personal relationship with Allah	47
	It is only the different name (same God)	49

T5	**Q:** Do you think the Christian doctrine of the Trinity is polytheism (belief in multiple gods)? [The Christian doctrine of the Trinity believes that the one God includes God the Father, God the Son (Jesus Christ), and God the Holy Spirit] ❏ **A** Trinity doctrine is polytheism. ❏ **B** Trinity doctrine is not polytheism. Any comment?	

Q	Comments	Participant Reference Numbers↓
T5	Is an unpardonable sin in Islam.	1
	It is a three-god theory.	2,5
	I do not understand this doctrine (trinity) I am confused.	3
	It is a sin to make someone equal with Allah	4
	We Muslims cannot make anyone equal to Allah	6
	Making someone equal to God is unpardonable sin	7
	This doctrine is making someone equal to God	8
	Some sorts of polytheism. I am confused about this Christian doctrine	9
	I do not understand it	10,13
	I do not understand trinity. To me it is a three-god idea	11
	I am not sure	15
	I do not understand the trinity.	16,24,25
	It is confusing to me	17,29
	I believe there are not (cannot be) three gods. Trinity is polytheism	18
	As long as they don't worship three gods, it is OK.	19
	I do not understand the trinity doctrine. But as long as they do not worship 3 gods, it is OK to me.	20
	I am not sure about that.	21
	I am not familiar with the trinity	23
	Not sure	26
	I do not know	30
	I do not understand the trinity concept. Sometimes I think it is a three-god concept. I am confused.	31
	I have no idea of the trinity	36

Q	Comments	Participant Reference Numbers↓
T5	I am not sure	37
	I am not aware of that	39
	It is very critical	41
	When Christians claim that Jesus Christ is God, it is *Shirk* (unpardonable sin in Islam)	45
	Three gods	47
	I am not sure about this doctrine	49
	It is very complex.	50

Q	

T6	Q: Do you believe that Jesus Christ is divine or merely a prophet?
	   ❑ **A** Divine (Jesus was God).
	   ❑ **B** Had divine power or wisdom.
	   ❑ **C** Merely a prophet with no real divine power (godly power).
	   Any comment?

Q	Comments	Participant Reference Numbers↓
T6	He was given power by God to do some miracles like other prophets.	1
	All prophets have divine power, including Muhammad	2
	Same like other prophets (Jesus had divine power)	3,4
	He was simply a messenger	5
	Allah granted him some power to do some miracles only	6
	All prophets have divine power.	7
	He was not God, but had godly character, which many prophets had	9
	He was given power by God like other prophets. The same power was given to Muhammad	12
	To me he (Jesus) was not merely a prophet	16
	He was merely a prophet, but divine power was given to him	17
	He was simply a prophet	18,20
	He is simply a prophet and human being	22
	I believe Jesus Christ was divine, but their (Muslim) perception can be changed.	27
	He (Jesus) was a mighty prophet of God.	36
	Allah gave him power. He did not have his own.	41
	Only to do miracles	47
	He was a prophet and messenger of God only	48
	God gave him power only to do miracles. It was not by his own.	49

T7	Q: Do you believe that Jesus Christ actually died on the cross? Or do you believe he did not actually die, but only swooned (fainted and appeared to be dead)? Or do you believe that it was not actually Christ who was killed on the cross, but some other person who appeared like him (cf. Surah 4:157)? Check all boxes you agree with below: ☐ A Yes, he died on the cross. ☐ B He did not die, but Allah lifted him up. ☐ C He only fainted, and appeared dead. ☐ D Someone else who appeared like him died on the cross. ☐ E Not sure what I believe about this. Any comment?	
Q	**Comments** **Participant Reference Numbers↓**	
T7	To accept crucifixion of Jesus is humiliation of God (Allah)	1
	God did not allow anybody to harm his prophet	2
	Someone else died for him, and he only fainted – both are false beliefs	4
	Allah could not allow this. Allah is the mighty God.	6
	Because in Islam there is substitution theory	7
	Surah 4:157 is confusing to me (substitution theory)	12
	According to Surah 4:157 (someone else took his place)	15
	Surah 4:157 – I agree with this Surah	17
	Being an Ahmadiyya Muslim, I believe that (Jesus fainted & appeared to be dead).	31
	Being Ahmadiyya, I believe Jesus fainted and appeared dead. Swoon theory	36
	I am convinced of this based on Surah 4:157 (someone else)	49

T8	Q: Do you think that the Christian Bible (the Holy Book) has been corrupted? ☐ A Corrupted. ☐ B Not corrupted. Any comment?	
Q	**Comments** **Participant Reference Numbers↓**	
T8	Various translations makes confusion, but I do not think original text is changed.	1
	No need of numerous translations.	2
	It is same as original text	3
	Corrupted by translation, without original meaning	4
	Different meanings in different versions	5
	I am not sure about the original text, but corrupted by translation	6
	Corrupted by translation, original meaning gets changed.	7
	It is corrupted in some ways by translation	8

Q	Comments	Participant Reference Numbers↓
T8	Text is not corrupted. By translation, interpretation is corrupted	10
	Translation makes problems	12
	Translation makes confusion. Translation makes different meaning	13
	Yes, some kind of corruption is there. It is not much textual corruption but interpretation.	16
	It lost originality because of translation	17
	Many translations give different meanings	18
	Translations make confusion	19
	But translation can lose the real and original meaning	21
	In one translation (language) there are many versions. The Qur'an is not like that. I am confused.	22
	Various translations makes confusion. Which one is wrong and which one is right.	28
	Some translations are confusing to me. It may lose original meaning.	31
	The text is not corrupted, but I think translation or versions are corrupted.	36
	Translation makes problem	37
	Different translation gives different meaning. It gives confusion.	38
	It is the translation of different languages. It loses original meaning in translation. Several versions in one language.	41
	Somewhat corrupted by translation	43
	Different translations and versions give different meaning, and it gives confusion	44
	So many translations. Many words are different meaning. Lost original	45
	It is a problem of translation into different languages.	46
	I think translations corrupt the meaning.	47
	Through various translations in different languages, original language is changed	49
T9	Q: Do you think that Sufi "veneration of Saints and Shrines and spiritual guides (pirs)" are the influence of Catholicism? ❐ Yes, they are the influence of Catholicism. ❐ No, they are not the influence of Catholicism. Any comment?	
Q	Comments	Participant Reference Numbers↓
T9	It started from Arabia.	1
	There is some influence of Catholicism	2
	Islam permits that. *Hajjis* venerate Muhammad's tomb in Medina during *Hajj*.	4

Q	Comments Participant Reference Numbers↓
T9	Sufis were there among the prophet Muhammad's close aides, but somehow they were mixed with animistic ideas later on	6
	Maybe. Because there are some similar practices'	7
	There are many similar practices	8
	The same practice is in Catholicism	10
	I am not sure.	11,15,28
	I am not sure	5,31
	Many similarities.	23
	I think it is the influence of paganism	49

T10	Q: What is your opinion about the Sufi belief that humans can have a personal relationship with God? ☐　A I believe a person can have a personal relationship with God. ☐　B I do not believe a person can have a personal relationship with God. 　　Any comment?

Q	Comments Participant Reference Numbers↓
T10	God is spirit; how can we have relationship with him? An unseen God.	1
	God is all above. Humans cannot have relationship with him.	2
	I believe a person can have personal relationship with God, but it is a spiritual relationship	3
	Allah is above all, he is not human (no relationship possible)	4
	God is not human. He cannot have relationship with humans.	5
	We are human and Allah is divine.	6
	It is a spiritual relationship (not physical)	7,10,14
	Spiritual only	8,13
	God is above all, he is not human.	12
	God and human is different	45
	He is far above. Humans cannot have relationship with him.	49
	By obeying his all commands is also making personal relationship	50

T11	Q: From the Muslim perspective, is Christianity a religion of infidels? ☐　A Yes, all Christians are infidels. ☐　B Most Christians are infidels. ☐　C Some Christians are infidels. ☐　D No, Christianity is not a religion of infidels. 　　Any comment?

Q	Comments	Participant Reference Numbers↓
T11	Many Americans are infidel, because of their practices and behavior	1
	Because they believe Jesus Christ is the Son of God.	2
	Some American Christians who lead unethical lives (are infidel)	3
	They believe that Jesus is God (therefore infidels)	5
	Because they adopted some pagan ideas	6
	When I see some Christian accept many pagan ideas	7
	But Christians act as infidels	8
	According to the definition of infidel, Christians are not.	12
	Trinity doctrine looks like paganism	44
	Their social practices are like infidels	47
	Many Americans are infidels.	49
	Those who worship idols, they are infidels only. I believe Christians do not do that. (not infidels)	50
T12	Q: Do you think the practices of Folk Islam are against the teachings of the Qur'an and Hadith? ❏ Yes. ❏ No. Please explain:	

Q	Comments	Participant Reference Numbers↓
T12	It is a mixture of paganism	1
	It has pagan influence.	2
	Folk Islam is popular. It teaches Qur'an and Hadith	3
	As long as they are strict on *Shahadah* (Islamic confession)	4
	It is animistic	5
	Because of syncretistic practice	6
	It is against Islamic shariah law	7
	As long as it is not indoctrinated	8
	It is contextualized practice	9
	Those who practice folk Islam, they are simple(minded); they practice indigenous culture	10
	There is an influence of paganism. The Qur'an does not support this.	11
	But some practices, for example magic, sorcery are against the Qur'an	12
	Yes, because it is related with paganism and Animism	15
	Some practices are, such as sorcery, magic, in the name of Allah	16
	Sorcery, magic and using the Qur'anic verses are not good practice	18
	Yes, some practices are against the teachings of the Qur'an.	23
	Because of animistic influence and pagan influence	43

Q	Comments	Participant Reference Numbers↓
T12	There are many folk practices, such as sorcery, magic that are against the teachings of the holy Qur'an	48
	Folk Islam is a popular Islam in South Asia. It is along the line of the Qur'an and Hadith	49
	Some practices are very bad.	50

| T13 | Q: Do you think Folk Islam is intermingled with Sufism in South Asia and was introduced by Sufi Missionaries?
 ❏ Yes.
 ❏ No. Any Comment? |

Q	Comments	Participant Reference Numbers↓
T13	I don't like Sufism	1
	Folk Islam is a practice of spirit worship	2
	Because of Folk Islam, Islam spread rapidly in South Asia	3
	Because of Folk Islam, many Hindus became Muslim	4
	It was introduced by some false teachers for their own interest	5
	Sufi missionaries did not introduce that. The people who were converted into Islam, they introduced that.	7
	Yes, they did it, because of the methodology of spreading Islam in India	8
	No, it was introduced later on	15
	Only to spread Islam.	49

| T14 | Q: Do you think *pirs* are mediators between God and human beings?
 ❏ Yes.
 ❏ No. Any Comment? |

Q	Comments	Participant Reference Numbers↓
T14	There is no mediator in Islam	1,2,6
	There is no mediator in Islam	8,15
	There are some *pirs* who are bad	3
	Many *pirs* act like they are mediators.	4
	Only Muhammad is mediator.	5
	We do not need a mediator or via	7
	We do not need a mediator between man and Allah	10
	There are many bad *pirs* who exploit people. I do not believe in them	11
	Many *pirs* are not genuine.	12
	They act like that. They deceive people	13
	There are many bad *pirs* nowadays	16

Q	Comments	Participant Reference Numbers↓
T14	Some are good *pirs* and some are bad *pirs*	17
	They act like that, but I do not trust these *pirs*.	18
	They are saints. They are close to Allah, but very few can be genuine *pirs*.	36
	They act like that, but they are not (mediators)	48
	Some bad *pirs* who act like that.	49
	I do not believe in *pirs*. We should have direct access to Allah.	50

Q		
T15	**Q:** Do you think South Asian Muslims are more open to Christianity because of the influence of syncretism practiced by Sufis? □ Yes. □ No. Please explain.	

Q	Comments	Participant Reference Numbers↓
T15	Many practices of Christianity such as using instrumental music in worship and meditation	1
	Because of cultural identity. Same culture	2
	Sufism has more tolerance (of other religions)	3
	Because it tolerates other religions	4
	Many religious practices are similar	5
	They are not radical like Arab Muslims. They are more tolerant in nature.	6
	It is mixed with Hinduism, Buddhism, and Animism.	7
	It is a mixture of Hinduism and Islam	8
	There is syncretistic ideas which make them more liberal.	49

Q		
T16	**Q:** Do you agree with the view of Deobandi Sunni fundamentalists that Western culture is associated with Christianity? □ Yes. □ No. Any Comment?	

Q	Comments	Participant Reference Numbers↓
T16	Colonialism and Western Christianity went together.	1,2
	Some Western cultures are associated with Christianity, but there are many good stuffs there.	4
	The British colonial power introduced Christianity in the name of education	5
	I am not sure about that	6, 7
	Many Western cultures are associated with Christianity	8

Q	Comments Participant Reference Numbers↓	
T16	There is no connection with Christianity. Religion and culture are different.	11
	Some Western cultures are related with Christian values.	12
	To some extent	17
	Not all Western culture is associated with Christianity	18
	Some Christian values are there	21
	Christian missionaries came under the protection of colonial powers	47
	Many Western culture are associated with Christianity	49

| S1 | Q: Do you believe that American cultural practices are based on Christian values and teaching? (Such as living together outside of marriage, homosexuality, abortion, etc., legal in the United States) ☐ Yes. ☐ No.   Any comment? |

Q	Comments Participant Reference Numbers↓	
S1	I am surprised when I see the Christian Church tolerate this practice	1
	I see many Christians practice those.	2,3
	Many American cultural practices are based on Christian values except all these	4
	Christianity is the dominant religion in America	5
	Churches do not have a strong voice against this practice	6
	Christian churches tolerate it	7
	Christian churches are accepting it.	8
	In America, Christians have very weak voices	12
	I have seen many confessing Christians even church-going people are practicing these.	22
	These practices are among Christians, not among Muslims.	35
	Some are based on Christian values, but not these	41
	I notice those who call themselves Christian, but they are not practicing what Christianity teaches.	43
	Christian churches tolerate this	44
	I do not understand why Christian churches are not having strong voices against these.	45
	Many cultural practices are based on Christian values, but these are not based on Christian values.	46
	I do not think these are based on Christian values, but nowadays Christians tolerate this	47

Q	Comments Participant Reference Numbers↓
S1	I do not understand why many Christians are practicing these	48
	I don't think Christianity teaches those, but I know many Christians practice those.	49

Q	Comments
S2	Q: Do you believe racial discrimination in the United States comes from the influence of Western Christianity (doctrine and teaching)? ☐ Yes. ☐ No. Any comment?

Q	Comments Participant Reference Numbers↓
S2	Most Western Christians are racist. Racism was introduced in America by the European colonial powers who were also Christian	1
	It was imposed by the white European Christians who first came here and invaded the land of native Indians (American) and then slavery	2
	Church leaders discriminate	3
	Christianity originally did not teach that, but Western Christians do.	4
	It is practiced in the church.	5
	Racial discrimination is in the church	6
	Historically it is true that Puritans killed many Indians (American) Christian churches supported slavery	7
	It was practiced historically	8
	It is not Christian doctrine and teaching, but practice.	9
	I have seen racial prejudice in the church	10
	Discrimination was always there from the beginning	12
	Slavery practiced among Christians (earlier time)	13
	Not directly, but some Christian influence is there.	16
	Racial discrimination and religion is different.	24
	It is yes and no both, because it started from the time of slavery and slavery was introduced by Christians.	31
	Christians were having slaves.	41
	It was at the beginning of American history when Puritans came to this country, they badly treated native Indians (American)	43
	Because there is always the anti-Muslim attitude	44
	In the church there is the practice of racial discrimination	46
	It was there at the beginning when immigrants first came from Europe to America they killed Indians (American Indians)	47

Q	Comments	Participant Reference Numbers↓
S2	Many Christians are racist	48
	There is discrimination in the church	49
	When black people in America are persecuted by white people, I am surprised. Both claim that they are Christian.	50

S3	**Q:** Are individualistic emphases in American family and society a result of Christian influences? ☐ Yes. ☐ No.　Any comment?

Q	Comments	Participant Reference Numbers↓
S3	There are many individualistic ideas in Christian doctrines.	1
	Individualistic attitudes and too much privacy	2
	No communalistic idea like South Asian culture	3
	Too much concern for privacy is individualism	4
	There is too much demand for privacy	5
	Christians in many churches are individualistic	6
	Christians are very individualistic	7
	American Christians are very individualistic; more concerned about privacy	8
	I think it is a cultural practice	12
	It is a cultural practice	15
	America was founded on Christian principles and Christian society is individualistic.	22
	Too much privacy.	47
	Individual benefit is the main focus in the society, but not community focus.	49

S4	**Q:** Is the free mixing of men and women, and gender equality in western society a Christian emphasis? ☐ Yes. ☐ No.　Any comment?

Q	Comments	Participant Reference Numbers↓
S4	It is a Christian emphasis. Free mixing gives opportunity to women to enjoy too much right in America. There should be a balance	1
	This practice of gender equality grants too much rights to women and in many cases it is abused.	2
	It is not a Christian emphasis, but in practice it is.	3
	It is practiced in the church.	4

260

Q	Comments	Participant Reference Numbers↓
S4	Western society is influenced by Christianity	5
	Unethical and sexual promiscuity in the churches; churches tolerate	6
	It is inside the church. Christian churches tolerate sexual promiscuity	7
	It is practiced in the Christian churches, and churches tolerate sexual promiscuity	8
	In my country (Bangladesh), I saw in Christian society, women have more freedom and liberty compared to Muslim society.	11
	At the church, seating arrangement proves that Christianity supports that	12
	Gender equality is a good practice. Muslims in America should support that	15
	It has become a cultural practice, but there should be balance	41
	It is there in the church. There are some woman pastors and ministers, sitting arrangement for women participants.	43
	It is not Christian emphasis but practice	44
	But Christians practice this	47
	It is widely practiced in the church	49

Q		
S5	**Q:** Do you think the prevailing Christian attitude in American society is anti-Muslim? ☐ Yes. ☐ No. Any comment?	

Q	Comments	Participant Reference Numbers↓
S5	Most Christians think Islam is a terroristic religion.	1,2,
	Especially after 9/11 there is anti Islam, but some Muslims are responsible for that.	3
	Anti-Muslim have always been there. Americans like cultural diversity but not in religion	4
	Often Muslims are responsible for that (anti-Muslim attitudes)	5
	Islamophobia is everywhere and present administration is anti-Muslim	6
	Hate crimes against Muslims are increasing day by day, because of Donald Trump's Muslim ban	7
	There are a large number of people (in America) who are not anti-Muslim.	8
	There is a strong prejudice among Christians in America that Muslims are terrorists. To some extent, Muslims are responsible for that.	12
	Most Americans have prejudice against Muslims	15
	Yes, there are some, but all people are like that	20

Q	Comments	Participant Reference Numbers↓
S5	Many prejudices against Muslims. Christian churches do not welcome Muslims	41
	There is a strong Islamophobia and prejudice against Muslims in America	43
	It is all along (always has been)	46
	Prejudice against Islam is very strong	47
	Islamophobia is very strong, especially after 9/11. Present U.S. administration, and even president, is anti-Muslim	49

Q		
S6	Q: Do you think social integration into mainline American society compromises a Muslim's convictions and makes them appear to embrace Christian ideals? ☐ Yes. ☐ No.　Any comment?	

Q	Comments	Participant Reference Numbers↓
S6	Because American society is influenced by Christian ideas and teaching. (social integration)	1
	Because there are many Christian ideas practiced in American society. Alcoholism is one of them.	2
	Social integration is needed in order to uplift Muslim society in America, otherwise they will be like frog in a well.	3
	To some extent it is true.	4
	Many practices in mainline American society is anti-Islam	5
	To integrate into American society, Muslims must compromise	6
	It will be compromised with some unethical practices	7
	Integrating into mainline American society is a compromise of our faith as Muslims	8
	Our Islamic faith and conviction is more important	9
	If I do not compromise my faith, nobody can change it	10
	We have to be careful about our faith. Integration is possible.	12
	Since we are in America, for our children's sake we need to integrate into American society	15
	We as Muslims have to keep our faith. We can integrate – is not a problem.	41
	Muslims will get bad influences from American society (if we integrate)	43
	Muslim immigrants need that in order to uplift themselves	44
	I believe that every Muslim should maintain their Islamic identity. Islam is the first (not America)	45

Q	Comments	Participant Reference Numbers↓
S6	Because mainline American society practices are against Islam	47
	We need to be careful. Without integrating Muslims will find difficulties and other benefits.	49
S7	**Q:** Do you think Christianity believes in women's rights and does that compromise Muslim beliefs? (Women's rights are rights that promote a position of legal and social equality of women with men.) ☐ Yes. ☐ No. Any comment?	

Q	Comments	Participant Reference Numbers↓
S7	Islam grants women's rights. Prophet Muhammad was the one who first introduced it; even forced (Arabian) society to do that.	1
	Because Islam also gives rights to women. But, in Islam it is balanced. Here is America women want to sit on the head of men	2
	There is women's rights in Islam, but here in America women have dominant attitudes.	3
	Too much rights for women. Women have dominant attitude.	4
	In Islam women have rights, but it is balanced. Women do not dominate over men	5
	Islam also supports Women's rights, but in American too many women want to dominate	6
	What is going on in American in the name of women's rights is very bad. It is too much.	7
	It is not women's rights, it is liberal feminism	8
	Although in Islam, women have no equal rights, but Islam gives some kinds of rights to women.	10
	There is too much women's rights in America.	12
	Islam also supports that.	15
	In Islam rights of women are recognized. But it has to be modified in the context of the 21st Century.	30
	But too much rights (of women)	41
	The Qur'an is very clear about women's rights.	44
	Islam also grants women's rights, but America too much	47
	In Islam there is women's rights, but it should be balanced.	49

Q	Comments	Participant Reference Numbers↓
S8	**Q:** Do you believe Christianity supports women wearing dress that is sexually provocative? ☐ **A** Yes. ☐ **B** No. ☐ **C** Not sure. Any comment?	

Q	Comments	Participant Reference Numbers↓
S8	Christianity tolerates sexual promiscuity, and silently supports it.	1,2,3,4
	Christian women's dress in church can be provocative.	5
	It is practiced in the church and churches do not speak against it.	6
	When I see it is happening in the church, then it becomes true to me	7
	When I see it happening in the church, then I am surprised.	8
	But I get confused when Christian women come to church with sexually provocative dress.	9
	These are the women who are immodest. Only they do this.	12
	Modesty is important.	13
	I have seen women with immodest dress at the church	14
	Many Christian women I know do that	17
	Some Christian women I know wear that type of dress, especially in summer time which is very awkward looking	18
	But, many Christian women wear that kind of dresses, even at the church	19
	It is not Christianity. No modesty in the church.	43
	It is not Christianity, but churches tolerate sexual promiscuity.	44
	It is part of American culture which is very bad. Modesty is very important.	45
	Christians practice this even at the church, especially summer time.	47
	I am surprised to see this practice in the church.	49

Q	Comments	Participant Reference Numbers↓
S9	**Q:** Do you believe body piercings and tattoos reflect Christian endorsement? ☐ A encourages them. ☐ B discourages them. ☐ C tolerates them. ☐ D I am not sure. Any comment?	

Q	Comments	Participant Reference Numbers↓
S9	It is a pagan and animistic idea and influence.	1,2
	It is an evil practice	3,5
	I think it is Animism.	4
	I think it is Animism. I do not understand how Christianity can tolerate it. Muslims do not like it	6

Q	Comments	Participant Reference Numbers↓
S9	I think it is a pagan practice and many Christians are having tattoos	7
	I am surprised that many of my Christian friends are having tattoos	8
	I think it is an animistic practice.	13
	I have seen many Christians have tattoos	30
	I see many church-going Christians with piercings	34
	It is an evil practice.	41
	I think it is Animism	43
	Many practicing Christians are having tattoos (disapproves it)	45
	In my opinion it is an evil practice.	49

Q		
E1	**Q:** Do you think the weak voice from some Christian churches in Greater Boston against homosexual practice and same-sex marriage implies silent support and sympathy towards these practices? ❏ Yes. ❏ No. Explain.	

Q	Comments	Participant Reference Numbers↓
E1	Churches should strongly publicly protest. (same sex marriage)	1,2
	Very weak protest from churches; no public protest	3,4,5
	Christians should publicly protest and Muslims will join in protests	6
	There is no public protest from Christian churches and no delegation from churches to their state government.	7
	There is no public protest from the Christian churches. They are compromising	8
	When Christian women protest against this in Kentucky, not many churches came to stand by her.	9
	Churches do not protest strongly in public	10
	Here in America, the separation of the church and state, everyone has their own choice and the State protects this freedom	11
	There is no strong public voice from the churches. We do not know who is supporting and who is not supporting.	12
	Churches are not protesting publicly, while Muslim society condemns that.	13
	Silent approval.	27
	They (Christian churches) do not protest publicly.	41
	There is no protest publicly	44
	Many Christians may not like this, but not any strong public voice	47
	There should be a strong public protest in the street from the churches in Greater Boston.	49

Q		
E2	**Q:** Do you think that Christians teach that living together outside of marriage is OK? ☐ Yes. ☐ No. Any comment?	
Q	**Comments**	**Participant Reference Numbers**↓
E2	When I see many Christians are doing that, then I am convinced that the church tolerates it.	1
	But I am surprised when I see practicing Christians living together.	2
	It is sad that Christians practice it.	3
	Christians tolerate it, very sad.	4
	In many Christian societies in America it is practiced. Churches tolerate that.	5
	Many churches tolerate it. Before marrying, boys and girls date and live together.	6
	Christian pastors (imams) are not strongly teaching about that.	7
	I have many Christian friends who live together. It is sin.	8
	It cannot be in Christian teaching, but many Christians practice it	9
	I get confused when I see my Christian friends practicing this	10
	Many Christians are practicing this.	11,12,15
	Weak voice of Christians	13
	But many Christians practice that (living together) whom I know	16
	Some of my Christian colleagues who are church-going practice that	17
	Many Christians practice that. I know them personally	18
	They may not teach, but they tolerate this bad practice	19
	I am not sure, but I have many Christian friends who practice that	22
	Many Christian families are practicing that.	23,26,28
	Christians tolerate this practice	38
	Many Christians practice this	41
	I am not sure, but many Christians practice it.	43
	Christians are practicing it. Churches are having very weak voices against it. It is very unethical.	45
	Many Christians are doing that	47
	Many Christians practice this and churches also tolerate it.	48
	I am surprised to see Christians are practicing this.	49
	Many Christians practice that. There is no strict discipline in churches in Greater Boston.	50

E3	Q: Do you think that Christians teach that legalized abortion is OK?	
	☐ Yes.	
	☐ No. Any comment?	

Q	Comments	Participant Reference Numbers↓
E3	But, they have the lame excuse that it is a court decision. Church should strongly protest publicly. (abortion)	1
	I think Christianity does not teach that. Christian churches tolerate it	2
	But, Christians accept it.	3
	Do not protest it, in fact many Christians practice it	4
	Because in America, women have more voice. They accept this decision.	5
	Christians do not have a strong voice against it.	6,14
	Many Christians say they are pro life, but not advocating for it much publicly. It is hypocrisy and compromising.	7
	They have weak voices.	8,18
	It is a sin.	9
	I have seen many of my Christian friends are practicing this	10
	It is legalized, so anybody can take the opportunity, but I think abortion is not good.	11
	Christians tolerate it	12
	Christians do not openly protest	17
	Many Christians support that	19
	Christian voices are not strong enough on that issue	26
	Christians tolerate it.	38
	But no strong protest (public) from Christians. I appreciate (those who publicly protest against abortion.)	41
	I am not sure	43
	There is no strong Christian voices.	44
	No strong Christian voice, killing unborn babies.	47
	Many Christians believe that.	48
	While there is no strong public protest, I think Christians tolerate it.	49
	Many Christians have weak voices on this issue.	50

E4	Q: Do you believe it is a Christian practice to approve an unmarried couple becoming parents? ☐ Yes. ☐ No. Any comment?	
Q	**Comments**	**Participant Reference Numbers↓**
E4	It has become a common practice in American culture and this country's culture has Christian influence.	1
	It has become a common practice among many Christians, but among Muslims it is not there. Christian churches are not teaching against it	2
	I know many of my Christian friends live together.	3
	Christian churches tolerate it.	4
	I am surprised when I see many Christians doing that.	5
	Christians do not have a strong voice against it.	6
	I am surprised when I see Christians are practicing this. I have two Christian friends who are not married, but having children.	7
	This is common among Christians.	8
	There is no strict discipline regarding this in Christian churches.	10
	I am confused when I see Christians are practicing that	11
	Many Christians practice it	12
	It may not be a Christian practice, but many Christians are doing that	13
	Many church-going unmarried people are practicing that.	14
	But there is no strong Christian teaching against that	16
	I am not sure about that, but I am surprised when I see some Christians are having babies without marriage	17
	In my neighborhood, I know some Christians are becoming parents outside marriage	18
	There is silent approval. Lot of single mothers in the church	19
	I have seen many Christians having children without marriage	20
	Many of my Christian friends are becoming parents without marriage	22
	It is also practiced in Christian families but less in number	23
	Many church-going Christian couples (are) becoming parents.	26
	It is not the teaching of the Bible, but many Christians practice it	28
	Christian churches have no discipline	38
	Churches tolerate it.	41
	Christians are practicing that. Churches are not taking any disciplinary action.	43
	Many Christians are becoming parents without marriage; it is very bad	45
	I have many Christian friends who practice it	47

Q	Comments Participant Reference Numbers↓	
E4	I do not believe that Christianity teaches, but among Christians it is common.	48
	I don't think Christianity teaches that, but tolerates that.	49
	Christian churches are not encouraging them to marry. Even old age, they are not married.	50

Q	Comments	
E5	**Q:** Do you believe that Christianity approves the common American practice of drinking alcohol and wine at social gatherings? ☐ Yes. ☐ No. Any comment?	

Q	Comments Participant Reference Numbers↓	
E5	Even at the church, many Christians bring alcohol.	1
	It is a common practice for socialization	3
	It is not Christianity, but a common practice for Christians in America	4
	Christians when they gather, drink alcohol	6
	Without alcohol, no social gathering, even among church people it is going on.	7
	For socialization, alcohol is important here in America.	8
	In my experience at a church gathering it was practiced	12
	It is a cultural practice and has become a custom	15
	It is not related with Christianity or any religious practice	31
	It is customary	41
	Even at the church, Christians drink wine and alcohol	47
	Christians practice this	49

Q	Comments	
E6	**Q:** Do you think the recent ruling of the Supreme Court, legalizing homosexual marriage throughout the United States was a result of Christian (Church) influence? ☐ Yes, strongly influenced by Christian church. ☐ No, it is a secular court. Any comment?	

Q	Comments Participant Reference Numbers↓	
E6	Church should have a strong voice to protest this decision	1,12
	There is no protest against this ruling (supreme court, gay marriage)	2,3
	Christians have very weak voices to publicly protest .	4,5
	Christian churches are reluctant on this issue. They could publicly protest it, even in front of the Supreme Court.	6
	In Washington DC, I know some Christian lobbyists are in favor of this (gay marriage)	7

Q	Comments	Participant Reference Numbers↓
E6	Christian churches do not have a strong public voice	8
	It is a liberal court (Supreme Court). It is a legal matter.	24
	Churches could protest it publicly	41,49
	Churches should protest it publicly	44
	Christians should come out at the street and protest	47

Appendix E
Glossary

Definitions

Islam: John L. Esposito in *The Oxford Dictionary of Islam* defines the term Islam: "The term Islam is derived from the Arabic root s-l-m, which means submission or peace." (Esposito 2003, 144)

> John Bowker defines the term *Islam* in *The Oxford Dictionary of World Religion*:
>
> The religion of allegiance to God and to his prophet Muhammad, the religion (*din*) which God always intended for his creation, but which is derived in its present form from the prophetic ministry of Muhammad (c.570–632), and the revelation mediated through him, the Qur'an. (Bowker 1977, 479)

John L. Esposito describes the term *Muslim* in *The Oxford Dictionary of Islam:*

> **Muslim:** One who submits to the will of God. The plural form, *muslimun*, refers to the collective body of those who adhere to the Islamic faith and thus belong to the Islamic community of believers (ummah). To demonstrate that one has become a Muslim, one must recite the *shahadah*, witnessing that there is no God but Allah and Muhammad is the messenger of God. The English term *Muslim* is used as an adjective attributing religious characteristics (e.g., Muslim faith), whereas *Islamic* generally connotes broader cultural meanings (e.g., Islamic art, Islamic literature). (Esposito 2003, 217)

Hadith: John Esposito in the *Oxford Dictionary of Islam* points out:

> **Hadith:** Report of the words and deeds of Muhammad and other early Muslims; considered an authoritative source of revelation, second only to the Quran (sometimes referred

to as sayings of the Prophet). Hadith (pl. *ahadith*; *hadith* is used as a singular or a collective term in English) were collected, transmitted, and taught orally for two centuries after Muhammad's death and then began to be collected in written form and codified. They serve as a source of biographical material for Muhammad, contextualization of Quranic revelations, and Islamic law. (Esposito 2003, 101)

Christianity: Christianity is the religion of Christians who believe in Jesus Christ as the Son of God and spiritual Savior. It is a religion based on the life and teachings of Jesus contained in the Bible and related beliefs and practices.

A Christian is defined by Trent C. Butler in the *Holman Bible Dictionary*:

> **Christian:** an adherent of Christ; one committed to Christ; a follower of Christ. Believers ... were called Christians because their behavior, activity, and speech were like Christ. ... A Christian is one ... whose daily life and behavior ... is like Christ. (Butler 1991, 252)

Angelo Di Berardino points out in the *Encyclopedia of Ancient Christianity*: " ...from the name 'Christian,' the apologists drew positive expositions of the connection between the philological meaning of the word 'good, beneficent' and 'their style of life'." (Angelo 1994–2013, 504)

Gospel: M. Eugene Boring describes the etymology and defines the term gospel:

> **Gospel:** The modern English word *gospel* is derived from the old English *g'odspel,* a combination of g'od (good) and *spel or spiel* (news, tidings). The ambiguity of its later written form led to a false etymological explanation of *g'odspel* in terms of "God" and "story, narrative," as though the English word meant "a story about God." In the New Testament, gospel is never used for a written document, but is the comprehensive term for the good news of God's saving act in Jesus Christ, communicated in a variety of images and concepts. (Boring 2007, 629)

South Asia: South Asia is located in the southern part of Asia and is comprised of seven countries: India, Pakistan, Bangladesh, Sri Lanka, Nepal, Bhutan, and Maldives. South Asians are people who are geographically located in or have emigrated from these seven countries.

South Asian Muslims: Muslims from South Asian countries (India, Bangladesh, Pakistan, Nepal, Bhutan, Sri Lanka, Maldives). Of the seven countries in South Asia, only Pakistan, Bangladesh, and Maldives are predominantly Muslim. The others include Muslims in their population.

NGO: An abbreviation which stands for "Non-Governmental Organization." Peter Willets, Professor of Global Politics, City University, London in his article, "What Is a Non-Governmental Organization," stated:

> The term, "non-governmental organization" or NGO, came into currency in 1945 because of the need for the UN to differentiate in its Charter between participation rights for intergovernmental specialized agencies and those for international private organizations. At the UN, virtually all types of private bodies can be recognized as NGOs. They only have to be independent from government control, not seeking to challenge governments either as a political party or by a narrow focus on human rights, non-profit-making and non-criminal. (Willets 1996, 1)

Surah: Arabic word which is translated as chapter of the Qur'an. John L. Esposito points out, "Usually translated as 'chapter.' The Qur'an is divided into 114 surahs, arranged by descending length rather than chronological order." (Esposito 2003, 307)

Sunna or Sunnah: Traditional account of what Muhammad did and said. It is an established belief-custom. Timothy C. Tennent defines *Sunna*: "In Islam, a reference to the examples of the Prophet which give guidance to the Islamic community and eventually were written down in collections known as Hadith and which inform Islamic law (Shari'ah)." (Tennent 2002, 256)

Shirk: The Arabic word translated as unpardonable sin. Timothy C. Tennent defines the word *Shirk*, "A grievous sin in Islam referring to polytheism or attributing 'partners' to Allah." (Tennent 2002, 256)

Shariah or Shari'ah: The Arabic term refers to Islamic law. Bruce A. McDowell and Anees Zaka describe shariah as, "The constitution of the Islamic community, the divine will applied to every situation in life." (McDowell and Zaka 1999, 302)

Tahrif: The Arabic word means corruption of the text. Norman L. Geisler and Abdul Saleeb define Tahrif as, "The Islamic doctrine that the original text of the Bible has been corrupted." (Geisler and Saleeb 1993, 315)

Caliph: The Arabic word translated as ruler. John Esposito states caliph is a "Term adopted by dynastic rulers of the Muslim world, referring to the successor to the Prophet Muhammad as the political-military ruler of Muslim community." (Esposito 2003, 49)

Sunni: The term derives from the Arabic word Sunna (see above). One of the major sects or branches of Islam. John L. Esposito defines the word Sunni:

> The name is derived from the Sunnah, the exemplary behavior of the Prophet. All Muslims are guided by Sunnah, but Sunnis stress it, as well as consensus (ijma; the full name of Sunnis is Ahl al-Sunnah wa'l-ijma, people of the Sunnah and consensus). (Esposito 2003, 306)

Shi'ite: The party of Ali, Muhammad's son-in-law and the fourth caliph of Islam; one of the main branches or sects of Islam. Norman L. Geisler and Abdul Saleeb describe this group as "The major Islamic sect that believes, in contrast to Sunnis, that Muhammad's son-in-law, Ali, was the true successor to Muhammad in the leadership of the Islamic community." (Geisler and Saleeb 1993, 314)

Sufism: Islamic mysticism. Phil Parshall defines Sufism as " …the embracive influence of mysticism within Islam." (Parshall 2002, 26)

BIBLIOGRAPHY

Abdalati, Hammudah. 1975. *Islam in Focus*. Indianapolis: American Trust Publications.

Abdul-Haqq, Abdiyah Akbar. 1980. *Sharing your Faith with a Muslim*. Minneapolis, MN: Bethany House.

Ahmad, Aziz. 1964. *Studies in Islamic Culture in the Indian Environment*. Oxford: Clarendon.

Ahmad, Ghulam Mirza. 2003. "Jesus in India." *Islam International Publications*. Accessed Sept. 26, 2016. http://www.alislam.org/library/books/Jesus_in_india/index.html/.

Ajijola, Alhaj A. D. 1978. *The Essence of Faith in Islam*. Lahore, Pakistan: Islamic Publications.

Ali, Khan. 2016. "How is Cultural Integration Defined?" *Qura Blog*, April 29. Accessed April 29, 2017. https://www.quora.com/How-is-cultural-integration-defined.

Ali, Yusuf Abdullah. 2000. *The Holy Qur'an: English Translation, Commentary and Notes with Full Arabic Text*. Ware, Hertfordshire: Wordsworth Editions.

Alix, Philippon. 2012. "When Sufi Tradition Reinvents Islamic Modernity. The Minhaj-ul Qur'an, a Neo-Sufi order in Pakistan." In *South Asian Sufis: Devotion, Deviation, and Destiny*, edited by Clinton Bennett and Charles M. Ramsey, 111–21. Bloomsbury: Bloomsbury Publishing.

American Anthropological Association. 1974. "Acculturation and Assimilation: A Clarification," *American Ethnologist* 1, no. 2 (October):351–67. Accessed May 4, 2017. http://users.clas.ufl.edu/ marilynm/Theorizing_Black_America_Syllabus_ files/Acculturation_ and_Assimilation_A_Clarification.pdf.

American Heritage College Dictionary. 1993. "Prejudice." Accessed Feb. 13, 2017. https:www.thoughtco.com/what-is-racial-prejudice2834953.

Andrae, Tor. 1960. *Muhammad the Man and His Faith*. New York: Harper and Row.

Answering-Islam.org. 2014. "Why Do Muslims Believe the Text of the Bible Has Been Corrupted?" Accessed Feb. 27, 2017. http://www. answeringislam.org /Bible/jrwhy.html.

Anwar, Zeenat. 1995. "But we are Americans Now! Our youth, our families and our future." In *At Home in the Hijra South Asian Muslims in the United States*, edited by Yvone Yazbeck Haddad, 252. Florida: University Press.

Asani, Ali S. 2005. "Sunni Islam." In *Encyclopedia of Religion*, 2nd edition, vol. 7, edited by Lyndsey Jones, 4644. Detroit, MI: Thomson Gale.

Attride-Stirrling, Jennifer. 2001. "Thematic networks: an analytic tool for qualitative research." *Sage Publication* 1, no. 3 (December):385–405. Accessed Jan. 12, 2016. https://www.researchgate.net/ publication/249730897_Thematic_ Networks_An_Analytic_Tool_for_ Qualitative_Research.

Azumah, John. 2008. *My Neighbour's Faith: Islam Explained for Christians*. Grand Rapids, MI: Zondervan.

Baker's Evangelical Dictionary of Biblical Theology. 1996. "Homosexuality." Accessed April 5, 2017. http://www. Biblestudytools.com/dictionaries/ bakers-evangelical-dictionary/homosexuality.html.

Bechtel, Kenneth J.1996. "Women's Rights in the American Century." UMBC Center for History Education. Accessed April 2017. http://www.umbc.edu/che/tahlessons/lessondisplay.php?lesson=71.

Bell, Richard and William Montgomery Watt. 1970. *Introduction to the Qur'an*. Edinburgh: University Press.

Bennett, Clinton and Charles M. Ramsey, eds. 2012. *South Asian Sufis: Devotion, Deviation, and Destiny*. Bloomsbury: Bloomsbury Publishing.

Berry, J. W., and D. L. Sam. 2015. "Multicultural Societies." In *the Oxford Handbook of Multicultural Identity*, edited by Veronica Benet-Martinez and Ying-Y Hong, 103. New York: Oxford University Press.

Billion Bibles.org. "Tahrif." 2017. Accessed Feb. 28, 2017, http://www.billionbibles.org/sharia/tahrif.html.

Blessing, Michelle. 2010. "Meaning of Family." *Lifestyle Blog*. Accessed April 2017. http://family.lovetoknow.com/about-family-values/meaning-family.

Bongoyok, Moussa. 2008. "Islam and Receptivity to Jesus." In *From Seed to Fruit*, edited by J. Dudley Woodberry, 297–310. Pasadena: William Carey Library.

Boring, M. Eugene. 2007. "Gospel." In *The New Interpreter's Dictionary of the Bible*, vol. 2, edited by Katharine Doob Sakenfeld, 629. Nashville, TN: Abingdon Press.

Bowker, John, ed. 1977. "Sufis." In *Oxford Dictionary of World Religions*. Oxford: Oxford University Press.

Braswell, George W. 1996. *Islam: Its Prophet, People, Politics and Power*. Nashville, TN: Broadman and Holman.

Bridge Initiative, Georgetown University. 2015. "What is Islamophobia?" Accessed April 4, 2017. http://bridge.georgetown.edu/what-is-islamophobia.

Bukhari. *Hadith*. 1970. Riyadh, Saudi Arabia: Darussalam.

—. *Hadith*. 1970. Riyadh, Saudi Arabia: Darussalam.

Butler, Trent C., ed. 2003. *Holman Illustrated Bible Dictionary*. Tennessee: Holman Bible Publishers.

Cagaptay, Soner. 2010. "Muslims vs. Islamists." *Hurriyet Daily*, January 27. Accessed April 12, 2017. http://www.washingtoninstitute.org/policy-analysis/view/muslims -vs.-islamists.

Caner, Mehmet Ergun, and Emir Fethi Caner. 2002. *Unveiling Islam*. Grand Rapids: Kregel.

Center for Race and Gender, University of California. 2016. "Defining 'Islamophobia," *Islamophobia Studies Journal* 3, no. 2 (Spring): unpaginated. Accessed April 14, 2017. https://crg.berkeley.edu/research-projects/islamophobia-research-documentation-project/.

Cesari, Jocelyne, ed. 2007. "Ahmadiyya movement" In *Encyclopedia of Islam in the United States*. West Port: Grandwood Press.

Chastain, Warren. 1981. "On Turning Muslim Stumbling Blocks into Stepping Stones." In *Perspectives on the World Christian Movement*, edited by Ralph D. Winter and Steven C. Hawthrone, 145–48. Pasadena, CA: William Carey Library.

Chowdhuri, Halim Flora. 2009. "Bengali, Bangladeshi yet Muslims." In *Living our Religions: Hindu and Muslims South Asian American Women Narrate Their Experience,* edited by Anjana Narayan and Bandana Purkayastha, 220–21. Virginia: Kumran Press.

Collins Dictionary.com. "Sectarianism." Accessed Oct. 25, 2017. https://www.collinsdictionary.com/us/dictionary/english/sectarianism.

Congressional Reference Service Report: The Islamic Traditions of Wahhabism and Salafiyya, 110th Congress, 2008, Rs21695.

Cragg, Kenneth. 1959. *Sandals at the Mosque.* London: SCM.

Craig, William Lane. "The Concept of God in Islam and Christianity." Lecture, Annual Convention of the National Religious Broadcasters, Reasonable Faith, Nashville, TN, September 18, 2007.

Di Berandino, Angelo. 2014. *Encyclopedia of Ancient Christianity.* Accessed March 18, 2017. https://www.ivpress.com/encyclopedia-of-ancient-christianity.

Dictionary.com. "Sectarianism." Accessed Oct. 25, 2017. http://www.dictionary.com/browse/sectarianism.

Douglas, Cathy. 2010. "Examining America's Cultural Values: Individualism." *Nayajeevan,* July. Accessed Feb. 2, 2017. http://www.nayajeevan.org/index.php?option=com_content&view=article&id=25:examining-americas-cultural-values-individualism&catid=3:articles&Itemid=8.

Duran, Khalid, and Daniel Pipes. 2002. "Face of American Islam: Muslim Immigrants." *Middle East Forum.* Accessed May 2016. www.danielpipes/441/faces-muslim-immigration.

Ellis, Carl. 2001. "Islam and African American Community." In *The Gospel for Islam,* edited by Roy Oksnevad and Dotsey Welliver, 39. Wheaton: EMIS, a division of the Billy Graham Center.

Elwell, Walter A., ed. 1996. *Baker's Evangelical Dictionary of Biblical Theology.* Accessed May12, 2017. www.biblestudytools.com/dictionaries/bakers … dictionary/homosexuality.html.

Esposito, John L., ed. 2003. *The Oxford Dictionary of Islam*: Oxford: University Press.

Farlex Dictionary of Idioms. 2015. "Public Display of Affection." Accessed April 24, 2017. http://idioms.thefreedictionary.com/ public+display+of+affection.

"FBI: Hate Crimes Spike Sharply Against Muslims." Ansari Azadeh, aired November 2016, on Cable News Network, accessed April 28, 2017. http://www.cnn.com/2016/11/14/us/fbi-hate-crime-report-muslims/.

Frontline Analysis. 2014. "Saudi Time Bomb?" PBS, interview with Mai Yamani, Vali Nasr, Maher Hathout, and Ahmed Ali. Aired November 15 on WGBH. Accessed Feb. 12, 2017, http://www.pbs.org/wgbh/pages/ frontline/shows/saudi/ analyses/.

Geisler, Norman L., and Abdul Saleeb. 1993. *Answering Islam: The Crescent in the Light of the Cross*. Grand Rapids, MI: Baker Book House.

George, Timothy. 2002. *Is the Father of Jesus the God of Muhammad?* Grand Rapids, MI: Zondervan.

Ghattas, Rauf, and Carol B. Ghattas. 2009. *A Christian Guide to the Qur'an*. Grand Rapids, MI: Kregel.

Gilchrist, John. 1999. *Facing the Muslim Challenge: A Handbook of Christian-Muslim Apologetics*. Claremont/Cape Town, South Africa: Life Challenge Africa.

—1999. "Origins and Sources of the Gospel of Barnabas." *Answeringislam. com*. Accessed Aug. 26, 2016. http://www.answering-islam.org/ Gilchrist/barnabas.html.

—1988. *The Textual History of the Qur'an and the Bible*. Villach, Austria: Light of Life.

Goddard, Hugh. 1996. *Muslim Perceptions of Christianity.* London: Grey Seal.

—1994. "Modern Pakistani and Indian Muslim Perceptions of Christianity." *Islam and Christian- Muslim Relations* 5, no. 2):165–68.

Gowing, Peter G., and William Henry Scott, eds. 1971. *Acculturation in Philippines.* Quezon City, Philippines: New Day.

Gracy, Celeste, and Jeremy Weber. 2014. "World Vision Reverse Decision to Hire Christians Same-Sex Marriages." *Christianity Today,* March. Accessed Sept. 25, 2016. http://www. christianitytoday.com/ct/2014/March-web-only/world-vision-reverse-decision-gay-same-sex-marriage-html.

Granfield, David. 1969. *The Abortion Decision.* Garden City, NY: Doubleday.

Green, Samuel. 2004. "The Gospel of Barnabas." *Answering-Islam. org.* Accessed 26 June, 2016. http://www.answering-islam.org/Green/barnabas.html.

Griffin, Aurora C. 2011. "The Philosophical Argument for Life." *The Harvard Crimson Blog.* Accessed June 14, 2017, http://www.thecrimeson.com/article/2011/11/29/abortion-fetus-logic-natural/.

Haar, ter Gerrie, ed. 2011. Religion and Development: *Ways of Transforming the World.* London: C. Hurst.

Haddad, Wadi Z. 1995. "A Tenth-Century Speculative Theologian's Refutation of the Basic Doctrines of Christianity: Al-Baqillani (d. A. D. 1013)." In *Christian-Muslim Encounters,* edited by Yvonne Yazbeck Haddad and Wadi Z. Haddad, 82–94. Florida: University Press.

Hanson, John H. 2007. "Jihad and the Ahmadiyya Muslim Community: Nonviolent Effects to Promote Islam in the Contemporary World." *Nova Religio: The Journal Alternative and Emergent Religions* 11, no. 2

(November):77–93. Accessed January 2017. http://www.jstor.org/stable/10.1525/nr.2007.11.2.77.

Hashmi, Arshi Saleem. 2012. "Issues of Women's Rights in South Asia." *SA Global Affairs Blog.* Accessed April 13, 2017. http://www.ndu.edu.pk/fcs/CVs/arshi_cv.pdf.

Hayek, Michael. 1961. *Al-Masih Fial-Islam.* Beirut, Lebanon: Catholic Press.

Hermansen, Mercia, and Mahruq F. Khan. 2009. "South Asian Muslim American Girl Power: Structures and Symbols of Control and Self-Expression." *Journal of International Women's Studies* 11, no. 3/7 (November):89. Accessed April 4, 2017, http://vc.bridgew.edu/ehi/viewcontent.cgi?article=1150&context=jiws.

Hesselgrave, David J. 1991. *Communication Christ Cross Culturally.* Grand Rapids, MI: Zondervan.

Hiebert, Paul G. 2001. *Anthropological Reflections on Missiological Issues.* Grand Rapids: MI: Baker Books.

Hobbs, Herchel H. 1971. *The Baptist Faith and Message.* Nashville, TN: Convention Press.

Ibrahim, Alhojailan Mohammad. 2012. "Thematic Analysis: A critical Review of its Process and Evaluation." *West East Journal of Social Sciences* 1, no.1 (December):39–46. Accessed June 2016. http://fac.ksu.edu.sa/sites/ default/files/ta_thematic_analysis-dr_mohammad-alhojailan.

Islam, Maidul. 2012. "Limits of Islamism: Ideological Articulations of Jama't-e-Islami in Contemporary India and Bangladesh." DPhil Thesis. University of Oxford.

Jadeed, Iskandar. 2010. *The Gospel of Barnabas: A False Testimony.* Rikon, Switzerland: Good Way.

Jones, Lindsey. 2005. *Encyclopedia of Religion*, 2nd ed. Accessed Sept. 10, 2016. http://isites.havard.edu/fs/does/icb.topic 980619.files/ asian%20 islam%20in%20south%.

Kabir, Shahriar. "The Ultimate Jihad." 2013. DVD, *Bangladesh, South Asian People's Union against Fundamentalism and Communalism, Impress Telefilm*. Accessed Feb. 10, 2017, http://www.youtube.com/ watch?v=qarRpm9ltmy.

Kane, Herbert J. 1978. *A Concise History of the Christian World Mission*. Grand Rapids, MI: Baker Book.

Keay, John. 2000. *India: A History*. New York: Atlantic Monthly Press.

Khalidi, Tarif., ed. 2001. *The Muslim Jesus*. Cambridge: Harvard University.

Khan, Ismail Muhammad. 2011. "The Assertion of Barelvi Extremism." *Hudson Institute*. Accessed March 10, 2017. www.hudson.org/ research/9848-the-assertion-of-barelvi-extremism.

Khan, Mussarat, and Kathryn Ecklund. 2012. "Attitudes Toward Muslim Americans Post-9/11." *Journal of Muslim Mental Health* 7, no.1:1–16. Accessed May 24, 2017, http://quod.lib.umich.edu/cgi/p/pod/dod-idx/ attitudes-toward-muslim-americans.

Khan, Zafarul-Islam. 2013. "Sectarianism and its local and regional complexities—a South Asian Perspective." *Milli Gazette*, April. Accessed March 12, 2017. http://www.milligazette.com/ news/6778-communalism-in-south-asia.

Kramer, Martin. 2003. "Coming to Terms: Fundamentalists or Islamists?" *Middle East Quarterly*10, no. 2, Spring. Accessed Feb. 12, 2017. http://www.meforum.org/541/coming-to-terms-fundamentalists-or-islamists#ftnref4.

Lawson, Todd. 1991. "The Crucifixion of Jesus in the Qur'an and the Qur'anic Commentary: A History of Survey Part." *Bulletin of Henry Martin Institute of Islamic Studies* 10, no. 2: 43–62.

—2009. *The Crucifixion and the Qur'an: A Study in the History of Muslim Thought.* Oxford: Oneworld.

Levitt, Peggy. 2007. *God Needs No Passport.* New York: New Press.

Lindsell, Harold, ed. 1971. *Harper Study Bible.* (Revised Standard Version, revised edition). Grand Rapids, MI: Zondervan.

Lipka, Michael, and John Gramlich. 2017. "5 facts about abortion." *Fact Tank, Pew Research Center,* January. Accessed Feb. 1, 2017. http://www.pewresearch.org/fact-tank/2017/01/26/5-facts-about-abortion/.

Londsdale, Laura Ragg, ed. 1907. *The Gospel of Barnabas.* Oxford: Clarendon Press.

Lopez, Raquel. 2012. "Perspective on Abortion: Pro-choice, Pro-Life, and What Lies in between." *European Journal of Social Science* 27, no. 4 (January):511–17. Accessed May 10, 2017. https://pdfs.semanticscholar.org/bbc/b17b6616460 d58ecb0efable31da8507329a.pdf.

Lukes, Steven M. 1971. "The Meaning of Individualism." *Journal of the History of Ideas* 32, no. 1 (January to March):45–46. Accessed April 26, 2017. https://www.jstor.org/stable/2708324?seq=1#page_scan_tab_contents.

Luzbetak, Louis J. 1963. *The Church and the Culture.* Techny, IL: Divine Word.

Masih, Abd Al. 1996. *The Main Challenges for Committed Christians in Serving Muslims.* Villace, Austria: Light of Life.

Masri, Fouad. 2014. *Connecting with Muslims.* Downers Grove, IL: IVP Books.

Masud, Kazi Anwarul. 2015. "Communalism and India." *South Asia Analysis Group Blog.* Accessed Feb. 21, 2017. http:?www.southasiaanalysis.org/node/1711.

McDowell, Bruce A., and Anees Zaka. 1999. *Muslims and Christians at the Table.* New Jersey: P&R Publishing.

McNee, Peter. 1976. *Crucial Issues in Bangladesh.* Pasadena, CA: William Carey Library.

Meacham, Jon. 2009. "Culture: The End of Christian America." *Newsweek,* April 4. Accessed April 6, 2017, http://www.newsweek.com/meacham-end-christian-america-77125.

Merriam-Webster Student Dictionary and Thesaurus. 1996. "Family." Accessed April 26, 2017, http:www.merriam-webster.com/dictionary/family.

Merriam-Webster Dictionary.com 2017. "Acculturation." Accessed May 6, 2017. https://www.merriamwebster.com/dictionary/acculturation.

—2017. "Assimilation." Accessed Feb. 18, 2017. http://www.merriam-webster.com/dictionary/assimilation.

—2017. "Docetism." Accessed Jan. 25, 2017. http://www.merriam-webster.com/dictionary/docetism.

—2017. "Family." Accessed Jan. 29, 2017. http://www.merriam-webster.com/dictionary/family.

—2017. "Individualism." Accessed Jan. 30, 2017. http://www.merriam-webster.com/dictionary/individualism.

—2017. "Sociology." Accessed Oct. 21, 2017, http://www.merriam-webster.com/dictionary/sociology.

Milad, Milani. 2011. "Representations of Jesus in Islamic Mysticism: Defining the Sufi Jesus." *Literature & Aesthetics* 21, no. 2:59. Accessed March 2017. http://openjournals.library.usyd.edu.au/index.php/LA/article/viewFile/5761/6460.

Mohammad-Arif, Aminah. 2002. *Salaam America: South Asian Muslims in New York*. London: Wimbledon Publishing.

Mohler, R. Albert 2017. "The Gathering Storm: Religious Liberty in the Wake of the Sexual Revolution." *twitter.com/albertmohler*, March 21, 2017. Accessed April 4, 2017. https://albertmohler.com/2017/03/21/gathering-storm-religious-liberty-wake-sexual-revolution/.

Morey, Robert A. 1992. *The Islamic Invasion: Confronting the World's Fastest Growing Religion*. Oregon: Harvest House.

Morris, William, ed. 1978. *The American Heritage Dictionary of the English Language*. Atlanta: Houghton Mifflin.

Mowdudi, Abu'l A'la. 1992. *Towards Understanding of the Qur'an* (vol. 2). Leister: Islamic Foundation.

Mozaffari, Mehdi. 2007. "What is Islamism? History and Definition of Concept," abstract, *Totalitarian Movements and Political Religions* 8, no. 1 (February):17–33. Accessed March 24, 2017. https://www.researchgate.net/publication/ 249036288_what_is_islam_History_and_Definition_ of_a_Concept.

Mufasir, Sulaiman Shahid. 1980. *Jesus, A Prophet of Islam*. Indianapolis: American Trust Publications.

Murphy, Carle. 2015. "Most U.S. Christian groups grow more accepting of homosexuality." Pew Research, *Factank: News in the numbers,* December 18. Accessed March 12, 2017. http://www.pewresearch.org/fact-tank/2015/12/18/most-u-s-christian-groups-grow-more-accepting-of-homosexuality/.

Nasr, Hossein Sayyed. 2009. "We and you Let us meet in God's Love: Christians and Muslims are both beckoned by their respective religions to seek peace." *Islamica* 21 no. 69. London: Islamic Society, London School of Economics and Political Science.

Nazir-Ali, Michael. 1987. *Frontiers in Muslim-Christian Encounter.* Oxford: Regnum Books.

Nicholson, Reynold A. 1996. *The Idea of Personality in Sufism.* Delhi: Idarah-i-Adabiyat-i-Delhi.

Nurbakhsh, Javad. 1983. *Jesus in the Eyes of the Sufis.* New York: Khaniqahi Nimatullahi Publications.

O' Brian, Matthew. 2016. "The Important Difference Between Assimilation and Integration." Immigrationreform.com Blog, September 29. Accessed Oct. 28, 2017. http://immigrationreform.com/2016/09/29/the-important-difference-between-assimilation-and-integration/.

Omar, Irfan A. 1996. ed. 2007. *A Muslim View of Christianity: Essays on Dialogue by Mahmoud Ayoub.* Maryknoll, New York: Orbis Books.

Parshall, Phil. 1983. *Bridges to Islam.* Grand Rapids, MI: Baker Book House.

Patel, Aakar. 2012. "Pakistan's Blasphemy Law." *Express Tribune,* August 26. Accessed Feb. 28, 2017. http://tribune.com.Pk/story/426498/Pakistans-blasphemy-law/.

Paul, Smith. 2013. "A British Agent." *Facebook,* April 25. Accessed April 15, 2017. https://www.facebook.com/ouralahazrat/posts/101520 09125621095.

Pew Research Center. 2013. "Tablighi Jama'at." *Religion and Public Life,* September 15. Accessed April 28, 2017. http://www.pewforum.org/2010/09/15/muslim-networks -and-movements-in-western-europe -tablighi-jamaat/.

—2013. "Kings Dream remains an Elusive Goal; Many Americans see Racial Disparities." *Social and Demographic Trends*, August 22. Accessed April 28, 2017. http://www.pewsocialtrends.org/2013/08/22/kings-dream-remains-an-elusive-goal-many-americans-see-racial-disparities/.

—2015. "America's Changing Religious Landscape." *Religion and Public Life,* May 12. Accessed April 29, 2017. http://www.pewforum.org/2015/05/12/americans-changing-religions-landscape/.

—2015. "The American Family Today." *Social and Demographic Trends*, December 17. Accessed April 27, 2017. http://www.pewsocialtrends.org/2015/12/17/1-the American-family-today/.

Piper, John. 2014. "World Vision: Adultery No, Homosexual Practice Yes." *Desiring God*, March 25. Accessed Oct. 20, 2016, http://www.desiringgod.org/blog/ posts/world-vision-adultery-no-homosexual-practice.yes/.

—2013. "We Know They Are Killing Children—All of Us Know." *Desiring God*, January 22. Accessed April 3, 2017. https://www.desiringgod.org/articles/we-know-they-are-killing-children-all-of-us-know.

Plummer, Robert L. 2010. *40 Questions about Interpreting the Bible*. Grand Rapids, MI: Kregel Publications.

Pluralism Project, Harvard University. 2009. "Islam in Greater Boston." Accessed February 2017, http://pluralism.org/landscape/boston/islam.

—2009. "World Religions in Greater Boston." Accessed April 15, 2010, http://id.lib.harvard.edu/aleph/012320343/catalog.

Poston, Larry. 1992. *Islamic Da'wah in the West: Muslim Missionary Activity and the Dynamics of Conversion to Islam*. Oxford: Oxford University Press.

Puri, Luv. 2009. "The Past and the Future of Deobandism." *Combating Terrorism Center,* November 3. Accessed Feb. 17, 2017. https://www.ctc.usma.edu/posts/the-past-and-future-of-deobandi-islam.

Purkayastha, Bandana. 2009. "Conclusion: Human Rights, Religious, Gender." In *Living our Religions: Hindu and Muslim South Asian American women narrate their experiences.* Edited by Anjana Narayan and Bandana Purkayastha, 73. Virginia: Kumran Press.

Richard, Lawrence O. 1982. *Illustrated Bible Handbook.* Nashville: Thomas Nelson.

Roy, Olivier. 1994. *The Failure of Political Islam.* Cambridge, Massachusetts: Harvard University Press.

Saal, William J. 1998. *Reaching Muslims for Christ.* Chicago: Moody Press.

Sayed, Ibrahim B. 2012. "Same Sex Marriage and Marriage in Islam." *Islamic Research Foundation International Inc.* Accessed Feb. 22, 2017. http://www.irfi.org/ articles/articles_151_200/same_sex_marriage_and_marriage_i.html/.

Schaff, Philip. 1910. *History of the Christian Church*, vol. 3. Grand Rapids, MI: Eerdmans.

Schwartz, Seth J., Jennifer B. Unger, Byron L. Zamboanga, and Jose Szapocznik. 2010. "Rethinking the Concept of Acculturation Implications for Theory and Research." *Am Psychol, Journal of PubMed Central* 65, no. 4 (July): 237–51. Accessed May 3, 2017. https://miami.pure.elsevier.com/en/publications/rethinking-the-concept-of-acculturation-implications-for-theory-and-research.

Sell, Randall L. 1997. "Defining and Measuring Sexual Orientation for Research." *Springer Link* 26, no. 6 (December):643–58. Accessed May 12, 2017. http://eknygos.Ismuni.it/springer/686/355–74pdf.

Sevea, Iqbal Singh. 2012. *The political Philosophy of Muhammad Iqbal: Islam and Nationalism in late Colonial India.* Cambridge: University Press.

Shenk, David W. 1981. "The [Sufi] Mystical Orders in Popular Islam." Unpublished paper.

Shushtery, A. M. A. 1938. *Outline of Islamic Culture*. Bangalore, India: Bangalore Press.

Sikand, Yogindar. 2007. "The Tablighi Jama't in Bangladesh." *South Asia: Journal of South Asia Studies* 22, no. 1 (May 8):101–23. Accessed Feb. 22, 2017. http://www.tandfonline.com/doi/abs/10.1080/00856409908723362.

—2000. "Islam And Caste Inequality Among Indian Muslims." Countercurrents.org, February 15. Accessed April 11, 2017. http://countercurrents.org.sikand150204.html/.

Singh, Rajib. 2014. "Bhakti and Sufi Movement in India." Important India.com, January 17. Accessed March January 20, 2017. http://www.importantindia.com/9517/bhakti-and-sufi-movement-in-india/.

Small, Luis Mario. 2009. "Ethnography." *Sage Journal* 10, no. 1 (March 1):5–38. Accessed Feb. 12, 2017. http://journal.sagepub.com/doi/pdf/10.1177/1466 13810809 95861963.small%20M.%20L.%20L.%20 (2009)%20How%2.

Smith, Cantwell Wilfred. 1957. *Islam in the Modern History*. New York: American Library Mentor Books.

Smith, Jane I. 1999. *Islam in America*. New York: Columbia University Press.

Southern Poverty Law Center. 2010. "Ten Ways to Fight Hate: A Community Response Guide," February 15. Accessed April 26, 2017. https://www.splcenter.org/ sites/default/files/d6_legacy_files/downloads/publication/ten_ways_to_fight_hate_2010.pdf.

Stand ford Encyclopedia of Philosophy. 2013. "Liberal Feminism." Accessed April 20, 2017. https://plato.stanford.edu/entries/feminism-liberal/.

Subhan, John A. 1938. *Sufism: Its Saints and Shrines*. Lucknow: Lucknow Publishing.

Sweetman, J. W. 1954. *Islam and Christian Theology*. London: Lutterworth Press.

Tennent, Timothy C. 2002. *Christianity at the Religious Roundtable: Evangelism in Conversation with Hinduism, Buddhism, and Islam*. Grand Rapids, MI: Baker Academic.

The Free Dictionaries by Farlex. "Cohabitation." Accessed May 14, 2017, http://www.the freedictionay.com/cohabitation.

Upadhyay. R. 2010. "The Legacy of Sayed Ahmad Barelvi in India." *Eurasia Review: News and Analysis*, October 30. Accessed March 11, 2017. http://www. eurasiareview.com/30102010-the-legacy -of-syed-ahmad-barelvi-in-india/.

Voskuil, Dennis N. 1987. "Individualism and Evangelism in America." Accessed Oct. 22, 2017. https://repository.westernsem.edu/pkp/index. php/rr/article/download/ 1088/1180.

Wacker, Grant. 2000. "Religious Liberalism and the Modern Crisis of Faith." *National Humanities Center, Duke University Divinity School*. Accessed Nov. 6, 2017. http://nationalhumanitiescenter.org/tserve/ twenty/tkeyinfo/liberal.html/.

Webster's New Universal Unabridged Dictionary. 2nd ed.. 1979. New York: Simon and Schuster.

Welch, Alford. 1977. "Death and Dying in the Qur'an." In *Religious Encounters with Death*, edited by Frank E. Reynolds and Earl H. Waugh. University Park, 183–89. Pennsylvania: Pennsylvania State University Press.

Woods, Martin. 2011. "Interviewing for Research and Analysing Qualitative Data: An Overview." Accessed Feb. 12,1917. https://

pdfs.semanticscholar.org/e45e/ ef2aa012980d773daef54f137d2ff4 9c44ba.pdf.

Younkins, Edward W. 1998. "Individualism and Freedman: Vital Pillars of True Communities." FEE Foundation for Economic Education Blog, January 1. Accessed on March 23, 2017. http://fee.org/freeman/ detail/individualism-and-freedom-vital-pillars-of-true-communities.

Zoba, Murray Wendy. 2000. "How Muslims See Christianity." *Christianity Today* 44 (March 1):1. Accessed April 5, 2017. http://www. christianitytoday.com/ct/2000/marchweb-only/31.0c.html.

INDEX

S

Salam 38
Sindh 26
Sufism 4, 9, 23, 24, 25, 26, 27, 28, 29,
    30, 31, 33, 34, 35, 37, 52, 55,
    116, 192, 207, 210, 211, 227,
    228, 231, 234, 237, 243, 256,
    257, 274, 287, 291
Syncretism 4, 23, 28, 29, 30, 192,
    212, 213, 234, 237, 243, 257

T

Tablighi Jama'at 4, 6, 16, 17, 18, 19,
    29, 45, 52, 116, 233, 287

Tafsir 80
Tahrif 105, 106, 108, 109, 110,
    274, 277
Tawhid 57, 58
Thematic Approach xxvii, 198
Trinity 54, 57, 58, 59, 60, 61, 62, 96,
    106, 190, 203, 227, 235, 236,
    242, 250, 255

Z

Zaydi 80

CPSIA information can be obtained
at www.ICGtesting.com
Printed in the USA
BVHW041001230720
584428BV00008B/87